TOMART's
illustrated
DISNEYANA
catalog and price guide

VOLUME FOUR — SUPPLEMENT EDITION

by Tom Tumbusch

Edited by Bob and Claire Raymond

**Consultant David R. Smith, Archivist
The Walt Disney Company**

Color Photography by Tom Schwartz

TOMART PUBLICATIONS
division of Tomart Corporation
Dayton, Ohio

*To Charles,
Sorry I was in California when the meeting was at your home. Hope to get there soon. Everybody there said they had a great visit
Tom Tumbusch*

To Pete Smith

William H. G. "Pete" Smith joined the Disney merchandise licensing organization in New York in 1950. He became Director of U. S. licensing in 1960 and headed the office until his retirement in 1986. Pete Smith died February 7, 1987.

ACKNOWLEDGEMENTS

Here is Volume Four. Hopefully you will see several improvements. One reason is the number of letters received suggesting improvements and/or providing additional information. I would like to thank these individuals plus the many collectors and dealers who have permitted me to photograph their Disneyana items. Special thanks for help on this edition go to Bob Lesser, Harvey and Jan Kamins, Richard Kamins, Ted Hake, Harry Hall, Jim Silva, Bob Coup, John Koukoutsakis, Joe Sarno, Dave and Elaine Hughes, Keith Schneider, Harry Matesky, Jerry and Mona Cook, Morris Hamasaki, Bill Shishima, Evie Wilson, Jean Toll, Charles Sexton, Ralph Simpson, Jack and Leon Janzen, Howard Brenner, Karl Price, Kim and Julie McEuen, Ray Walsh, Ron Aubry, Irene and Bill Young, Sue and Lee Kazee, Roger Le Roque, Nick Farago, Barbara DeHays, Al Konetzni, Maxine Evans, Greg Shelton, George McIntyre, Von Crabill, Peter Hawke, Henry Mazzeo, Jr. and George Hagenauer for their help.

A special thanks also to Rick Lenhard and his crew at Boldruler Typesetters for excellent service and cooperation in providing the typography. Central Printing in Dayton and Carpenter Lithographers in Springfield, Ohio for printing and binding. Production help thanks are also in order for Warren Miller, Jim Tromley, and the staff at Printing Preparations, and to Brock Hull at Hull Paper Co.

Everyone who enjoys the color photography joins me in thanking Tom Schwartz and his assistant, Fred Boomer, for their work setting up and photographing all the items shown in color.

A very special tip of the mouse ears goes to Bob Molinari who provided pages of additions and corrections from his vast knowledge of Disneyana. For this and sharing his collection for photos to be seen in this and future editions . . . thanks a Vernon Kilns' ostrich worth.

And to the editors — collectors Bob and Claire Raymond, and Dave Smith, Archivist, The Walt Disney Company and Paula Sigman, Assistant Archivist — for guidance and all the time they spent reviewing, correcting, and otherwise improving the manuscript, I extend my personal gratitude.

For their moral support and guidance outside the field of Disneyana I am deeply indebted to Stan Freedman, Marilyn Scott, Pete Trohatos, Dave Gross, Rebecca Trissel, and Kim Yost.

Lastly, a very special thanks to my children — Amy who helped in many ways and had to put up with a dad who works a lot on weekends, and son, Tom, who once again did all the keystroke work on this book, plus helped in many other projects required to put it all together.

Tom Tumbusch
September, 1987

Tomart's Illustrated DISNEYANA Catalog and Price Guide will be updated on a regular basis. If you wish to be notified when the supplements become available, send a self-addressed stamped envelope to Tomart Publications, P. O. Box 2102, Dayton, OH 45429.

Library of Congress Catalog Card Number: 85-51198

ISBN: 0-914293-04-4   Printed in U.S.A.

FOREWORD

Volume Four is the first supplement edition to *Tomart's Illustrated DISNEYANA Catalog and Price Guide*. Most of the items listed herein have been identified since the original three volumes were published. However, there are some corrections and additions to previously published data. Where an item is pictured for the first time, for example, the column listing is repeated with a current value estimate.

This edition has been made possible by the success of the first three books. The contribution of additional information couldn't have been more supportive. This edition represents a broader collective effort of many people who share an interest in Disneyana.

Prices for the items listed reflect the current market as of publication. It does not, however, list update prices on all previously published items. This will be done when the original books are revised and reprinted.

An alphabetical list of Disney licensees appears at the rear of this volume. Each listing includes the manufacturer's name, city, years licensed and categories of items produced. The list includes over 200 additional licensees discovered in old files when Disney's New York licensing offices moved to a new location in 1986. This expanded alphabetical listing of manufacturers should also help locate the classification where a particular item can be found. Unfortunately the original three volumes and this one will now need to be checked to determine if an item is included.

The number of Disneyana collectors continues to grow. Membership in both The Mouse Club and The National Fantasy Fan Club for Disneyana Collectors is increasing.

There was a time when only items produced prior to 1955, in particular those of the 30's, were considered collectible. In more recent years, attractive limited edition items have contributed to the growth of the Disneyana hobby. The amount of new "collectible" merchandise is almost staggering, but eventually it all seems to be sold. In fact, many people collect mainly newer items. Therefore, limited editions and other new items actively collected have been included in these volumes.

The goal of this work continues to be twofold: 1) To identify and classify, and 2) to provide an estimate of value. In regards to the latter, it should be noted that price guides are out of date the day they roll off the press. Prices go up and down — and may vary from one area to another. The price ranges shown in this book are, however, relative to each other at the time of publication. In that context, with condition taken into account, prices can be adjusted for local demand factors and changes in market trends.

This book is a compilation of major Disneyana sources and the experience of the author. The manuscript has been reviewed by David R. Smith, Archivist, The Walt Disney Company, and by Disneyana experts, Claire and Bob Raymond. Specialized collectors have been consulted on their areas of expertise.

Disney characters and theme park graphics are, of course, copyrighted by The Walt Disney Company.

With the continued support of the collectors and sellers of Disneyana, the work of finding and publishing additional items of Disneyana will go forward. Thank you, everyone — meeting and working with each of you is a large part of what makes it all worth while. If you like Tomart's DISNEYANA series, please express your thanks to the wonderful, helpful people listed in the acknowledgements.

WHAT IS DISNEYANA?

Any item associated with The Walt Disney Company or its affiliated operations, past or present, is considered to be Disneyana. The degree to which any item of Disneyana becomes collectible depends on many factors. What is utilitarian today will become collectible tomorrow. Certainly some segments of the total Disneyana spectrum are more popular than others. Even infringement items (those items not authorized or licensed by Disney) are also collected on a selected basis.

People who buy Disneyana can be categorized into four groups:

1) Consumers who purchase items as a toy, game, doll, etc. to be used, discarded or sold in a garage sale.

2) Admirers who purchase a Disney piece because it appeals to them as a souvenir or a small piece of art they can own. It is bought with the intent to preserve and perhaps display as they would any object of art.

3) Collectors who purchase a piece of Disneyana to add it to a collection. These people may collect only plates, figures, records, or items from the 30's. They may confine their interest to several specialities or collect everything marked with a Disney copyright. Collectors buy Disneyana for their personal enjoyment and, perhaps, for investment.

4) Dealers and investors who buy Disneyana with the intent of realizing a profit from their knowledge and interest.

Many who buy Disneyana as utilitarian toys know they sell well at garage sales and flea markets. And, of course, the other three types of purchasers are interdependent on each other as buyers, sellers, and traders in the secondary market.

WHAT DISNEYANA IS INCLUDED?

All identified products produced on a U.S. license and selected Canadian licenses are included. Many of these products were produced in England, Germany, Japan, Mexico, France or other countries, but were distributed in the U.S.

There are tens of thousands of items produced under licenses granted in about every country on Earth. It is known that all early records of William B. Levy, Disney's first foreign licensing agent, were destroyed. Examples brought into this country by collectors and dealers suggest, however, the volume of merchandise items probably exceeded the total produced under U.S. licenses, especially for the very early years (1930-34).

Only a few examples of foreign licensed merchandise are included in Tomart's Illustrated DISNEYANA series. There are several reasons, including — the void of information on what was produced, the difficulties monitoring rarity and values outside the U.S. and Canada, currency fluctuations, and general collecting interest in such items. Most collectors realize items never sold in this market are obviously "rare" to find, but may be commonly available and purchased at a much lower cost in the countries of origin.

WHY COLLECT DISNEYANA?

Collecting anything — stamps, old bottles, primitive tools or baseball cards — has many self-satisfying rewards. Finding a rare or perfect condition piece in some junk shop is exciting. Every antique shop or flea market provides the thrill of the hunt and the chance to meet others who share a collecting interest.

Each item in a collection becomes a trophy the collector has found, bought, won in an auction, or otherwise traded to obtain. To collect is to succeed at your own pace under whatever terms and goals you set for yourself. Collecting provides a comfortable niche in a highly competitive world — one that the collector controls — as opposed, for example, to job or other pressures they cannot. And every collector "knows" that if they lose interest, they "can get more" than they paid when the collection is sold. Unfortunately, such assumptions are not always the case.

Everything is collected by somebody. The number of what many might consider to be "odd-ball" collector's items can be confirmed in any collecting journal. However, ask any antique/collectibles dealer about the most popular collecting categories. They'll tell you that Disneyana is among the strongest — and growing.

WHAT MAKES DISNEYANA SO COLLECTIBLE?

Disneyana items are particularly attractive as collectibles. Some of the major reasons are as follows:

1) Disneyana is art. In most cases, it is good art that often reflects the popular culture of the era in which it was produced. Older pieces are recognized as art and are exhibited in some of the world's most famous museums . . . and in a growing number of toy and children's museums. Even the Smithsonian Institution is planning a popular culture museum. Yet, Disneyana is art anyone can own.

2) Disneyana has been produced in large quantities since the 20's. There are millions of Disneyana items floating around out there to keep intriguing the collecting interest. Disneyana is found worldwide.

3) Disneyana is associated with Walt Disney, one of the world's best known and respected individuals. Even though a minute portion of Disneyana was created by him, Walt Disney continues to be a major driving force behind his company's characters long after his death in 1966.

4) Disneyana is still being produced. Some items are being manufactured as limited editions. Many are marketed by mail, thus creating a larger market for Disney collectibles with each passing day. Likewise, visitors to Disney theme parks are exposed to more and more collectible merchandise and the Disney collecting interest. As older items increase in value, many collectors specialize in more modern pieces. The result — nearly anyone can collect some type of Disneyana that is interesting art and has a reasonable prospect of growing in value.

5) Disneyana brings high prices at major auctions. More people are learning there is a solid base for value as a result of this exposure. They also became familiar with items they would like to own and seek out dealers in Disneyana. There are full-time dealers all across the country that make a large part of their living

buying and selling Disneyana. However, it takes knowledge and experience to succeed in such a venture. Speculating in Disneyana is risky. Buying Disneyana as an investment generally leads to a small bank account and a large inventory that is difficult to liquidate for actual value.

Whatever your interest in Disneyana, be assured you are in good company. Movie personalities, industrialists, government officials, and people in all walks of life collect various forms of Disneyana. Yearly sales of old and new Disneyana items are estimated to exceed $400 million.

HOW TO USE THIS BOOK

Tomart's Illustrated DISNEYANA Catalog and Price Guide was designed to be an authoritative and easy to use collector's guide. It utilizes an identification and classification system designed to catalog Disneyana.

No one, including the Disney Archives, can list all of the hundreds of thousands, perhaps millions of different Disneyana items that have been produced since the 1920's. However, this system contains the framework in which they may be organized. This is the first supplement edition of material not contained in the original three volume set. This is just the beginning. The hope is that the Tomart Disneyana series will become even more authoritative with each succeeding edition.

The format is a classification system — one similar to the yellow pages of a telephone book. If you want to locate a book, handkerchief, or umbrella, just look under those headings in the proper volume. In some cases, you will find a cross index reference to help locate the listing of interest. A classification index is included in Volume Three. Certain classifications such as Books are divided into smaller groups. An explanation of these groups is found, in this case, under the broad heading of "Books."

Common usage and collecting focus were the main guidelines used in establishing classifications. Cross references and special notes are used throughout to help direct the reader.

Manufacturers and the years they were licensed are incorporated into each classification. Only licensees not included in the original volumes are listed at the individual classifications in this supplement edition.

The classification format is standardized for the most part. However, if there was a better way to communicate more information in less space, a different approach was used.

Items are listed by year at each classification. Each item is assigned a reference code number consisting of one letter and four numbers. Use of these numbers in dealer and distributor ads and collector's correspondence is encouraged. Permission for such use to conduct buying, selling, and the trade of Disneyana in lists, letters or ads is hereby granted.

The identity code numbers also serve to match the correct listing to a nearby photo. Usually, there is a listing for every photo, but unfortunately, not all items can be depicted. In certain vast classifications, such as "Advertisements," a cross section of available material is used for illustration. No specific ads are listed. There should be no duplication of identity code numbers between Volume Four and the original three books (except for relisting due to a correction or new photo). These will be merged together when volumes are updated.

THE VALUES IN THIS PRICE GUIDE

This book is a collector's and dealer's guide to average prices, in a range of conditions. The real value of any collectible is what a buyer is willing to pay. No more. No less. Prices are constantly changing — up and down.

Many factors have a bearing on each transaction. Not the least of these are perceived value, emotional appeal, or competitive drive for ownership.

Reference to the Volume One section on "Values" provides a more detailed rationale on prices. What it all boils down to is the two ways Disneyana items are sold . . . pre-priced or by auction to the highest bidder.

This book reports market prices based on items sold at leading antique shows and flea markets, as well as toy and antique advertising shows from Boston to Glendale, CA. No attempt has been made to report auction prices.

Collectors who buy at shows can generally purchase for less. Often, they have first choice of items offered for sale; sometimes at exceptional bargain prices. But they also incur substantial time and travel expenses.

Mail and gallery auctions are preferred by collectors who don't have the time or the ability to visit major shows. Money spent and current resale value also tend to be of less concern to the auction buyer. The winning bidder must outlast the others who have an emotional fix on ownership or perhaps need the specific piece to "complete" a collection.

It's difficult to say who actually spends more money in pursuit of their collecting interest . . . the show goer or the auction buyer. This much is sure. There are substantial costs involved beyond the money spent on collectibles by the show goer not normally considered in the "price" and higher overhead costs that must be covered in mail or gallery auction sales where the "price" includes everything.

INFORMATION ON COLLECTING DISNEYANA

There are new Disneyana publications and the quality of the existing ones continues to hit new heights. Here is a run down on what's currently available and how to subscribe.

The Mouse Club Newsletter is mailed to members as part of $17 per year dues. It contains information on collecting, Disney events and artists, theme parks, and club news, plus buy, sell, and trade ads. Obtain membership information from The Mouse Club, 2056 Cirone Way, San Jose, CA 95124.

Fantasy Line, published by The National Fantasy Fan Club for Disneyana Collectors, is distributed to members who pay $15 annual dues. The publication features articles on theme park activities, newer collectibles, collecting Disneyana, Disney artists, events and club news. Also contains collectors' ads. Get membership information by writing P. O. Box 19212, Irvine, CA 92713.

The Disneyana Collector is published by Grolier Enterprises, Inc., Sherman Turnpike, Danbury, CT 06816. This Disney licensed mail order company specializes in limited edition collectibles. The newsletter contains feature articles and general interest collecting information, along with ads for Grolier products. Contact the company to get on the mailing list.

The "E" Ticket features articles on Disney and other theme parks. A good specialized publication. To obtain copies of this newsletter, contact The "E" Ticket, 20560 Alaminos Dr., Saugus, CA 91350.

Collector's Showcase, P. O. Box 6929, San Diego, CA 91350; *Antique Toy World,* 394 Belle Plaine, Chicago, IL 60618; *Antique Trader* P.O. Box 1050, Dubuque, IA 52001 and other antique publications occasionally feature articles and ads relative to Disneyana.

Christie's East, 219 E. 67th St, New York, NY 10021; Sotheby's 1334 York Ave. at 72nd St, New York, NY 10021 and Phillips, 406 E. 79th St, New York, NY 10021; publish catalogs for periodic Disneyana and comic art gallery auctions.

Hake's Americana, P. O. Box 1444, York, PA 17405; The Collector's Book Store, 1708 N. Vine St., Hollywood, CA 90028; and Historicana, 1642 Robert Rd, Lancaster, PA 17601 publish mail auction catalogs containing Disneyana.

There is a growing list of toy, antique advertising and nostalgia shows where Disney related items can be purchased. The larger ones are listed in Volume One.

THE DISNEY TIME LINE

This section is intended to give collectors background and historical information useful in dating Disneyana items. It began in

Volume One with 1915, the year Walt Disney took his first art lesson in Chicago. It continued through the studio's first successes, the creation of Mickey Mouse, the birth of character merchandising, and the first three animated features — *Snow White and the Seven Dwarfs*, *Pinocchio*, and *Fantasia*.

In Volume Two the Disney Time Line continued with the abrupt changes the studio faced upon the declaration of World War II — including its support of the War effort, the development of the South American market, and the curtailment of animated feature films.

Volume Three picks up with *Cinderella*, the first animated feature in nearly eight years, highlights the early years in the company owned operation of character licensing, and continues to the sweeping new management changes taking shape in 1985.

1986

The new management team led by Michael Eisner and Frank Wells stepped up marketing and development. The name was changed to The Walt Disney Company on Feb. 6. The gift-giver machines introduced for Disneyland's 30th anniversary worked

overtime making every park guest a winner. Some won new GM cars. Most got a pin or free popcorn. The live action success, *Down and Out in Beverly Hills* (Jan. 31), was quickly followed by *Ruthless People* (June 27). *The Great Mouse Detective* (July 2), based on *Basil of Baker Street*, was the 26th animated feature produced, and the last begun by previous management. *Captain EO* finally opened at EPCOT and Disneyland after several delays (Sept. 18). Walt Disney World began celebrating its 15th birthday on Oct. 1 with a car/prize giveaway promotion similar to the one used at Disneyland the previous two years.

The studio underwent major remodeling. The once inconspicuous location was marked with a sign and Mickey on the water tower.

The Living Seas opened Jan. 15 at EPCOT Center.

Disney had returned to network TV the previous fall with two Saturday morning kid shows: *The Wuzzles* and *Disney's Adventures of The Gummi Bears*. The Disney Sunday Movie premiered Feb. 2.

The Disney characters were also invited to EPCOT Center and merchandise produced under foreign licenses is now sold at World Showcase shops, a practice instituted by the new management.

The Cinderella Castle Mystery Tour, Alice's Tea Party and American Journeys in Circle-Vision 360 opened in Tokyo Disneyland.

1987

The year began with the 60 hour "interplanetary launch" of Star Tours at Disneyland. A special free watch and 3 to 5 hour lines awaited visitors. The attraction was the first using the Lucasfilm *Star Wars* characters. A new copyright form — ©Disney — began showing up on merchandise.

The Euro Disneyland agreement was signed March 24th for a location near Paris, France. Opening is planned for 1992.

The 50th Anniversary of Snow White was the year long theme park and merchandise promotion. Disney Dollars were issued at Disneyland. Nearly $2 million worth $1 Mickey and $5 Goofy bills were printed.

Disney Dollars went on sale at Walt Disney World October 2. Disney Stores opened in Glendale and San Francisco malls.

Duck Tales, an animated series of 65 original episodes produced for the TV syndication market, began airing on Sept 18.

Tokyo Disneyland premiered *Captain EO* and Big Thunder Mountain Railroad.

And the future is already in the works.

The working titles of animated film projects currently in production are *Oliver and the Dodger* (animals retelling the *Oliver Twist* story), *Who Framed Roger Rabbit* (animated characters living in a live action world), and *The Little Mermaid* (currently in sound track and character development).

A log flume attraction based on the *Song of the South* characters will be the next attraction at Disneyland. Originally to be called Zip-A-Dee-Doo-Dah, the name was changed to Splash Mountain. Norway will open in EPCOT Center's World Showcase in April '88. Pleasure Island is coming to Walt Disney World Village at Lake Buena Vista, and may be the prototype for Disney themed mini-attractions to be built in major cities in the U. S.

Typhoon Lagoon and the Disney-MGM Studio Tour are also under development on the Florida property as separate gated attractions. Opening dates are projected for July '88. And Mickey Mouse is turning 60!

ESSENTIAL GUIDELINES TO THE DATA
AND PRICES IN THIS BOOK

At each new classification there is a brief overview of the material covered, followed by item listings. However, most classifications simply supplement listings found in the first three volumes. The best information currently available on manufacturers, items produced, and the years licensed begins on page 123. THIS INFORMATION IS NOT ALL-INCLUSIVE AND ERRORS UNDOUBTEDLY EXIST. The data is most reliable for the years 1934-50 and from 1970 to 1986, although it might not be precise. In some cases the possible error is the listing of a year licensed. More often it will be the absence of a year in which Disney products were made.

Price range estimates are based on the experience of the author as witnessed at major shows across the country. Auction results are not generally considered. (See page 5 for a more complete explanation of prices listed.) In cases where sufficient trade experience is absent, best guesstimates are provided. Where a price range refers to different size items, the high end refers to the largest size. The greater the price spread, the more valuable a strictly mint item. Also, in the case of a wide price range, "fine" grade items are worth substantially less than the average or mid-price shown. If the price range shown is 10-100, the fine value is around 40 not 50 to 55.

This sometimes flawed information is provided in the belief that available data will lead to improved scholarship in the future. Any collectors or former Disney employees having printed data or dated Disneyana material that clarifies this information are encouraged to send photos of items or photocopies of printed material to Tom Tumbusch c/o Tomart Publications, P.O. Box 2102, Dayton, Ohio 45429.

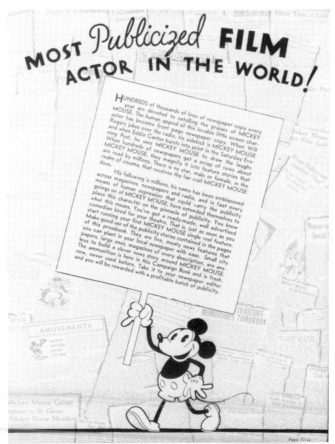

A2000 ADVERTISEMENTS, CLIPPED FROM MAGAZINES AND NEWSPAPERS

Found special ad for United China Relief in a few issues of *The New Yorker* featuring Donald, Hop Lo, and one of Mickey's rare appearances with 3-D ears. Ad proofs or reprints furnished by ad agencies or magazines also are included in this classification. The Walt Disney Company has now run several advertising sections in *Time-Life* publications to promote the theme parks.

A3000 ADVERTISING SIGNS

A wealth of old Disney advertising material continues to be discovered. The biggest single cache released in the last 2 years was a lot of over 40 different paper and cardboard bread signs. This material promotes the small Mickey Mouse bread cards; the Globetrotters map; Snow White bread, bread cards, Jingle Club and Guards of the Magic Forest; and Pinocchio bread cards and Circus cut-outs. Some milk bottle collars were also found with this material. The lot went through three dealers and asking prices are now $100 to $2500 per piece. However, a survey of collectors finds that most are not buying at these prices.

A3000

A4081

9

A4060

A4090

Framed Courvoisier cel and label

Unmarked studio cel and background

Cel sold at Disneyland's Art Corner

A4000 AMERICA ON PARADE

A4045	Plate, pewter	25 - 60
A4060	Shopping bag	4 - 10
A4081	Puzzle, tray	1 - 10
A4082	Puzzle, jigsaw	2 - 8
A4085	Bell	5 - 25
A4086	Colorforms set	1 - 5
A4087	Pillow/robe set	5 - 20
A4088	Placemat	1 - 5
A4089	Tray	4 - 2
A4090	Frameable Postcards (8), each	3 - 12

A4089

A4045

A5000 AMERICAN POTTERY COMPANY

While Vernon Kilns ceased production in 1942, the first American Pottery license was not granted until 1943. Selected pieces were produced from the Vernon Kilns molds at that time. No license was issued to Evan K. Shaw until 1945. American operated independently or as an isolated Shaw division for 2 years. Identical pieces were produced by Shaw until 1955, some still identified as American Pottery. See Evan K. Shaw.

A5500 ANIMATED AND OTHER STORE DISPLAYS

Pinocchio, made by National Displays of NYC, is dated 1940. Upper torso bows and turns, both arms move, head turns and eyes light up. Valued $600 — $3000.

Styrofoam Pinocchio and Jiminy cricket at Xylophone circa 50's. Valued $300 — $500.

Wood Centaurette from Fantasia made by W.L. Stensgaard & Associates (NYC/Chicago) 1940. Lettering on the underneath side of the base reads, "This unit is the property of Davenport Hosiery Mills and is loaned for the exclusive showing of Humming Bird Hosiery and is to be returned upon request or any time that you want to discontinue its use." Valued at 700-3000.

A7000 ANIMATION CELS AND BACKGROUNDS

Cels continue to lead Disneyana to new value heights at the New York auction galleries. The highest value realized at the press deadline exceeded $30,000 for a prominent *cel and background*. The most often seen asking price on 30's cels originally sold through Courvoisier Galleries is $1200, but sales or trades for less attractive cels are more often in the $600 to $800 range. Higher demand cels from Snow White, Pinocchio and Fantasia can command the $1200 figure or more in extra fine to mint condition.

Character images on Courvoisier cels were usually cut-out, mounted on a fresh, clean cel, matted over a printed background and framed. See example of white authenticating tag.

Cels from 1947 to around 1955 were not commercially sold, but many were kept by animators and distributed as gifts.

Disneyland sold cels at the Art Corner. These were authenticated by a gold seal on the reverse. Usually these were matted and sealed with no background. Art Corner cels purchased in the last three years at shows and conventions ranged in price from $30 to $90. Newly released cels at Disneyland and Walt Disney World are $125 and up. These are authenticated with an embossed seal on the cel material and are often matted against a printed line drawing background.

If you wish to purchase cels through the mail, two dealers with catalogs to contact are: Cel-ebration!, 45 Salem Lane, Little Silver, NJ 07739 or Gallery Lainzberg, 417 Guaranty Bldg., 3rd Ave. & 3rd St. S.E., Cedar Rapids, IA 52401.

Courvoisier Galleries cel from Snow White and the Seven Dwarfs with printed background-damaged and in need of repair

11

A8000

A8000

A8000

A8000

A8000

A8000 APPAREL

Apparel licensing, long the largest classification of Disney merchandise, has been boosted by Sears' Winnie the Pooh promotions and new lines for the theme parks. The phenomenally successful line of Mickey & Co. sportswear, accessories and shoes by J. G. Hook, Inc. continues to lead the way. Apparel manufacturers and their products can be found in the alphabetical list of licensees at the rear of this volume.

A8000

A8000

A8050 ASH TRAYS & COASTERS

A8066	Mickey on surfboard (plaster)	10 - 75
A8067	Mickey milk promotion	20 - 45
A8991	Cardboard coasters	1 - 10

A9000 AUCTION CATALOGS

The number of Disneyana auctions continue to grow. Older catalogs still fetch $5 to $20.

A8991

A8067

MICKEY MOUSE
"UNDIES"

Knitted Underwear for Girls and Boys

manufactured under exclusive license from Walt Disney

Mickey Mouse Undies are to be had in Vests, Panties, Bloomers and Union Suits for girls; Waist Union Suits for girls or boys; Union Suits for boys. Colors—white and pink. For ages 2 to 12. Also athletic 2-button shoulder Union Suits, athletic pull-over Shirts and elastic top Shorts for boys—in white. For ages 6 to 16.

The *Fabric* is genuine Diamond Mesh of fine combed cotton yarn, made in conformity with established Norwich Standards.

TO RETAIL - 25¢ to 50¢

Order from your wholesaler

NORWICH KNITTING CO.
• NORWICH, N. Y •

Sales Office, 346 Broadway, New York City

A8000

A9000

A9000

A9625

B1448

B1392

B1455

B1445

B1905

B1460

B2535

B1870

B2545

B1873

B2687-B2696

B2544

B2826

14

A9500 AWARDS AND CERTIFICATES

The theme parks are responsible for most of the certificates being printed. However, a unique one commemorated the first day Disney stock traded on the Tokyo exchange.

A9625	Tokyo stock exchange	5 - 25
A9650	Theme park certificates	2 - 20

A1350 BANKS

B1364	Telephone, candlestick or cradle type (N.N. Hill Brass)	35 - 170
B1392	Dumbo figural (Crown)	20 - 90
B1445	Donald's head	5 - 25
B1448	Mouseclubhouse Treasury bank (Mattel) w/Mousekey	8 - 45
B1455	Uncle Scrooge plastic premium made in Finland, but given to children opening accounts. Name of the US bank often appears on reverse of chest.	5 - 15
B1460	Character house & vehicle banks (6 dif), each	4 - 8

B1850 BLOTTERS

B1856	National Wallpaper Company	8 - 25
B1870	Additional Sunoco Gas and Oil	5 - 20
B1872	Sunheat heating oil	5 - 20
B1873	Complete Building Service	8 - 23

B1900 BOOK PLATES AND BOOKMARKS

B1902	Theater promotional bookmarks	3 - 15
B1905	Additional Antioch designs	1 - 8

B2501 BOOKS — ART AND ANIMATION

B2505	Fantasia (1940) w/dust jacket	50 - 400
B2535	The Fine Art of Walt Disney's Donald Duck (1981) Another Rainbow bound folio of paintings by Carl Barks	100 - 210
B2544	Snow White and the Seven Dwarfs & the Making of the Classic Film (50th Anniversary) Simon & Schuster	5 - 15
B2545	The Complete Story of Walt Disney's Snow White and the Seven Dwarfs (50th Anniversary reprint of B5285) Abrams	5 - 15

B2600 BIG LITTLE BOOKS, BIG BIG BOOKS, BETTER LITTLE BOOKS, WEE LITTLE BOOKS AND PENNY BOOKS

The entire series of all books in this classification is shown in Volume One. Except for the Penny Books. These were printed on a very cheap paper and are rarely found in fine or better condition. Several more have been found for photography. Value 5-25 each.

B2775 BOOKS — COLORING, PAINTING AND ACTIVITY

B2776	Mickey Mouse Pictures to Paint (1931) #210	15 - 150
B2813	Paint Book Animals from Snow White (1938) #606	5 - 40
B2814	Walt Disney's Brave Little Tailor Paint and Crayon Book (1938) #616	10 - 80
B2815	Farmyard Symphony Paintless Paint Book (1939) #652	10 - 50
B2826	Fantasia Paint Book (1939) #689	10 - 80
B2848	Walt Disney's Paint Book (1946) #646 (Incorrect cover shown in Volume One)	4 - 22
B2875	Pinocchio Coloring Book (1954) #2031	2 - 12
B2880	Uncle Scrooge Coloring Book (1955) Dell #130	10 50
B2883	Let's Go to Disneyland Coloring Book (1956) Dell #140	3 - 20
B2884	Goofy Dots (1956) #1413	1 - 8
B2887	Jimmie Dodd Magic Carpet Coloring Book (1957) #	2 - 10
B2891	Andy Burnett (1958) #1185	2 - 10
B2892	Walt Disney Presents Disneyland Coloring Book (1958) #1127	3 - 18
B2895	Walt Disney's Big Big Coloring Book (1959) Watkins-Strathmore #1871	2 - 10
B2896	Donald Duck Trace and Color Book (1960)	

B1872   B1856

A9650

B2505

B2813

B2776   B2815

B2848

B2875

B2880

B3161

B2884

B2887

B2891

B3197

B2892

B2895

B2896

B3198

B3136

B3310

B3317

B3D26

	#1661	2 - 20
B2900	Donald Duck Coloring Book (1963) Watkins-Strathmore #1861-3	2 - 8
B2915	Winnie the Pooh (1965) #1116	1 - 7
B2916	Bambi with fuzzy cover (1966) #1180	1 - 9
B2918	The Love Bug (1969) Hunts catsup give-away	2 - 8
B2922	Disneyland Coloring Book (1970) #1050	1 - 6
B2925	A Visit to Walt Disney World Coloring Book (1971) #1078	1 - 4

B3100 BOOKS — CUT OR PUNCH OUT

B3136	Sleeping Beauty Cut-Out Standups (1959)	5 - 20
B3161	Pinocchio (1961) Golden Giant	5 - 20
B3197	A Visit to Walt Disney World (1971)	3 - 10
B3198	Mickey Mouse Revue (1971)	4 - 20

B3300 BOOKS — LINEN LIKE

B3310	The Wise Little Hen (1937) #888 (back cover shown in error in Volume One)	10 - 50
B3317	A Mickey Mouse Alphabet (1938) #889	15 - 50
B3331	Pinocchio (1940) #846 is not a Linen Like book as listed in Volume One.	

B3400 BOOKS — GOLDEN BOOKS — LITTLE, BIG, GIANT, AND TINY

Little Golden Books

B3D26	Peter Pan and the Indians	2 - 10
B3D70	Scamp's Adventure	1 - 8
B3D75	Manni the Donkey in the Forest World	1 - 8
B3D91	Pollyanna	1 - 6
B3D94	Donald Duck Private Eye	2 - 10
BD101	Pinocchio and the Whale	2 - 10
BD118	The Ugly Dachshund	1 - 8
BD145	Return to OZ Escape From the Witch's Castle	1 - 2

Big Golden Books listed in Volume One

BD145

BD146

BD147

Walt Disney's
Bambi

B3700

Walt Disney
TREASURY
21 BEST-LOVED STORIES

A GIANT GOLDEN BOOK

B3739

Walt Disney's
Pinocchio

BD148

BD149

Walt Disney's
CIRCUS

A BIG GOLDEN BOOK

B3702A

Walt Disney's
THE ADVENTURES OF
Mr. TOAD

A BIG GOLDEN BOOK

B3708

Walt Disney's
Savage
Sam

A BIG GOLDEN BOOK

B3768

GOLDEN PICTURE STORY BOOK 50¢
OF DISNEY DUCKS

Walt Disney's WONDERFUL
WORLD OF DUCKS
featuring
LUDWIG VON DRAKE

B3762

Walt Disney's
THE GREAT
LOCOMOTIVE
CHASE

WALT DISNEY LIBRARY

B3738

WALT DISNEY PRESENTS
LT. ROBIN CRUSOE,
★★★ U.S.N. ★★★
STARRING DICK VAN DYKE

B3790

A GOLDEN BOOK
WALT DISNEY'S
Bunny Book

B3769

GOLDEN TALL TOY BOOKS

Color and Wipe-Off Books with Magic Crayons. Each book is
based on an episode from the motion picture:

#10607 THE SWORD IN THE STONE $1 Retail
#10608 MERLIN'S MAGIC DUEL $1 Retail
#10609 CROWNING OF THE KING $1 Retail

Each contains a story in pictures and a box of Magic Crayons
to color each picture. The colors can be wiped off and the
pictures can be colored again.

Walt Disney's
Merlin
the Magician

#GF 222
29 CENTS

MERLIN THE MAGICIAN COLORING BOOK

CARTOON
50 YEARS OF
DIME-STORE
MEMORABILIA
BY
ROBERT HEIDE
& JOHN GILMAN
COLLECTIBLES

B4660

HOW'S YOUR "I.Q."
A quick automotive quiz,
entertaining and informative

B4026

BD146 Return to OZ—Dorothy Saves the Emerald City 1 - 2
BD147 The Black Cauldron — Taran Finds a Friend 1 - 3
BD148 Pinocchio 1 - 2
BD149 The Jungle Book 1 - 2
BD150 101 Dalmatians 1 - 2
B3A33 Sleeping Beauty Story and Paper Doll Book 2 - 20

Tiny Golden Library
Walt Disney's Tiny Movie series (with no #s)

B3660 Bambi Plays Follow the Leader 1 - 3
B3661 Bongo Stars Again 1 - 3
B3662 Bootle Beetle's Adventures 1 - 3
B3663 Brer Rabbit Plays a Trick 1 - 3
B3664 Cinderella's Ball Gown 1 - 3
B3665 Donald Duck's Wild Goose Chase 1 - 3
B3666 Dopey and the Wicked Witch 1 - 3
B3667 Dumbo's Magic Feather 1 - 3
B3668 Mickey's New Car 1 - 3
B3669 Pablo the Penguin Takes a Trip 1 - 3
B3670 Pinocchio's Surprise 1 - 3
B3671 Three Little Pigs Fool a Wolf 1 - 3

Big Golden Books

B3700 Bambi (1941) 4 - 35
B3702A Walt Disney's Circus (1944) marked "A Big Golden Book" 4 - 30
B3708 The Adventures of Mr. Toad (1949) 3 - 30
B3738 The Great Locomotive Chase (1956) 2 - 14
B3739 Treasury of 21 Best Loved Stories (c.1956) 3 - 18
B3762 Wonderful World of Ducks (1961) 2 - 12
B3768 Savage Sam (1963) 2 - 10
B3769 Bunny Book (1971) 2 - 12
B3790 Lt. Robinson Crusoe U.S.N. (1966) 2 - 10

B3800 BOOKS — PAPERBACK, POCKET SIZE

B3826 The Moon-Spinners (1964) Crest 1 - 2
B3850 The Wonderful World of Disney series (1975) Pyramid — Dr. Syn Alias the Scarecrow 1 - 3
B3854 Of Mice and Mickey (1975) Manor 1 - 2

B3900 BOOKS — POP-UP AND MECHANICAL

B3972 Mickey's Christmas Carol Golden Melody Book 3 - 10

B4000 BOOKS AND MAGAZINES — SPONSORED

B4026 How's Your "I-Q" (1941) Sunoco 4-28

B4500 BOOKS — REFERENCE

B4547 The Story of Walt Disney (1957) Holt 8 - 35
B4579 Mickey Mouse Club Scrapbook (1975) G & D 1 - 8
B4651 A Celebration of Comic Art and Memorabilia (1975) Hawthorn 8 - 50
B4598 The New Mickey Mouse Club Book (1977) G & D 1 - 6
B4660 Cartoon Collectibles (1984) Doubleday 1 - 15
B4663 Disney's World (1985) Stein and Day 2 - 10
B4665 Mickey Mouse Memorabilia (1986) Abrams 3 - 30
B4670 Official Overstreet Comic Book Price Guide (1987) Ballantine.Each annual volume is valuable to Disneyana collectors. The '87 edition has feature articles on Disneyana. 4-12

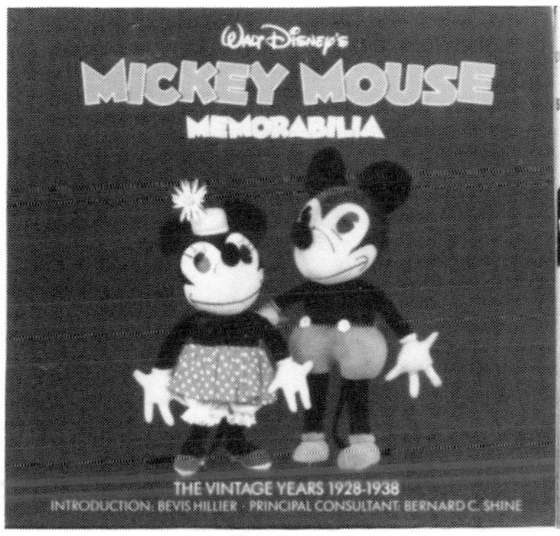

B4665

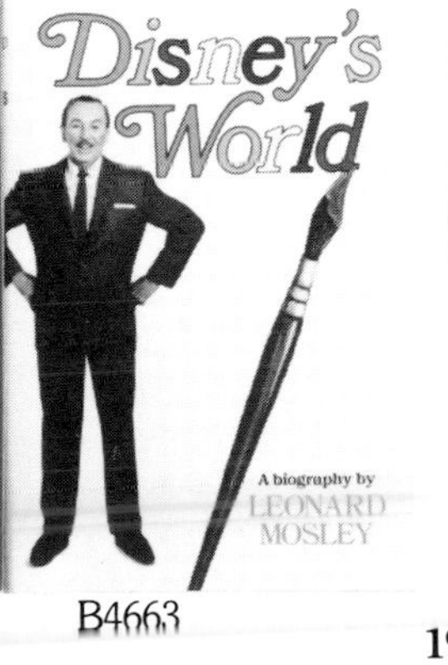

B4663

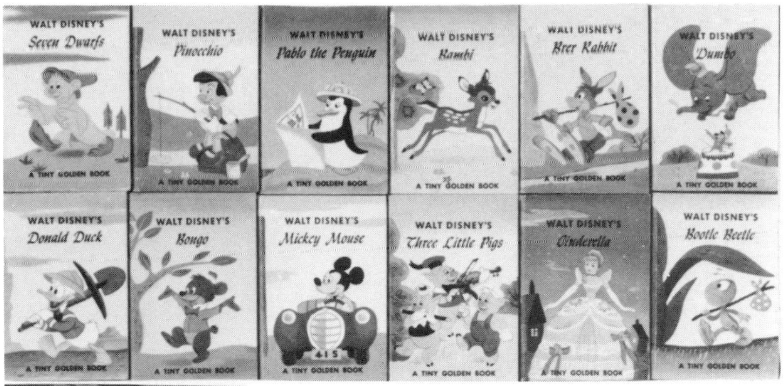

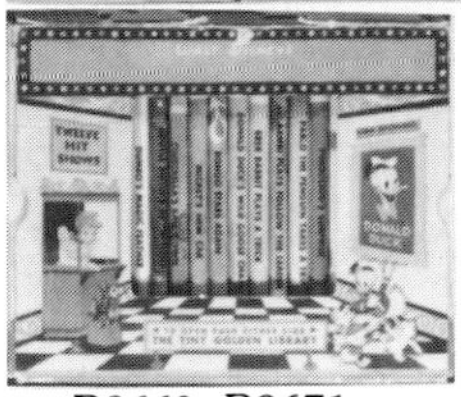
B3660 - B3671

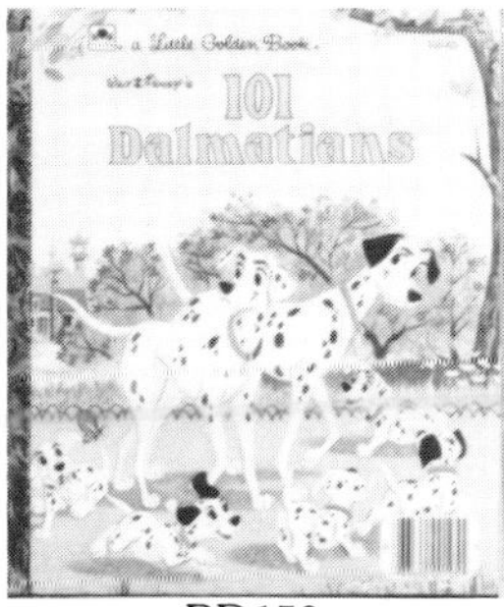

BD150

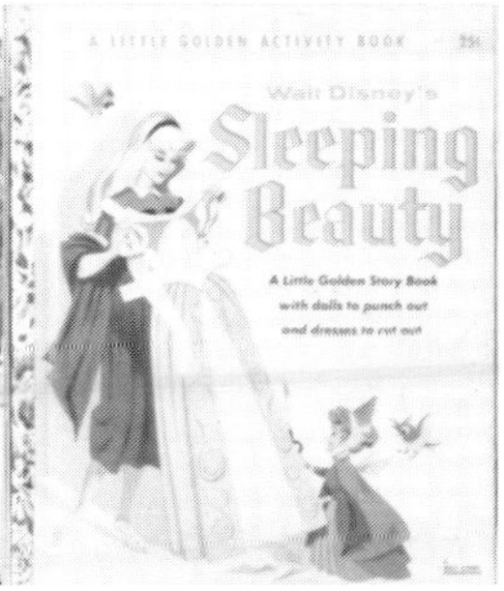

B3A33

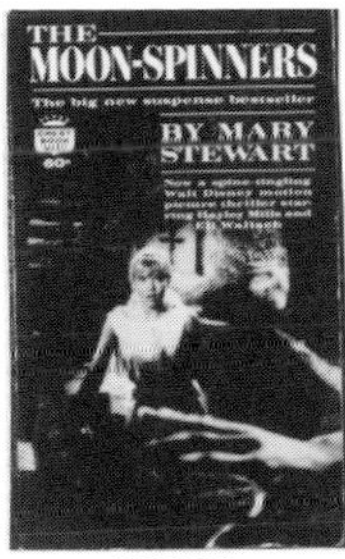

B3826

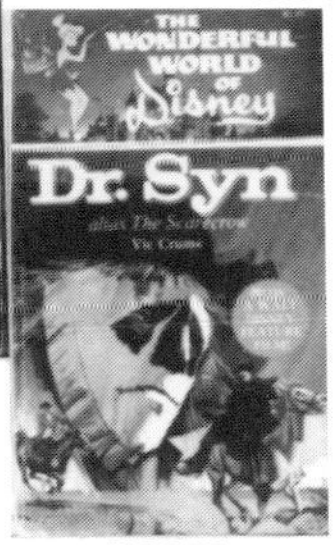

B3850

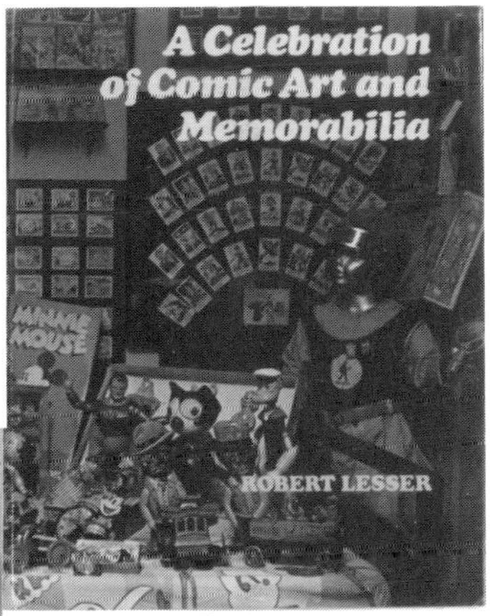

B4651

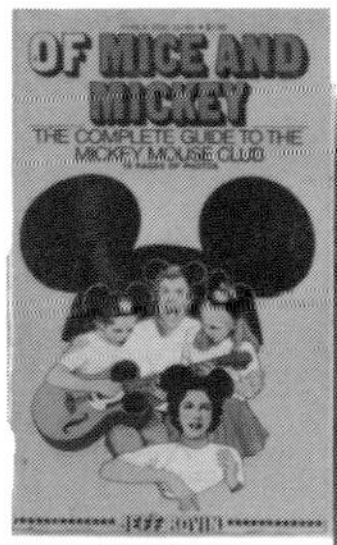

B3854

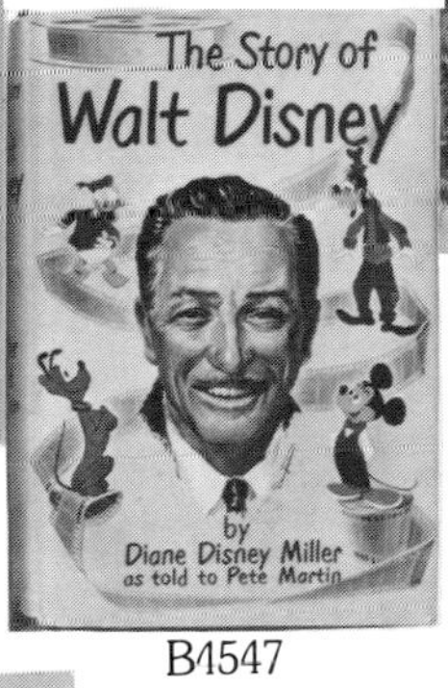

B4547

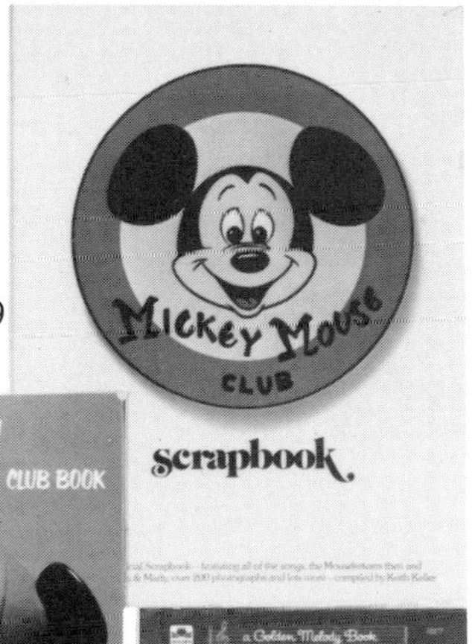

B4579

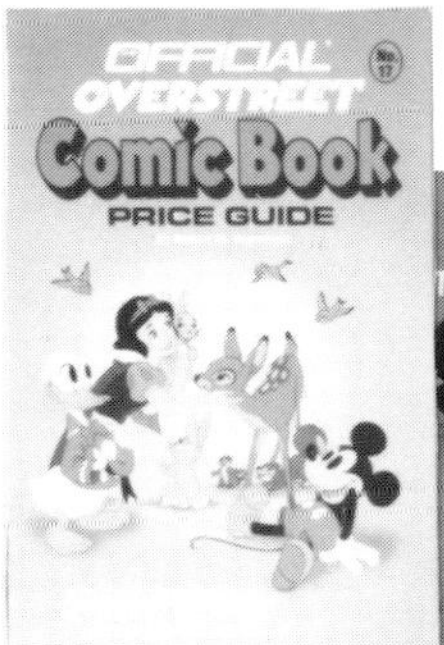

B4670

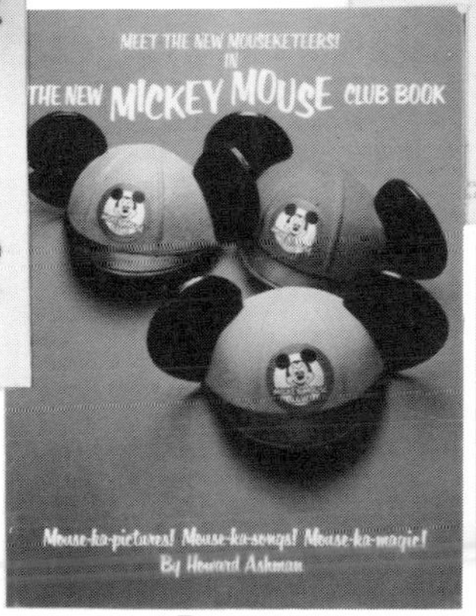

B4598

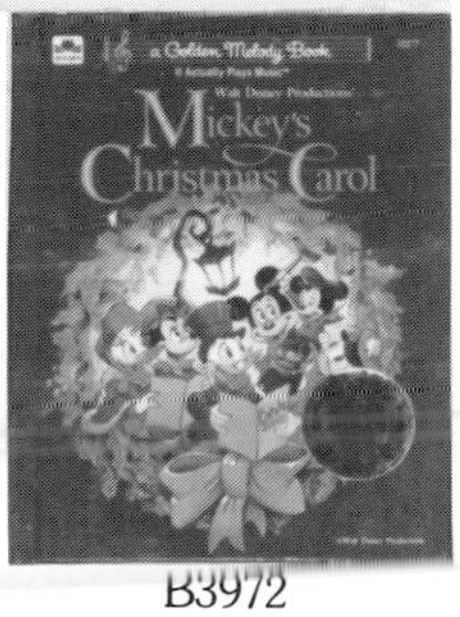

B3972

B4717

B4755

B4734

B4736

B5211

B5273

B5284

B4760

B5305

B5311

B5373

B5301

B5492

B5397

B5400

B5503

B5485

B5384

B4700 BOOKS — STAMP AND STICKER FUN

B4717	Peter Pan (1952) #2181	10 - 40
B4734	True-Life Adventures (Golden WD-4) 1955	3 - 12
B4736	Animals of Africa (Golden WD-7) 1956	2 - 10
B4755	Donald Duck Sticker Fun (1960) #2183	2 - 10
B4760	Mary Poppins Sticker Fun (1964) #1684	2 - 8
B4765	The Jungle Book Sticker Fun (1971) #1680	1 - 5
B4766	Disneyland Sticker Fun (1967) #2183	2 - 12

B5200 BOOKS — STORY

B5207	Mickey Mouse Illustrated Movie Stories (Canadian)	15 - 100
B5211	Mickey Mouse — Book #2 (1932) McKay	20 - 150
B5273	Mickey Mouse Has a Busy Day (1937) #1077	10 - 60
B5284	Pluto and the Puppy (1937) G & D	10 - 75
B5301	Brave Little Tailor (1938) #972	10 - 60
B5305	Snow White and the Seven Dwarfs from the Famous Movie Story, no#	10 - 50
B5311	Ferdinand the Bull (1938) Dell	5 - 30
B5315	Mickey Mouse Has a Party (1938) #798	10 - 50
B5317	Mickey Mouse in Numberland (1938) #745	15 - 60
B5373	Walt Disney's Version of Pinocchio #6880	15 - 60
B5384	Figaro and Cleo (1940) #1059	3 - 20
B5397	Pinocchio (1940) #846	8 - 60
B5400	Pinocchio (1940) Heath	4 - 20
B5412	Walt Disney's Version of Pinocchio (24 pages) 1940	4 - 25
B5485	Mickey and the Beanstalk (1947) G & D	3 - 20
B5492	Come Play with Donald Duck (1948) G & D	3 - 20
B5494	Come Play with Pluto Pup (1948) G & D	3 - 20
B5503	Dumbo of the Circus (1948) Heath	10 - 60
B5546	Donald Duck and the Hidden Gold (1951) Sandpiper	3 - 8
B5546	With dust jacket	5 - 20
B5547	Alice In Wonderland (1951) Sandpiper	3 - 10
B5547	With dust jacket	7 - 22
B5582	Stormy (1954) CC#2404	2 - 4
B5583	Beaver Valley (1954) TAT #2553	1 - 3
B5585	Living Desert (1955) S&S, Dust jacket	2 - 5
B5591	Davy Crockett and Mike Fink (1955) S&S #439	2 - 10
B5600	American Folklore (1956) no #	3 - 15
B5615	Mickey Mouse Club Treasure Mine (1956) #2918 Boxed set of 8 soft back titles — 7 reprints of 1949-50 Tiny Tales book, plus a new MMC	

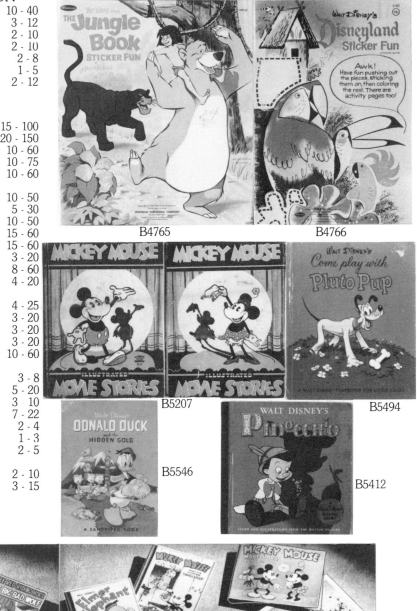

B4765 B4766

B5207 B5494

B5546 B5412

David McKay ad in 1936-37 Kay Kamen merchandise catalog. Books are listed in Volume One

Whitman ad in Kamen's 1940-41 catalog

B5585

B5582

B5583

B5624

B5674

B5669

B5600

B5591

B5629

B5692

B5681

B5640

B5687

B6550

B6550

B6550

B6550

B6550

B6550

title — Bongo, Mickey and the Beanstalk, The Three Orphan Kittens, Danny, Johnny Appleseed, Mickey Mouse's Summer Vacation, plus Corky and White Shadow, in box ... 25 75

B5624	Snow White and the Seven Dwarfs (1957) TAT #2578	1 - 3
B5629	Worlds of Nature (S & S)	2 - 10
B5640	Big Book (1958) #7196	2 - 15
B5669	Donald Duck Treasury (1960) S & S #12517	2 - 4
B5674	Babes In Toyland (Tip-Top) 1961 #2490	2 - 4
B5679	Huey, Louie and Dewey's Christmas Wish (Tip-Top) 1962 #2497	2 - 5
B5681	Ludwig Von Drake Dog Expert (Tip-Top) #2482	2 - 5
B5687	The Magic of Mary Poppins (1964) no #	3 - 15
B5692	A Visit to Disneyland (1970) Big TAT #2421	3 - 15

B6200 BOOKS — OTHERS

B6350	Lake Buena Vista 1986 & 1987 Telephone books, each	1 - 5
B6400	Autograph books, each	1 - 10
B6550	Early story books in English	5 - 70

B6350

B5615

B5679

B6400

B7103

B7121

B7100 BREAD CARDS AND PREMIUMS

Included in the large find of Kay Kamen advertising materials (see A3000 — ADVERTISING SIGNS) were several different manuals detailing how the bread and milk promotions worked. In each promotion there was an album, map or picture where the entire collection of bread "cards" could be pasted. The picture cards were tucked under a special wax-paper band around the outside of the loaf of bread. The Pevly Milk Co. and perhaps other dairies used 4-page promotional folders or other means to give away the picture cards.

Bottle collars were used for the Globetrotters promotion.

Albums for the large bread cards were available at the grocery store, but you had to request the collecting device thereafter. An additional 1938 promotion has been discovered - the *Mickey Mouse Travel Club News*. Bakeries still delivered to the home at that time and routinely used 4-page promotional folders to push new products and weekly specials. Mickey appeared in a syndicated promotion piece called *The Happy Home-Makers Weekly*. News about his travels to the various 48 states appeared on the

B7110

Pinocchio bread card album

B7114

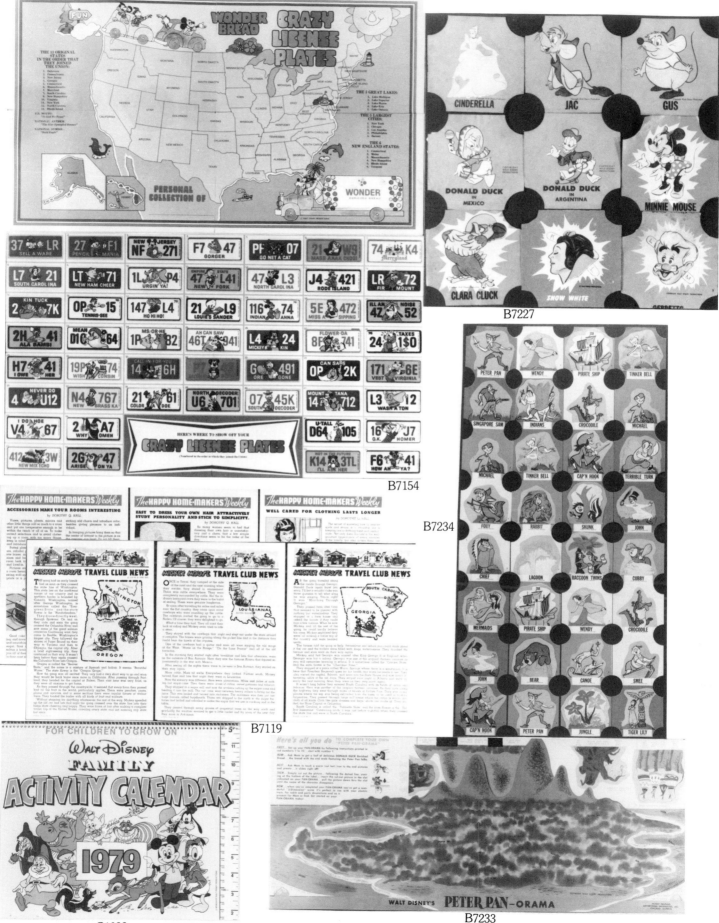

B7227

B7154

B7234

B7119

B7233

C1098

back panel of these 4-color folders. There were 22 different issues with 2 or 3 states appearing on some panels. The Snow White Bread promotion manual shows a wide variety of tie-in packaging for other products ranging from donuts to popcorn. (See — F8500 FOOD AND DRINK PRODUCTS) Also, see all 96 of the smaller Mickey Mouse bread cards in the color section.

B7103	Large bread card albums (2 different)	20 - 75
B7108	Small bread cards (2 1/2" x 4 1/4") each	2 - 8
B7110	Mail reply card for 48 page bread card album	5 - 15
B7114	Wax-paper band for Globetrotter promotion	6 - 45
B7119	Happy Home Maker/Travel Club News folders (1938), each	5 - 20
B7121	Snow White Jingle Club bread cards, each	4 - 12
B7126	Pinocchio bread cards (60) each	1 - 7
B7154	Crazy license plate poster, complete	2 - 15

B7200 BREADWRAPPERS AND END SEALS

B7227	Cinderella set (?) each	1 - 8
B7230A	Alice in Wonderland poster	3 - 20
B7231	Peter Pan Picture (not puzzle as listed in Vol. 1) Album	3 - 28
B7233	Peter Pan-orama punch out scene	5 - 35
B7234	Peter Pan-orama end seals (24) each	1 - 6

C1000 CALENDARS

C1080	Advent calendars (various years)	1 - 8
C1082	1972 Mickey Mouse (Buzza-Cardozo)	2 - 10
C1097	1978 Hallmark Mickey Mouse Magazine Covers	2 - 10
C1098	1979 Family Activity	2 - 10
C1108	EPCOT Center monthly construction each	1 - 5

C1080

B7230A

B7231

B7126

C1097

C1082

C1108

25

This page measures 4×5 but Goodness, gracious, sakes alive!---

Although it measured 8×10

You'd have to open it again

Hi

C2700

I hunted in the card shops AND AT FIRST I WAS DISMAYED FOR THIS SORT OF CARD I WANTED DIDN'T SEEM TO BE DISPLAYED

GIMME SOMETHING SORT OF SPACIOUS! DON'T BE BASHFUL · SHOOT THE WORKS! DON'T THEY MAKE 'EM ANY BIGGER? WAS MY PLEA TO ALL THE CLERKS

So they SEARCHED BENEATH THE COUNTERS and they hunted mighty hard and they did their best to find me JUST THE PROPER SORT OF CARD --

CAMERA OUTFIT

Here is Your MICKEY MOUSE CAMERA

INSTRUCTION BOOK

C1215

'TILL AT LAST THEY FOUND A DANDY! AND I SHOUTED, "THAT'LL DO!"

To make it "wide" enough to say this BIG, LONG WISH FOR YOU TODAY

C1564

'CAUSE IT TAKES A HEAP OF PAPER for this wish I'M WISHING YOU!

HAPPY BIRTHDAY

C2035

HAPPY BIRTHDAY

C2035

C1200 CAMERAS

C1215 Mickey Mouse Camera Outfit, complete in box	35 - 75
C1220 Mick-a-Matic (ear release)	10 - 60
C1221 Same as C1220, but with button shutter release	5 - 30
C1225 Mickey engineer	2 - 10

C1560 CANES

C1564 Wooden Mickey (Borgfeldt)	25 - 175

C2000 CARDS — GREETING

C2005 Hall Brothers, regular, each	6 - 20
C2025 Hall Brothers, pop-up, each	8 - 25
C2035 Hall Brothers, fold-outs, each	10 - 50
C2300 Saludos Amigos, each	5 - 15
C2500 50's cards, each	2 - 10
C2600 60's cards, each	1 - 8
C2700 70's cards, each	1 - 5

C2300

C2035

C5100

C5000 CASTING SETS AND FIGURES

A nice selection of 1968 Mini-Mold sets made by Yankee Homecraft Corp. were recently uncovered in an old warehouse. Individual mold sets for 24 different figures were found with the lot — including a set of 6 from Jungle Book.

C5100 Model-Craft set #9	10 - 50

Yankee Homecraft Corp. 1968

C5120 Snow White and the 7 Dwarfs Mini-mold set	10 - 35
C5121 Snow White and the 7 Dwarfs Mini-plaques moulding and color set	12 - 40
C5122 Character Mini-mold set	10 - 35
C5123 Individual molds for Mickey, Donald, Goofy, Huey, Pluto, Winnie the Pooh, Snow White and the 7 Dwarfs, Pinocchio, Jiminy Cricket, Bambi, Dumbo, Mowgli, Girl Cub, King Louie, Baloo, Sonny and Shere Khan, each	3 - 9
C5150 Walt Disney World Mickey Dough (1971)	6 - 20

C5500 CEREAL PACKAGES AND CUTOUTS

The author has received a request for a list of Post Toasties package backs. While these were numbered on an inside bottom flap, virtually all were cut off. In this edition we have begun the list. Anyone having other title(s) please send a photocopy of them to Tomart, P.O. Box 2102, Dayton, OH 45429.

Mickey and His Pals 1934
The Three Little Pigs Cutouts 1934
Mickey Mouse at Play 1934
Mickey, Minnie & Pluto 1934
Mickey Goes "A Hunting" 1934
"The Big Bad Wolf" (and Red Riding Hood) 1934
Mickey at the Circus 1934
Mickey Mouse in the Pet Shop 1934
Mickey Out West 1934
The Steeple-Chase 1934
Mickey Mouse in "Camping Out" 1934

C5121

WALT DISNEY'S Character MINI-MOLD SET

MAKES FIGURINES UP TO 8 INCHES TALL

7 FIGURINES TO MOLD AND PAINT
A NEW NO-HEAT METHOD

C5122

MINI MOLD — Mickey Mouse
MINI MOLD — Donald Duck
MINI MOLD — Goofy
MINI MOLD — Huey
MINI MOLD — Pluto
MINI MOLD — Winnie-The-Pooh

MINI MOLD — Mowgli
MINI MOLD — Girl Cub
MINI MOLD — King Louie
MINI MOLD — Baloo
MINI MOLD — Sonny
MINI MOLD — Shere Khan

MINI MOLD — Dopey
MINI MOLD — Sleepy
MINI MOLD — Grumpy
MINI MOLD — Bashful
MINI MOLD — Sneezy
MINI MOLD — Doc

MINI MOLD — Snow White
MINI MOLD — Happy
MINI MOLD — Pinocchio
MINI MOLD — Jiminy Cricket
MINI MOLD — Bambi
MINI MOLD — Dumbo

C5123

YANKEE HOMECRAFT CORP.

"Snow White Moulding & Coloring Set To Hang"

"Snow White Mini-mold Set"
With 8 Rubber molds.

Yankee Homecraft Corp.
East Natick, Mass. 01762 — Contact: Tony Ciroli

C5120

Post Toasties Corn Flakes
MADE OF CORN GRITS SUGAR AND SALT

POSTUM COMPANY, INC.
BATTLE CREEK, MICHIGAN

NET WEIGHT 13 OZS.
MADE IN U.S.A.

MICKEY THE CHEF

MICKEY MOUSE'S HOUSE

MICKEY GOES TO WORK

MICKEY MOUSE ON ICE

MICKEY MOUSE'S AIRPLANE

C5500

Mickey Mouse Learning How to Skate 1934

Mickey and Minnie Give a Party 1935
Mickey Mouse in the Good Old Summer Time 1935
Mickey the Athlete 1935
Mickey the Fire Chief 1935
Mickey Mouse's Band Concert 1935
Mickey the Chef 1935
Mickey's Vaudeville Show 1935
Mickey and His Pals at the Amusement Park 1935
Mickey's Service Station (story panel back) 1935
Mickey's Kangaroo (story panel back) 1935
Mickey Mouse's House 1935
Mickey Mouse and Pluto in Puppy Love (story panel back) 1935
Gulliver Mickey (story panel back) 1935
"Cock of the Walk" (story panel back) 1935?
Mickey Mouse Goes to Work 1935

Mickey Mouse the "G" Man (game back) 1936
Mickey Mouse Baseball Game! (game back) date?
Mickey Mouse in "The Orphans' Picnic" (story panel back) 1936
Mickey Mouse "On Ice" (story panel back) 1936
Mickey Mouse Presents Walt Disney's Three Little Kittens 1936
Mickey Mouse's Airplane (date?)
Mickey Mouse (on the farm) exact title and date missing
Mickey Mouse (big game hunting) exact title and date missing
Mickey Mouse The Sea Captain (date?)
Mickey Mouse and His Mousemobile (date?)
Mickey Mouse's Football Team (date?)
Mickey Mouse's Hot Dog Stand (date?)

Mickey Mouse in China 1937

Mickey Mouse presents his new friends Snow White and the Seven Dwarfs
Snow White and Prince at Wishing Well 1937
Snow White Guesses the Names of the Dwarfs 1937
The Dwarfs at Work in the Diamond Mine 1937

The Dwarfs Chase the Witch 1938
Snow White and Seven Dwarfs (date?)
Snow White, Prince, Forest Friends, Witch, & Cruel Queen (date?)
The Prince Wakes Snow White with a Kiss 1938
The Prince Takes Snow White to His Castle (date?)
Mickey the Traffic Cop 1938
Mickey Mouse's Radio Program (date?)

Mickey Mouse at the Playground 1939
Mickey Mouse presents The Fox Hunt 1939
Mickey Mouse's Parrot 1939
Mickey Mouse presents The Whalers 1939
Mickey Mouse presents Ferdinand the Bull
Ferdinand Under the Cork Tree & 4 others 1939
They Took Ferdinand Away in a Cart & 3 others 1939
Ferocious Ferdinand, Banderilleros, Mad Matador, Picador, & bulls 1939
Young Ferdinand, Swordbearer, Trumpeter, Matador & Mama 1939
Picador, Men w/ Funny Hats, Ferdinand Sits on Bee 1939
Ferdinand Loved to Smell Flowers, Senorita, & 3 others 1939

Mickey Mouse presents His Friend Pinocchio
Pinocchio, Foulfellow, Blue Fairy, Gideon & Coachman 1939

C5500

C5500

C6221

C6254

C6230

C6255

C6231

C6298

C6299

C6299

C6551

C6816

C7858

C6750

C6616   C6638   C6654

Have cut-outs for at least 2 more boxes w/ Pinocchio (2 more), Figaro, Cleo, Geppetto, Jiminy Cricket, Lampwick, Stromboli & Gendarme 1939
Blue Fairy Brings Pinocchio Back to Life & 3 others 1939
Geppetto, the Woodcarver, puts the finishing touches & 3 others 1939
Pinocchio, w/donkey ears, & Geppetto at Sea & 3 others 1939

Pinocchio Starts to School (story back) 1940
Pinocchio Joins the Show (story back) 1940
Jiminy Meets Pinocchio (story back) 1940

C6100 CHINAWARE

The Bavarian China pieces shown in the color section were imported by Schumann Brothers under a sub-license from George Borgfeldt from 1932-34. The four pieces were purchased for $150 in 1986. The top plate is marked, "Royal Paragon China Mickey Mouse Series . . . Made in England." It was purchased for $10 in Louisville, KY. It may have been imported for sale in the U.S. or purchased abroad.

C6200 CHRISTMAS CARDS — CORPORATE

There was not an official studio Christmas card for 1985, however, there have been a proliferation of cards from different corporate divisions in recent years. The Disneyland card for 1985 received the largest circulation.

C6221	1952 Peter Pan	12 - 50
C6230	1961 Babes in Toyland	8 - 40
C6231	1962 Wonderful World at Christmas	8 - 40
C6254	1985 Disneyland card (there was no studio/ corporate card for 1985)	1 - 8
C6255	1986 Lady and the Tramp	3 - 10
C6298	Tokyo cards, each	1 - 8
C6299	Executive and division cards, various, each	1 - 8

C6300 CHRISTMAS LIGHTS AND SHIELDS

Only the Noma Mickey Mouse and Silly Symphony sets were sold in US. However, a Snow White, a Pinocchio, and perhaps a Fantasia set were sold in Canada.

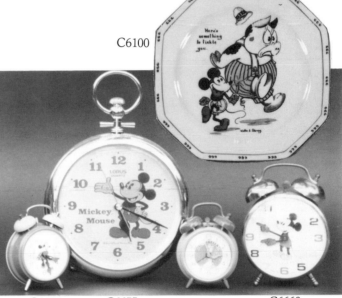

C6305

C6510 CHRISTMAS — MISCELLANEOUS

C6550	Santa bag	1 - 5
C6551	Stocking	2 - 9

C6600 CLOCKS

C6616	Bayard Snow White	25 - 120
C6638	Mickey Mouse alarm	30 - 150
C6654	Sleeping Beauty	20 - 110
C6655	More recent clocks	5 - 20
5660	Mickey (Bradley)	5 - 25
C6665	Bradley mini size alarm (Mickey, Minnie, Donald, Cinderella) each	5 - 25

C6750 CLOTHES HANGERS

A series of illustrated wood hangers produced by Alexander Asquine Inc. of Pittsburgh was manufactured in 1986. Mickey, Minnie, Donald and Pluto were featured. Value 2-7 each.

C6800 COINS AND MEDALLIONS

C6816	Walt Disney/Mickey 8oz bronze	50 - 100
C6827	Walt Disney World, souvenir, Mickey in center on reverse	3 - 4
C6849	Walt Disney World, 15 Years logo	5 - 6

C7000 COMIC BOOKS AND DIGESTS — NEWSTAND

Disney comic books had been on sale for over 45 years when publication ceased in 1984. Many of the older stories had been republished in miniature form over the years in the 57 issues of

C6303

C6100

C6665   C6655   C6660

C7000

C7800

31

C7015

C7062

C7011

C7030

C7037

C8071

C8208-C8211

Walt Disney Comics Digest (Jun 67 to Feb 76). In 1986, Gladstone Publishing div. of Another Rainbow, a company run by comic and art collectors, pumped new life (and distribution) into Disney titles. Gladstone is reprinting the best of older material done by US and Foreign publishers and developing some new stories. Gladstone also released a few Comics Digests.

Top investment grade comic books have largely been found. True mint copies are never really seen at antique or toy shows. What looks like new to most dealers or collectors would pale next to a mint copy. Prices in this guide ignore the investment grade books because preservation techniques would had to have been used since the day the issue was purchased new for it to survive in mint, investment condition. There is a chance you may find uncirculated comics Grandma hid in her cedar chest in Colorado or Arizona. Then you have something worthy of individual appraisal and the need for a dealer contact who knows top buyers. Otherwise, exposure to air, heat, and/or dampness have already accelerated the self-destructive acid in the paper.

C7000	Donald Duck (1938) Whitman/ K.K.Publications	40 - 200
C7011	Bambi (1942) #12	6 - 32
C7015	Bambi's Children (1943) #30	5 - 50
C7030	Mickey Mouse in Jungle Magic (1947) #181	8 - 30
C7037	Mickey Mouse and His Sky Adventure (1949) #214	10 - 100
C7038	3 Little Pigs and the Wonderful Magic Lamp (1949) #218	7 - 28
C7043	Donald Duck in Voodoo Hoodoo (1949) #238	10 - 100
C7045	Mickey Mouse and the Black Sorcerer (1949) #248	
C7047	Donald Duck in Luck of the North (1949) #256	10 - 100
C7062	Donald Duck in No Such Varmint (1951) #318	8 - 80
C7064	Donald Duck in Old California (1951) #328	7 - 75
C7074	Donald Duck in a Christmas for Shacktown (1951) #367	6 - 60
C7600	Gladstone Disney titles	1 - 2
C7800	Walt Disney Comics Digests	1 - 25
C7858	Gladstone Comics Disney Digest Titles	1 - 2

C7950 COMIC BOOK SUBSCRIPTION PREMIUMS, PROMOTIONS, AND ACKNOWLEDGEMENTS

C7955	Walt Disney Comics and Stories mailers	5 - 45

C8000 COMIC BOOKS — PREMIUM AND GIVEAWAY

C8071	Dumbo Weekly (1-16, 1941) each	3 - 18
C8208-		
C8211	Cheerios Set Y, each	2 - 10
	(Except "Donald Duck's Atom Bomb")	8 - 75
C8230-		
C8237	Wheaties Set A, each	2 - 10

C7038   C7043   C7045

C7064   C7074   C7047

C7600

C7955

C8230-

C8308

-C8237

C8839

C8838

C9250

C9250

C9274

C9275

C8919

34

C8308	New Adventures of Peter Pan presented by Admiral (1953)	5 - 20

C8800 CONSTRUCTION SETS

C8838	Mickey Mouse Plastic Construction Bricks (1954) Practi-Cole Products, Inc.	4 - 32
C8839	Mickey Mouse Club Krazy Ikes (1955) Whitman	5 - 35

C8900 COOKIE BOXES AND PREMIUMS

C8903	Mickey Mouse Comic Cookies box	30 - 180
C8919	Stauffer's Disney Cookies, small	.25 - 1

C9000 COOKIE JARS

C9121	Winnie the Pooh Collection figural	8 - 40
C9131	Chef Mickey	10 - 25

C9121   C9131

C9200 COSTUMES AND PLAY OUTFITS

C9250	Mickey (1947) Ben Cooper	4 - 40
C9250	Dumbo (1947) Ben Cooper	3 - 27
C9274	Mouseketeers play outfit, boy's or girl's (1955) Eddy	4 - 40
C9275	Explorers Club Outfit (1955) Eddy	4 - 40

C9350 CRAFT SETS

C9366	Snow White Wood Burning set	8 - 45
C9381	Character String Art kits	5 - 20
C9393	Mickey Mouse Shrinky Dinks	1 - 3

C9400 CRAYON AND COLORING SETS

C9401	Crayons (1934) Marks Bros., set of 8	5 - 25
C9420	Magic Pictures (40's) Jaymar	4 - 22
C9449	Mickey Mouse Club — 12 Coloring books and crayons (1955) Whitman, boxed set	3 - 30
C9455	Annette Coloring Box (1962) Whitman	4 - 35

C8903

C9366

C9420

C9381

C9393

C9455

D2020

D2021

D2025

C9750

D4066

Disneykings

D4060

Mickey Mouse Club 12 Coloring Books

C9449

ROLYkins

D4086

Disney Fun Pals

D4110

LOUIS MARX & CO.
200 Fifth Avenue
New York, N. Y. 10010
Contact: C. E. Hjelte

"Snow White
and the Seven Dwarfs"
Figurine Picture Book

Suggested retail price
$1.98

D4068

C9750 CRICKET NOISE MAKERS

A fairly large quantity of these early "crickets" were found in an old lodge hall. There were only six different in the over 70 pieces found. They are Mickey playing the sax, drum, clarinet, violin, triangle and banjo. They sold briskly at $150 per set.

D2000 DECALS

D2020	Mickey or Donald product decals, 30's, each	3 - 20
D2021	Character product decals, 40's	2 - 12
D2025	Meyercord, Snow White, each	2 - 15

D3575 DISNEY DOLLARS

This classification is prompted by The Walt Disney Company decision to issue their own paper currency for use at Disneyland. Approximately $2 million worth of $1 bills featuring Mickey and $5 bills sporting Goofy were issued. The company promises to redeem them in U.S. dollars upon demand. If successful at Disneyland, use may be expanded to other theme parks. Actually, this type of "script" money has been in existence since Disneyland opened in 1955. Ticket coupons and passports have always been good for admission or use anytime. When individual attraction tickets were eliminated, the company began redeeming them for the cash value paid.

The first Disney Dollars were the ones distributed at Mickey Mouse Club meetings held in theaters in the early 30's. Redemption, however, was limited to ice cream cones. There was "funny money" Mickey play bucks printed on each Disney newspaper comic page and some interesting 30's play money that you needed to keep about 45 years before any value was recognized.

The first theme park Disney Dollar was printed at Disneyland in 1964. Walt Disney World Recreation Coupons (1971) were designed to promote the expanded Disney concept of family entertainment and the vast sports facilities throughout the Walt Disney World complex. They were amazingly similar to the "new" design for the Mickey buck. They were numbered and signed by Roy Disney, but were not redeemable in cash. Who wouldn't like to have a whole handful now?

D3577	Mickey Mouse Cone dollars	2 - 12
D3578	Dollars cut from Sunday newspapers, each	.50 - 1
D3580	Mickey Mouse play money, 30's, each	1 - 5
D3584	Disneyland 1964 issue	?
D3585	Walt Disney World recreation coupons, each	2 - 15
D3587	Disney Dollar announcement flyer	.25 - .50
D3588	Disneyland $1 bill (1987)	1 - ?
D3589	Disneyland $5 bill (1987)	5 - ?

D4000 DISNEYKINS

Variations in Marx Disneykins products continue to be discovered. In addition to those mentioned in Volume One are a line of Disneykings that are similar to Disney Fun Pals in size. They were used in at least one "Figure Picture Book." There were several different Ludwig Von Drake sets, a special premium set of 7 Jungle Book characters, plus a number of additional characters beyond the original 34.

D4024	Additional figures including — Bongo, Big Bad Wolf and 3 Little Pigs, Tortoise, Hare, Queen of Hearts, Dumbo clown, Princess Aurora, Prince Phillip, Flora, Fauna, Merryweather and Maleficent, each	2 - 20
D4060	Disneykings, Mickey, Donald, Goofy, Pluto, Daisy, Dewey, Minnie, Bambi, Snow White, Dopey, Alice, March Hare, Mad Hatter, Pinocchio, Figaro, Geppetto, Pecos Bill, Panchito, Blue Fairy and Captain Hook, each	1 - 8
D4066	Ludwig Von Drake sets, each	4 - 15
D4068	Snow White and the Seven Dwarfs Figurine Picture Book (1968)	8 - 30
D4070	Jungle Book premium set — Mowgli, Baloo, Bagheera, King Louie, Colonel Hathi, Sonny and Shere Kahn, set of 7	12 - 40
D4086	Rolykins, ball bearing, set of 6 on card	6 - 25
D4110	Disney Fun Pal sets, each	6 - 18

D5000 DISNEYLAND

D5004	Monsanto Hall of Chemistry fold out booklet (1956)	6 - 40
D5006	Give-away map/guide folders	

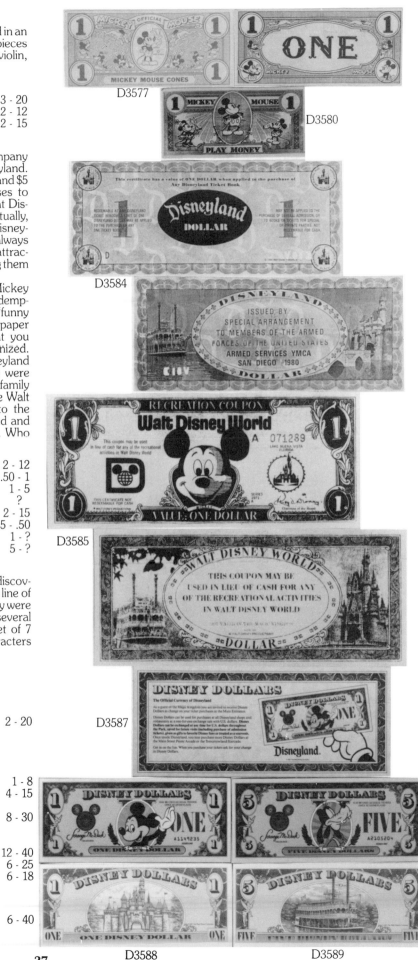

D3577

D3580

D3584

D3585

D3587

D3588

D3589

D5004

D5043

D5041

D5014

D5006

D5037

D5025

D5007

D5073

D5021

D5038

D5515

D5700

A — 1955 or 56	7 - 40
B — 1957, 58 or 59	5 - 30
C — 1960 - 65	3 - 18
D — 1966 - 75	2 - 8
E — 1976 - 87	1 - 4

D5007 Autopia drivers licenses, each — 1 - 8

D5014 Gate flyers
— promoting newest attractions — The Columbia, Alice in Wonderland and the Grand Canyon (1958) — 3 - 12
— Enchanted Tiki Room and Below Decks (1964) — 2 - 10

D5021 Plastic Home of the Future (1960) 2-color — 3 - 25

D5022 Walt Disney's Guide to Disneyland (1961) red — 5 - 22

D5025 Monsanto Home of the Future (1963) 4-color — 4 - 25

D5037 Schwinn Take A Trip to Disneyland (1966) — 3 - 25

D5038 Grad Nite Albums, each — 2 - 20

D5041 Walt Disney's Pirates of the Caribbean (1968) — 5 - 22

D5043 Adventure thru Inner Space post card cover booklet — 5 - 25

D5073 It's A Small World souvenir booklet (1978) — 1 - 8

D5140 Your Trip to Disneyland (record and map, 1955) Mattel — 5 - 50

D5142 Map of Tom Sawyer Island (1957) original version lists "Tom and Huck's Tree House" as the "highest point in Disneyland." Later version (but also copyrighted 1957) deletes such mention, and uses dark green shading to make trails stand out. — 2 - 10

D5350 Main Street light post signs — 35 - 200

D5510 Press tickets
— Captain EO — 3 - 12
— Star Tours — 3 - 12

D5515 Cast tickets
— Star Tours — 2 - 10

D5650 30th Year hats (5 different — one for each land) each — 2 - 8

D5700 1986 Gift Giver Ticket — 1 - 2

D5703 Designated attraction tickets, each — 1 - 10

D5703

D5140

D5022

TOM SAWYER ISLAND

D5142

D5510

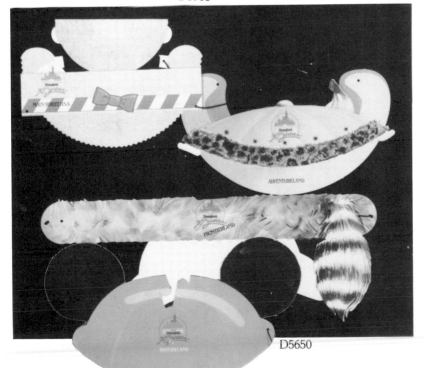

D5650

Disneyland paper bag ©1958

39

D6109

D6540

D6542

D7842

D7853

D7848

D6863-D6868

D7855

D8503

D6100 DOLLS

D6109	Charlotte Clark Donald (signed)	100 - 500
D6200	Dean Rag Book Co., 5" and 9" Mickey dolls	40 - 400
D6376	Seven Dwarfs, 15" size (1938), Knicker-bocker, each	30 - 145
D6540	Pinocchio and the Blue Fairy (1951), Duchess	20 - 80
D6541	Snow White (1951), Duchess	10 - 45
D6542	Cinderella (1951), Duchess	10 - 45
D6543	Alice In Wonderland (1951), Duchess	10 - 50
D6620	Baby Princess Sleeping Beauty (1959)	8 - 35
D6863-		
D6868	Mickey Costume series (c.1975) Durham, Super Mickey, Chef, Drum Major, Ring Master, Sailor and Cowboy, movable arms and legs, heads turn, each	8 - 20
D6880	Mickey and Minnie, with stands (1985), Applause, each	10 - 40
D6881	Mickey/Minnie wedding or Mouseketeers (1986), ea., Applause	8 - 20

D7800 DOLLS — PAPER

All paper dolls listed below were published by Whitman. Some code numbers in this section have been changed.

D7842	Annette in Hawaii (1961) #1969	5 - 20
D7848	Annette Movie & TV Doll (1962) boxed	7 - 25
D7850	Hayley Mills in Summer Magic (1963) #1966	6 - 23
D7853	Annette Cut Out Doll (1964) #1953	5 - 18
D7855	Mary Poppins 4 Paper Dolls (1964) #1982	5 - 18
D7857	Hayley Mills in That Darn Cat (1965) #1955	5 - 15

D8500 DRAWING SETS AND MATERIALS

D8501	Marks Brothers Pantograph #954	50 - 300
D8503	Mickey and Minnie's Merry Moments stencil outfit (Spear's) c. 1931	40 - 150
D8504	Mickey Mouse Art Set (Dixon) #2670	20 - 130

D6376

D7850

D7857

D8504

D8501

E1501

E1504

E6427

E6425

E6117

THE LIVING SEAS
Grand Opening
January 15, 1986

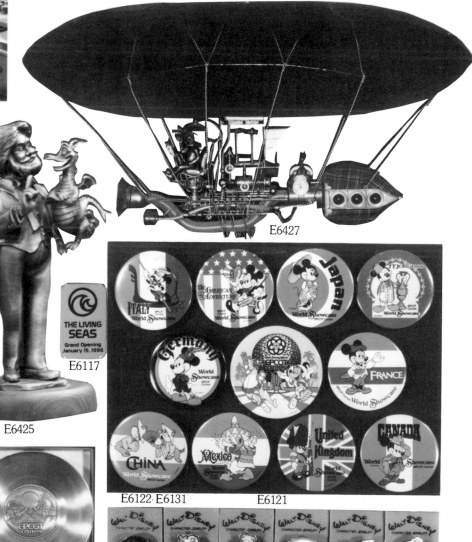

E6122·E6131   E6121

E5000

E6799

E6233

E1500 EASTER EGG DYE — TRANSFER AND DECORATION SETS

E1501	Transfer — O's Album (Paas)	8 - 60
E1504	Man — Egg — Kins punch-out book (Pass)	8 - 60
E1542	Egg Art — Fantasia (Sun Hill) contains Mickey and Bambi's combined sets but none from Fantasia	2 - 10
E1543	Mickey Mouse Easter Egg Color Kit (Sun Hill)	1 - 4

E5000 EMPLOYEE PUBLICATIONS

Additional examples from the Disneyland Line, Walt Disney World's Eyes and Ears, and EPCOT Center Today.

E6000 EPCOT CENTER

Merchandise has come to *EPCOT Center* in a big way under the new Disney management. Disney characters are now part of the EPCOT show and began appearing on merchandise in 1986. World Showcase shops began selling products produced on foreign licenses about the same time. Great Britain, Japan and Germany have taken the greatest advantage of this opportunity. A major effort to tie characters to the World Showcase pavilions began in 1987.

E6019	Wood plates (4), each	2 - 5
E6117	The Living Seas — Grand Opening pinback	5 - 25
E6118	The Living Seas pinback	1 - 3
E6121	Character pinback, 3", pink	1 - 3
E6122-6131	World Showcase pinbacks, each	1 - 2
E6232	Kitchen Kabaret, set of 8 cloisonne pins, each	1 - 3
E6233	Figment cloisonne pin set (6), each	2 - 4
E6240	Future World or World Showcase, cloisonne pin	2 - 4
E6325	World Showcase Mugs, Ceramic (10), each	2 - 4
E6326	World Showcase Mugs, Plastic (10), each	1 - 3
E6327	World Showcase cardboard coasters (10), each	1 - 3
E6425	Dreamfinder and Figment figure, bronze	100 - 250
E6427	Dream Machine with Dreamfinder and Figment, selling price	4,500
E6510	Plush characters in costumes (12) each	4 - 20
E6572	Let's Tour EPCOT Center Stamp Book and Album	2 - 7
E6573	Your EPCOT Center Memory Album and Stamp Book	2 - 7
E6799	Candy dish	2 - 7

E1542

E1543

E6572

E6573

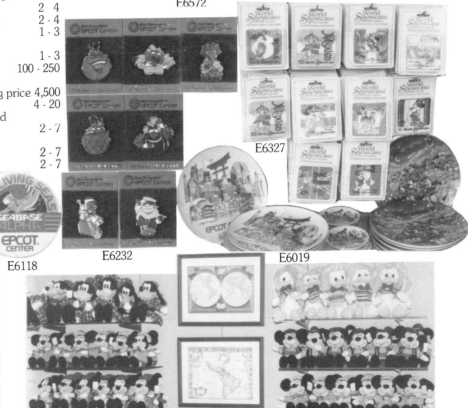

E6327

E6232

E6019

E6118

E6510

E6240

A HARDEE HAPPY BIRTHDAY TO MICKEY!

F2061

MELAMINE SNACK SET

with THERMOPLASTIC MUG

F2064

E6326

WALT DISNEY'S Sleeping Beauty AND PRINCE

Complete with HORSE and ACCESSORIES

F5722

StoryKins Make Your Fairy Tales Come True....

F5737

A DISNEYLAND TOY

F5649

F3030

Walt Disney's OFFICIAL ★ Johnny Tremain and HORSE

SET INCLUDES
SADDLE · SADDLE BAGS · LANTERN
PISTOL · RIFLE · POWDER HORN · HAT
STIRRUPS · STIRRUP STRAPS · REINS
DISPATCH CASE · BELT and BRIDLE

F5721

Walt Disney's Donald Duck's "express" HAND DECORATED

GOOFY   DONALD DUCK'S EXPRESS   PLUTO

F5730

F6005

OFFICIAL Walt Disney's Zorro Rider and Horse in Lifelike Detail

SET INCLUDES
HORSE · ZORRO RIDER
SADDLE · BRIDLE · REINS
CINCH STRAP · SWORD · WHIP
MASK · CAPE · HAT

LOUIS MARX & CO. INC., GLEN DALE, W. VA.

Z5034

Two original boxes for Snow White and the Seven Dwarfs porcelain bisque figurines. Sets came in five different sizes.

44

E8000 EURO DISNEYLAND

The second Disney theme park to be built outside the U.S. was set in an agreement signed March 24, 1987. The location is near Paris, France. Opening is planned for 1992. A French language pre-opening brochure using art from previous theme parks has been prepared and is still available. It also includes a preliminary map of the park layout.

F2000 50TH BIRTHDAY — MICKEY MOUSE

F2061	Pepsi coloring contest sheet	1 - 2
F2064	Melamine snack set	3 - 10
F2080	Purse	3 - 10

F3000 FIGURES — CELLULOID

F3027	Donald 7″, long bill, moveable arms and legs	50 - 200
F3030	Mickeys on celluloid bridge, wood base	30 - 120
F3032	Two walking Mickeys on celluloid base, large one hollow	20 - 80

F5500 FIGURES — PLASTIC

Plastic figures are another hot area of Disneyana. In addition to Disneykin type figures (See D4000), Louis Marx & Co. produced unpainted, but finely detailed Disney figures in a wide range of sizes. Many are listed on page 44 of Volume Two. In addition, there were three large horse and rider sets — Zorro (also came in two smaller sizes), Johnny Tremain, and Sleeping Beauty and Prince. There was a Peter Pan boxed set of 5 figures and other sets packaged in plastic bags. Linemar did a 12″ Babes in Toyland soldier set and Auburn did some special sets for Disneyland. Vanity Fair Electronics Corp. produced *StoryKins* sets of plastic figures accompanied by thin red plastic records. Snow White has combable hair and the figures of the Seven Dwarfs had bristle like beards. Mattel produced 12 clear crystal-like hard plastic figures under the name of *Little Treasures* in 1975.

F5635	Peter Pan boxed set	15 - 70
F5638	Lady and Tramp	6 - 25
F5649	Auburn Disneyland sets, each	15 - 60
	Zorro on horse w/all accessories (See Z5034)	
F5721	Johnny Tremain and horse w/all accessories	15 - 55
F5722	Sleeping Beauty and Prince, horse w/all accessories	15 - 80
F5724	Babes in Toyland flexible soldiers (Linemar)	10 - 50
F5730	Donald Duck's Express and figures (1968)	7 - 32
F5737	StoryKins Snow White and Doc	5 - 25
F5738	StoryKins remaining 6 Dwarfs	5 - 25
F5800	Little Treasures clear hard plastic figures of Mickey, Donald, Tinker Bell, Bambi, Thumper, Flower, Snow White, Dopey, Doc, Pinocchio, Jiminy Cricket and Figaro, each	1 - 3
F5812	Little Treasures packaged sets (4), each	5 - 20

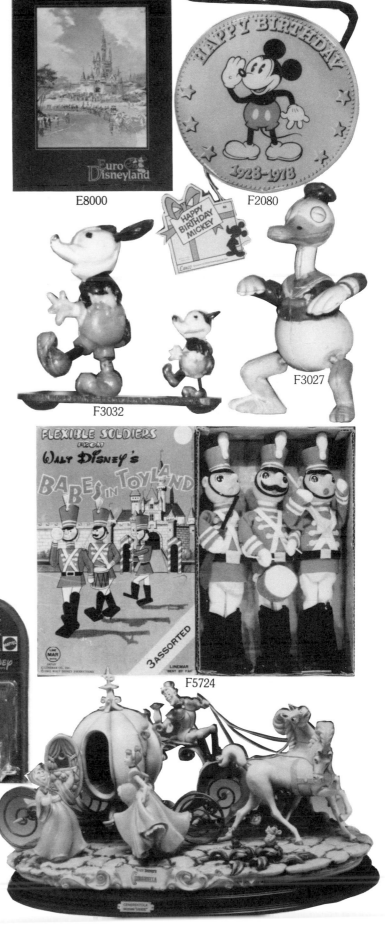

F3032

F3027

F5724

F5812

F6000 FIGURES — PORCELAIN BISQUE

The market for bisque figures is brisk. Many of the 30's figures appear to be purchased for return to Japanese collectors. The Royal Orleans Christmas '80 and '81 figures were liquidated for $1 each in the Ohio area in 1986. No great quantities of the larger figures seemed to pop up. The Capodimonte series continues to be expanded. Original purchase prices have also been increased. A large scene from Alice in Wonderland has been issued. Individual figures of Donald Duck, Snow White and each Dwarf, Pinocchio, Mickey as the Sorcerer's Apprentice, and Peter Pan have been added.

Capodimonte porcelain scenes, mini-scenes and individual figures from Italy continue to be sold at Disney theme parks and selected dealers in the U.S. Alice in Wonderland and Peter Pan have been produced in addition to the ones pictured above and Cinderella on the previous page.

Christmas bisques from Grolier continue and the theme parks began issuing a new series in 1985 based on the studio Christmas card 50 years previous. The first two were one year off, but the series got in sync with the 1987 Snow White issue.

F6000	Mickey, 1″	25 - 75
F6005	Mickey riding in canoe	80 - 500
	Grolier Christmas bisques	
F6500	Mickey, Minnie and Pluto at Lampost, 1979	25 - 60
F6501	Lady and Tramp, 1980	15 - 30
F6502	Santa and Mickey (short run), 1981	35 - 100
F6503	Dumbo pulling sleigh, 1982	15 - 35
F6504	Scrooge Christmas Surprise, 1983	15 - 30
F6505	Happy Birthday Donald, 1984	15 - 30
F6506	Mickey and Donald as Santa's Helpers, 1985	15 - 30
F6507	Musical "We Wish You A Merry Christmas", 1986	20 - 35
	Disneyland/Walt Disney World Christmas bisques	
F6550	1985 Based on 1934 Studio Christmas card	25 - 85
F6551	Individual Mickey and Minnie from F6550, each	10 - 18
F6552	1986 Based on 1935 Studio Christmas card	25 - 40
F6553	1987 Based on Snow White card, one of 2 for 1937	New 75
F6554	Individual figures from 6553, each	2 - 4

F6500   F6502   F6503

F6551   F6550   F6552

F7000 FIGURES — RUBBER

The 1934 Kay Kamen merchandise catalog shows the Seiberling 3 Little Pigs and Big Bad Wolf came in two versions - with only minor paint and fully decorated. Later editions show only the full paint version. It matters little since most of both types have already disintegrated. There was also a set of flat, 4 color Snow White and the Seven Dwarfs from Seiberling.

F7048	Seiberling Snow White and the Seven Dwarfs, flat with 4 color transfers, set in box	75 - 350
F7048A	Individual figures from F7048, each	10 - 30

F7048

F7450 FILM PROMOTION MATERIALS, MISC.

In addition to the posters, press books, publicity kits, advertisements and stills elsewhere classified, there have been thousands of special promotional pieces. These have been produced for consumers, the press, and/or the theater trade. There were

F7450

mailers, booklets, merchandise, pop-ups, and other unique promotion pieces. The examples included for demonstration include school study pieces for *Fantasia*, a bound pre-booking scenario for *Make Mine Music*, an advertising merchandise mailer for *Melody Time*, a "flasher" card for *Trenchcoat*, and a pop-up mailer for *Mickey's Christmas Carol*. These items were all purchased for prices of $20 or under. Values must be judged on the individual items, based on uniqueness, the film and buyer appeal.

F7500 FILMS, SLIDES AND VIEWERS

F7521	Pepsodent's Snow White Moving Picture Machine (cardboard viewer) 1938 premium	40 - 160
F7555	Super 8 and Super 8 sound home movies	3 - 25

F7900 FLOWER VASES AND PLANTERS

Several unusual planters have been uncovered. A sample of a Dennison unit was finally found. This was a rectangular ceramic vessel faced with a cardboard Donald Duck. Two of the unidentified pieces might be Leed's but no available reference identifies them as such.

F7922	Bambi figural	10 - 40
F7930	Mickey w/package	7 - 35
F7931	Pluto w/basket	5 - 20
F7935	Dancing Donald (Dennison)	6 - 30
F7940	Nodder Donald in boat	7 - 35
F7947	Donald pushing cart (Breckner)	5 - 20

F7521

F7930

F7931

F7940

F7935

F7922

F7947

F7450

F7555

48

F8500 FOOD AND DRINK PRODUCTS

F8524   Snow White and the Seven Dwarfs "Popt
       Corn" bag   8 32

F8525   Cake container, "do-nut" carton or bun
       wrapper, each   8 - 32

F8526   Snow White cake and pastry flour bag
       (Canadian)   1 - 2

F8566   Fun Spreads catsup, mayo, mustard, or relish
       packets, boxed   2 - 5

F8600 FOOTWEAR — SLIPPERS, SOCKS, SHOES, ETC.

Footwear has been a major Disney licensing classification since the early 30's. While not very collectible, photos of the products are still of some interest. Included are several not previously published.

F8526

F8524

F8500

F8525

F8525

F8566

F8600

F8600

57

F8600

F9040

F9039

F9041

G2010

MICKEY MOUSE
TIC-TAC-TOE
Game

DIRECTIONS

G1227

WALT DISNEY
One Hundred and One
Dalmatians
GAME

For 2 to 4 Players · Ages 7 to 10
Enjoy the Chase... Win the Race

G1235

WALT DISNEY
DONALD DUCK
CARD GAME

G2067

MICKEY MOUSE
Old Maid
Cards

WALT DISNEY
PRODUCTIONS ROBIN HOOD
GAME

G1260

WALT DISNEY'S JIG SAW
LOTTO

JIG SAW LOTTO

Walt Disney's JIG SAW LOTTO

G3007

An Electric GAME complete with battery!

WALT DISNEY'S
SLEEPING
BEAUTY

WALT DISNEY'S Peter Pan
A GAME of ADVENTURE

AN EXCITING
TRAVEL GAME FOR
TWO TO FOUR PLAYERS

Walt Disney's
Peter Pan

G1184

WALT DISNEY'S
Disneyland
GAME

2 to 4 Players   Ages 5 to 9

Featuring
the
Magic Whirl
Spinner

G1245

WALT DISNEY'S Sleeping Beauty

Sleeping Beauty

CARD No. 1

G2934

WALT DISNEY
CHARACTER

SCRAMBLE
INTERCHANGEABLE
PICTURES

MAKES 1000 DIFFERENT COMBINATIONS
EDUCATIONAL and ENTERTAINING

G3008

58

F9000 FRICTION TOYS

F9039	Mickey's airliner	45 - 195
F9040	Mickey Mouse sparkling jet	45 - 195
F9041	Mickey's cart	10 - 65

G1001 GAMES — BOARD

G1017	Walt Disney's Own Game Red Riding Hood (Parker)	12 - 50
G1029	Snow White Game, Tek toothbrush premium	20 - 50
G1032	Game Parade (American Toy Works)	20 - 70
G1184	Peter Pan — A Game of Adventure	5 - 25
G1196	Hardy Boys Treasure Game	5 - 22
G1226	Sleeping Beauty Castle, litho tin	5 - 28
G1227	Mickey Mouse Tic-Tac-Toe, litho tin	5 - 25
G1235	One Hundred and One Dalmatians	4 - 16
G1240	Mary Poppins Game w/magic wheel	4 - 18
G1241	Mary Poppins Carousel Game (Parker)	3 - 15
G1245	Disneyland (10 Anniversary) w/magic wheel	4 - 20
G1260	Robin Hood	2 - 10

G2000 GAMES — CARD

The Russell Manufacturing Co. ceased being a Disney licensee in 1986 ending a 41-year relationship. Whitman remains as the major supplier in this classification.

G2010	Mickey Mouse Old Maid Cards (3 designs)	6 - 35
G2067	Donald Duck Card Game (1st design)	5 - 25
G2000	Goofy Card Tricks (Whitman)	1 - 4

G2900 GAMES — ELECTRIC AND ELECTRONIC

G2933	Disneyland Electric Tours with Davy Crockett — 4 Games In One (Jacmar)	5 - 35
G2934	Sleeping Beauty — An Electric Game (Jacmar)	5 - 25

G3000 GAMES — PUZZLE

G3007	Jig Saw Lotto (Jaymar) small size	4 - 22
G3008	Character SCRAMBLE (Plane Facts)	5 - 35
G3019	Mickey Mouse Comic Picture Puzzle (Parker)	5 - 25

G1017

G1032

G1029

G2000

G1196

G1241

G2933

G3334

G3281

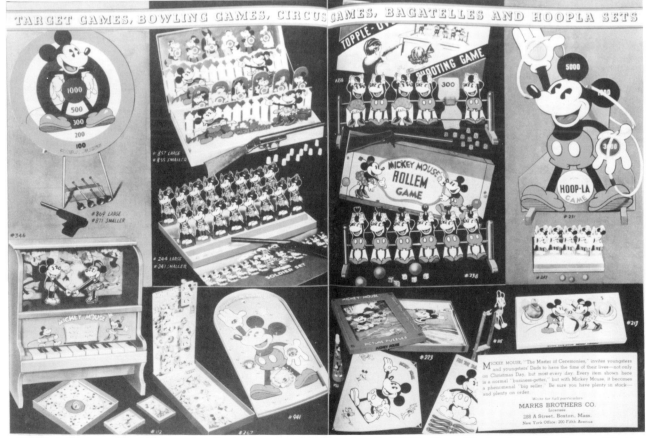

1935 Marks Brothers ad for skill games, plus other toys, games and puzzles — from the 1935 Kay Kamen Merchandise catalog. Items are listed in Volumes Two and Three.

G3200 GAMES — SKILL

G3281	Donald Duck Tiddley Winx (Jaymar)	5 - 25
G3291	Shooting Gallery (Lido)	5 - 25
G3334	Ludwig Von Drake Score-A-Matic Ball Toss Game (Transogram)	5 - 25
G3345	Donald Duck Fun Ball (Gardner)	4 - 18
G3358	Pinocchio Pic Ups	1 8

G5500 GOEBEL

The list of Disney Goebel figurines was the last section written in the first three volumes. The translated list arrived just in time for publication. The exact incised numbers have been determined for several more pieces. It is also fairly clear that only about the first 150 or so original issue pieces were sold in this country. A quantity of Tinker Bells (DIS 188) incised dated 1959 were imported in what remained of a 2,000 numbered edition firing. The source was Germany. The Disney theme parks are also selling new editions of many original mold Bambis and other figures. Some of the reissue Bambis have flies rather than the original butterflies on their tails. More pieces are coming out these days. Virtually all the pieces seen on the Goebel color page were found in less than a year at prices ranging less than quoted in Volume Two.

G6000 GOOD HOUSEKEEPING CHILDREN'S PAGES

The following is a list of all 125 monthly Good Housekeeping pages that appeared from April 1934 to Sept 1944 save Aug 1939 when no Disney page appeared. Values remain   1 4 for single color pages, 1-10 for featured sections from Snow White and the Seven Dwarfs or Pinocchio, and 1-6 for 2-color pages.

1934

Apr	The Grasshopper and the Ants
May	The Big Bad Wolf
June	The Wise Little Hen
July	The Flying Mouse
Aug	Peculiar Penguins
Sep	The Goddess of Spring
Oct	The Tortoise and the Hare
Nov	The Golden Touch
Dec	Water Babies

May 1935

G3291

G3358

Goebel Marks

Full Bee - 1950   Stylized - 1957

3 Line - 1964

Goebel
Goebel Bee - 1972

Goebel
Name - 1979 to date

G5099   G5100   G5122   G5075

G5111   G5120   G5101

1935

Jan	Mickey Mouse in The Band Concert
Feb	The Cookie Carnival
Mar	Mickey Mouse — Mickey's Garden
Apr	The Robber Kitten
May	Mickey Mouse — Mickey's Fire Brigade
June	Who Killed Cock Robin?
July	Mickey Mouse — Mickey's Magic Hat
Aug	Music Land
Sep	Cock of the Walk
Oct	Three Little Wolves
Nov	Mickey Mouse in On Ice
Dec	Broken Toys

1936

Jan	Mickey Mouse in Through the Mirror
Feb	Elmer Elephant
Mar	Mickey Mouse — Mickey's Rival
Apr	Mickey Mouse — Alpine Mickey
May	Mickey Mouse in Moving Day
June	Mickey Mouse — Mickey's Circus
July	The Three Mouseketeers
Aug	Toby Tortoise Returns
Sep	Mickey Mouse Presents Donald & Pluto
Oct	The Country Cousin
Nov	Mickey Mouse Presents Mickey's Elephant
Dec	More Kittens

1937

Jan	Mickey Mouse Presents Don Donald
Feb	Mickey Mouse Presents Mickey's Amateurs
Mar	Hiawatha
Apr	Mickey Mouse Presents Pluto's Quinpuplets
May	Mickey Mouse — Donald's Ostrich
June	Mickey Mouse Presents Clock Cleaners
July	Wynken, Blynken, and Nod
Aug	Mickey Mouse — The Boat Builders
Sep	Mickey Mouse — The Dog Show
Oct	Donald Duck — Lumberjack Donald
Nov	Snow White and the Seven Dwarfs — Part I
Dec	Snow White and the Seven Dwarfs — Part II

1938

Jan	Donald Duck — The Delivery Boy
Feb	Donald Duck — Antarctic Trappers
Mar	Mickey Mouse — Movie Makers
Apr	The Practical Pig
May	Donald Duck — Good Scouts
June	Mickey Mouse — Mickey's Parrot
July	Donald Duck — Donald's Golf Game
Aug	Donald Duck — Donald's Cousin Gus
Sep	Mickey Mouse — Beach Picnic
Oct	Mickey Mouse — Brave Little Tailor
Nov	Farmyard Symphony
Dec	Merbabies

1939

Jan	Donald Duck — Donald's Lucky Day
Feb	Mickey Mouse — Society Dog Show
Mar	Donald Duck — The Hockey Champ
Apr	The Ugly Duckling
May	Goofy and Wilbur
June	Mickey Mouse — The Pointer
July	Donald Duck — Sea Scouts
Aug	Note: No listing of Disney Page in Table of Contents for this Month
Sep	Donald Duck — Donald's Penguin
Oct	Pinocchio — Part I
Nov	Pinocchio — Part II
Dec	Donald Duck — Donald's Date

1940

Jan	Donald Duck — Officer Duck
Feb	Mickey Mouse — Ice Antics
Mar	Donald Duck — Donald's Elephant
Apr	Donald Duck — Billposters
May	Donald Duck — Donald's Vacation
June	Mickey Mouse — Bone Trouble
July	Mickey Mouse — Mickey's Magic Lamp
Aug	Donald Duck — Window Cleaners
Sep	Mickey Mouse — Mister Mouse Takes a Trip

Sep 1936

Mar 1937

Apr 1935

Apr 1938   Feb 1939

May 1934   Dec 1934

Oct	Donald Duck — Fire Chief
Nov	Donald Duck — Put-Put Troubles
Dec	Good Housekeeping Toy Festival

1941

Jan	Mickey Mouse — The Little Whirlwind
Feb	Mickey Mouse — Big-Hearted Pluto
Mar	Donald Duck — "Timber"
Apr	Goofy — "Goofy's Glider"
May	Donald Duck — "Golden Eggs"
June	Mickey Mouse — "A Gentleman's Gentleman"
July	Goofy — "Baggage Buster"
Aug	Mickey Mouse — "Canine Caddy"
Sep	Donald Duck — "Truant Officer Donald"
Oct	Pluto — "Lend A Paw"
Nov	Goofy — The Art of Skiing
Dec	Donald Duck — "Chef Donald"

1942

Jan	Mickey Mouse — "Mickey's Birthday Party"
Feb	Donald Duck — "Donald's Camera"
Mar	Goofy — The Art of Self-Defense
Apr	Mickey Mouse — "Symphony Hour"
May	Donald Duck — Donald's Garden
June	Goofy — El Gaucho Goofy
July	"Pluto At The Zoo"
Aug	"The Victory March"
Sep	Bambi — Part I
Oct	Bambi — Part II
Nov	Bambi — Part III
Dec	Mickey Mouse's Good-Neighbor Page — Lake Titicaca

1943

Jan	Mickey Mouse's Good-Neighbor Page — Jose Carioca
Feb	Mickey Mouse's Good-Neighbor Page — Pluto and the Armadillo
Mar	Mickey Mouse's Good-Neighbor Page — Pedro
Apr	Mickey Mouse's Good-Neighbor Page — The Cold-Blooded Penguin
May	Mickey Mouse's Good-Neighbor Page — The Pelican and the Snipe
June	Donald Duck in The Vanishing Private
July	Pluto Wins a Victory Through Air Power
Aug	Donald Duck — "Home Defense"
Sep	Goofy in "Victory Vehicles"
	New Tales From Old Mother Goose as told by Walt Disney
Oct	Mickey, Minnie & Donald — Fetch Water
Nov	Donald & Goofy — Pies
Dec	Mickey, Minnie & A Lamb

1944

Jan	Mickey, Minnie & Donald — Tarts
Feb	Mickey Mouse — Coo Coo Clock
Mar	Mickey, Minnie, Morty, Ferdy & Donald Three Pigs
Apr	
May	Minnie Mouse, Pluto & Spider
June	Mickey Mouse & Clara Cluck
July	Donald Duck & Nephews with Candle
Aug	Mickey Mouse & Figaro
Sep	Donald Duck as Humpty Dumpty

G9100 GUM CARDS, GUM WRAPPERS AND TRADING CARDS

G9101	Album for Gum Inc. 1-48	10 - 80
G9102	Album for Gum Inc. 49-96	10 - 90

G9101   G9102

H3000

G9759

H6000

J2074

H5975

J2051

K2000

H6000

H6000

G9205	Texas John Slaughter (?) Canadian, each	.50 - 1
G9255	Return to Oz Sticker set (44)	4 - 12
G9256	Return to Oz cards (24), set	3 - 8

G9700 GUNS, SWORDS AND OTHER PLAY WEAPONS

| G9759 | Sleeping Beauty Magic Bubble Wand (Gardner) | 5 - 25 |

H3000 HATS AND CAPS

In this volume are some hat lines from the late 40's plus the first squeak bill Donald Duck hat. The original was made of felt with plastic bill. In later versions the felt was replaced with plastic mesh.

H5975 HOME MOVIE TITLE CARDS

When Walt Disney Productions began to expand home entertainment marketing, home video was a few years off. Introduction of the Super 8 format gave a strong boost to home movie making and Disney film sales. Title cards for home movie making were used as a premium for those who purchased Disney films.

H6000 HOUSEHOLD GOODS, PRODUCTS AND MISCELLANEOUS

Some of the most esoteric uses of characters appear on household products. Items identified for this edition include — a promotion piece for a Snow White Laundry. (This 4-page flyer was included with Kay Kamen material recently uncovered, so there may have been an effort to create such laundries on a wide scale.) Shirt boards, c. 40's, used as stiffener for packaged, laundered shirts, set of 12, paid $4 each. Others were a switch plate cover from the early 50's, tissues from the 70's, air freshener and the recent Dixie cup promotions. Items in this classification rarely sell for more than 5 10.

H3000

H6000

J2000 JEWELRY (EXCEPT RINGS)

| J2051 | Mickey/Minnie mesh coin purse | 20 - 200 |
| J2074 | Box for Brier Mfg. Company Jewelry | 3 - 15 |

K2000 KEY CHAINS AND CASES

There were a number of "flasher" key chains. Most were Disneyland souvenirs, but one Mickey was from DELCO. These are valued 1-5. Virtually every new Disney promotion features a lucite key chain. These now go for .75-2.

K5000 KNIVES, POCKET

| K5060 | Jackknives (Richards of Sheffield), 5 designs, Mickey, Goofy, Donald, Baloo, Little John, each | 4 - 12 |

L1000 LAMPS, LAMPSHADES AND NIGHTLIGHTS

| L1073 | Ceiling globe | 15 - 50 |

H6000

K5060

K2000

L1073

H6000

L2000

L2000

L4600

L5000

L2000 LANTERNS, MAGIC AND SLIDES

The Mickey Mouse Toy Lantern Outfit was made by Ensign, Ltd., under an English license. Enough of them show up, however, to indicate Borgfeldt may have sold them in the U.S. The boxed set sells for 150-550 depending on the completeness and condition of the delicate glass slide sets and the magic lantern itself.

L4000 LETTERHEADS

A new promotional letterhead is created for virtually every Disney film, TV show or theme park promotional event. And, of course, each Disney operating company has a letterhead. Recent letterheads found blank or with letters or publicity material sell for around .25 to .50 each.

L4600 LICENSE PLATES

There was a 1971 "Walt Disney World Coming" plate and regular size auto license plates have been issued since 1976 at Disney theme parks. Disneyland has issued an annual plate since 1985. Value of the bicentennial plate is 3-15. Others are 1-5.

L5000 LOBBY CARDS

Selected lobby card sets have been sold at theme park Disneyana shops (as available) starting at $10 for complete 8 card sets in the envelope.

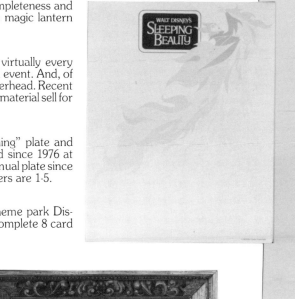

L4000

L5000

L4600

M2000

M2000

M2000

M2000

M2000

M3160

M3210 - M3260

M2000 MAGAZINES WITH DISNEY COVERS

The variety of magazines featuring Walt Disney characters on the cover seems endless. Values for magazines from the last 20 years is 1-8. Top values increase to 10-12 for good 50's and 60's issues, with 10-25 for top 30's and 40's material.

M3100 MASKS

M3103	Three Pigs, each	4 - 20
M3131	Wheaties — Mickey, Donald, Cinderella, Lucifer and Br'er Rabbit from set of 8, each	3 - 15
M3140	Mickey, 40's, cardboard	3 - 15
M3160	Mickey and Friends Playtime Masks	2 - 10
M3162	The Disney Book of Masks (Whitman)	1 - 3
M3165	Mickey, plastic (Ben Cooper)	1 - 4

M3200 MATCHES AND MATCH SAFES

There were two enameled match safe designs in the early 30's. Matchbooks from the studio commissary, the China Relief, and the Pepsi-Cola WWII insignia series offer examples from the late 30's and 40's. The vast majority of matchbooks have been generated by theme park events, shops, restaurants, and hotels. It is an area of Disneyana that offers a wide variety of graphics for little or no cost to theme park visitors.

M3203	3 Pigs match safe, orange or green enamel	10 - 40
M3204	Mickey/Minnie match safe	20 - 70
M3210	China Relief	2 - 8
	Pepsi Cola WWII insignia series (See W8000)	
M3220	Disneyland 50's or 60's	1 - 6
M3240	Disneyland 70's or 80's	.25 - 1
M3250	Walt Disney World or EPCOT	.10 - 1
M3260	Tokyo Disneyland	.25 - 1

M3900 MERCHANDISE CATALOGS

Catalogs from Kay Kamen and the Disney Merchandise Licensing Division provide the foundation of these books. Several other pieces have been acquired, and are listed below. Additions include licensee lists published for many years by the New York Disney office, the new Family Gift Catalogs being issued by the Mail Order Division and Merchandise Catalogs being prepared by the theme parks.

M3909	Envelopes for Kay Kamen catalogs	10 - 50
M3910	Merchandise Catalogs (Kamen)	175 - 600
M3919	Reproduction of 1935 & 1938 Catalogs	10 - 20
M3920	Merchandise division catalogs	5 - 20

M2000

M3131

M3909

M3919

M3162

M3140

M3910

M3980

M3103

M3165

M3920

M3955

M3980

M3980

M6415

N3000

M3920

| M3955 | Licensee lists | 1 - 10 |
| M3980 | Family Gift Catalogs or theme park merchandise catalogs | .25 - 1 |

M5000 MICKEY MOUSE EARS

| M5005 | Illustrated ears | 4 - 20 |

M5005

M5100 MICKEY MOUSE FAN CLUB

A new Mickey Mouse Fan Club was formed in 1986. Members receive newsletters, balloons, buttons (none special as yet) and other mailing stuffers of interest to young members. Obtain membership from — Mickey Mouse Fan Club, 5959 Triumph St., Commerce, CA 90040.

M5100

M6435

M6400 MOBILES

M6408	Pard Lady and the Tramp premium	5 - 25
M6415	Sleeping Beauty (plastic)	3 - 15
M6430	Peter Pan	2 - 7
M6435	Bedknobs and Broomsticks	1 - 5

M9000 MUSIC BOXES

M9122	Seven Dwarfs, each	10 - 25
M9179	Seven Dwarfs, each	10 - 30
M9190	Schmid ceramic music boxes, each	10 - 25

M9500 MUSICAL INSTRUMENTS

Whistles moved to W7920

M6408

N3000 NEWSPAPER COMIC STRIPS

The proof from King Features Syndicate shows how the daily strips are distributed in weekly installments. Also shown are 1957 examples from *A True Life Adventure* series distributed from March 14, 1955 to April 14, 1973.

M9122   M9179

M9190

M9190

N3000

O8001

P0415

P1235

P1238

P1262

P0505

O8000 OSWALD THE LUCKY RABBIT

Oswald the Lucky Rabbit was a character developed by the Disney Studio in 1927. His first film released was *Trolley Troubles*. In all, 26 titles were done by Disney before the copyright owner "hired" most of Walt's animators and went into production for himself. As a result of this crisis Mickey Mouse was created.

Oswald was the first Disney character merchandised on consumer products and thus played a historic role in Disneyana. There is, however, a complicating factor. Oswald merchandise was sold for many years after he ceased to be a Disney character and an Oswald comic was published until 1962. To further complicate matters, both the Disney and non-Disney films were distributed by Universal, the name in which all early Oswald character merchandise was copyrighted.

The Disney Oswald had longer, floppier ears than his successor, who was more generally known as *Oswald the Rabbit*. The positively identified Disney Oswald merchandise includes a pin back button, candy wrapper and display sign, celluloid figure and a stencil set. Merchandise known to exist, but uncertain to be Disney connected includes a Fisher Price paddle puppet, stuffed Oswald, and mechanical Oswald walking doll.

O8001	Stencil set (Universal Toy & Novelty Co.)	85 - 250
O8002	Pin back button (Philadelphia Badge Co.)	55 - 275
O8005	Candy wrapper (Vogan Candy Corp.)	?
O8006	Candy display sign (Vogan Candy Corp.)	?
O8010	Crib toy celluloid figure	35 - 160
O8015	Stuffed doll	30-90
O8018	Walking Oswald doll	200 - 400

P0400 PAINT BOXES AND SETS

P0415	Mickey Mouse paint set #204 (Marks Brothers)	45 - 300
P0468	Disneyland Color by Number Oil set	8 - 25
P0505	Mickey Mouse Club oil painting by numbers	6 - 20

P0800 PATCHES AND LABELS

P0808	Wornova Halloween costume patches, each	3 - 15
P0820	Theme park costume patches, each	5 - 25

P1200 PENNANTS

P1235	Disneyland 10th Anniversary	3 - 16
P1238	Disneyland 25th Anniversary	1 - 5
P1262	Walt Disney World 15th Anniversary	1 - 5

P1850 PIE BIRD

There was one Donald Duck ceramic pie bird known to the author. It doesn't appear in any merchandise catalogs. The piece has been seen nationwide and has been traced to a variety of estates. There are no marks to indicate the manufacturer, only the incised words "Donald Duck" on one side and "©Walt Disney" on the other. There have been many pie birds made for use in venting steam from the bottom of the pie during baking. Have seen this item priced from 50-150.

O8010
O8015

P0820
P0808
P1850

P2265 P2266 P2267 P2272 P2273 P2268 P2269 P2270

P2271 P2274 P2275 P2276 P2435 P2432

P0468

P2177

P2261

P2430

P2185

P2621

P2589 P2249 P2314 P2587 P2443 P2431

P2307 P2308 P2262 P2281

P2306 P2300 P2286 P2600 P2614

Coca-Cola carton promoting WDW 15th year pins

74

P1900 PINBACK BUTTONS, PINS AND BADGES

Pinback buttons and pins are a dominant collecting classification on the west coast, a mania in Southern California where it is not unusual for an item to be selling for $100 one day and $5 the next. The button boom has been around since 1984, but has failed to spread much beyond the immediate areas of Disneyland and Walt Disney World, the source of most buttons and pins. Collecting is further complicated by the number of reproductions and "privately" minted products. There are probably as many phoneys as there are Disney made or authorized pinback subjects. Some are quite interesting and worth having. This book attempts to stick with official issues, but it is hard to nail down certain pieces. Some legit issues are only used for a day or two.

There is a tendency toward more cloisonne pins. A series of such pins was used for the *Gift Giver Extraordinaire* promotion at Disneyland in 1986 and continued as part of the 15th Anniversary celebration at Walt Disney World in 1987. Coca-Cola also issued 60 different pins for the 15th year event. The promotion was offered to Coke bottlers nationwide, but was used differently in virtually every market where it appeared. Many bottlers did not participate. The pins were framed in sets of 60 for major Coke customers and for sale to Disney employees. They also came in a set of 24, three different sets of 8, and individually. Other anniversary celebrations, theme park events and attraction openings, ice shows, and character buttons for general retail sales summarize the new listings.

P2046

P2029

P2174

P2176

P2175

P2313   P2588   P2618

P2830

P2192

P2292   P2293   P2294   P2444

P2029	Bakery and grocer employee	70 - 350
P2046	Jiminy Cricket I'm No Fool About Safety tab	4 - 20
P2174	Disneyland Grad Nite '86 or '87	1 - 5
P2175	Walt Disney World Grad Nite '86 or '87	1 - 5
P2176	Grad Nite Pooh Bear buttons	1 - 7
P2177	Mickey's Christmas Carol	1 - 6
P2185	Cervantes Ties	2 - 15
P2191	FI-84 Rangers	2 - 10
P2192	Music Festival Program cloisonne pin	1 - 8
P2193	Videopolis	1 - 2
P2249	30th — Hollywood Bowl Concert	1 - 5
P2250	I Won a GM Car!	4 - 25
P2251	1986 Sword in the Stone	5 - 20
P2255	Disneyland 31st Birthday	1 - 4
P2260	Los Angeles Children's Museum Salutes Disneyland's 30th Anniversary Summer '85	2 - 10
P2261	Skyfest	2 - 8
P2262	Happy New Year ('86) Disneyland or WDW	1 - 5

Cloisonne pins from the Gift Giver Extraordinaire (P2265-2275)

P2265	Disneyland — Mickey beating a drum	2 - 8
P2266	Main Street — Mickey on an old time bike	1 - 2
P2267	Adventureland — Goofy in safari hat	1 - 2
P2268	New Orleans Square — Br'er Fox playing a sax	4 - 20
P2269	New Orleans Square — Mickey playing trumpet, gold lettering	3 - 12
P2270	Same as P2269, but with red lettering	1 - 4
P2271	Bear Country — Bear with guitar	1 - 2
P2272	Frontierland — Peg Leg Pete, with pointed star	3 - 12
P2273	Same as P2272, but with gold dots on star points to blunt them	1 - 2
P2274	Fantasyland — Mickey as Sorcerer's Apprentice	1 - 2
P2275	Tomorrowland Donald in space suit, with sharp point on lighting bolt	2 - 10
P2276	Same as P2275, but with point of lighting bolt rounded	1 - 2
P2281	Disneyland Circus Fantasy '86 or '87	2 - 8
P2284	Don't be late . . . Disneyland	5 - 25
P2286	Disneyland '86 Spring or Fall Tour, each	5 - 25
P2287	Win A Car — Grads Have More Fun At Grad Nite '86	3 - 15
P2288	Hands Across America — May 25, 1986	5 - 28
P2290	Totally Minnie	1 - 3
P2292	Captain EO, purple background	1 - 2
P2293	Captain EO, black background	1 - 2
P2294	Captain EO, cloisonne, black background, Disneyland or WDW	2 - 4

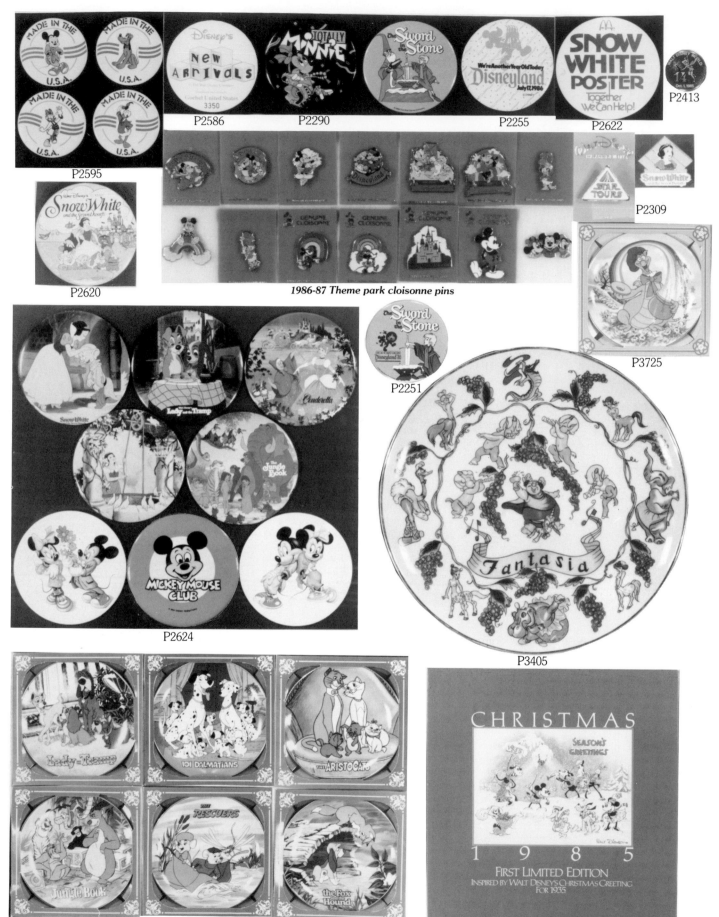

P2595

P2586

P2290

P2255

P2622

P2413

1986-87 Theme park cloisonne pins

P2309

P2620

P3725

P2251

P2624

P3405

P3730

P3740

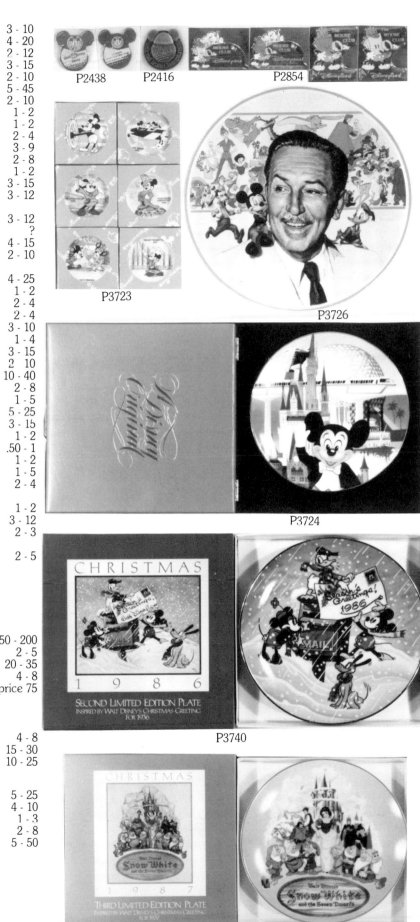

P2296	Captain EO, cloisonne, gold background	3 - 10
P2298	Captain EO, silver, hologram	4 - 20
P2300	Disneyland Comes to the Fashion Show Mall	2 - 12
P2301	Ogden Welcomes Mickey & Friends	3 - 15
P2302	Korean Festival Disneyland	2 - 10
P2305	Star Tours aviator wings, press giveaway	5 - 45
P2306	Star Tours black background	2 - 10
P2307	Star Tours, logo only	1 - 2
P2308	Star Tours, with Droids	1 - 2
P2309	Star Tours logo cloisonne	2 - 4
P2312	Grad Nite cloisonne	3 - 9
P2313	Disneyland Hotel Fantasia shop Mickey	2 - 8
P2314	Disneyland Hotel	1 - 2
P2412	Tour World Showcase Time Trial	3 - 15
P2413	Walt Disney World 14th birthday	3 - 12
P2414	Sport Goofy Trophy (TWA, Adidas, Coca-Cola)	3 - 12
P2416	WDW Golf Classic (11 different)	?
P2425	King Kamehameha is Koming	4 - 15
P2427	Crockett's Tavern	2 - 10
P2430	15 Years Happy Birthday Walt Disney World light-up	4 - 25
P2431	15 Years Walt Disney World	1 - 2
P2432	15 Years Happy Birthday cloisonne pin	2 - 4
P2435	Liberty Square cloisonne pin	2 - 4
P2438	WDW Golf Classic cloisonne pin	3 - 10
P2439	Team Mickey's Athletic Club	1 - 4
P2442	Happy 53rd Birthday, Donald (June 9, 1987)	3 - 15
P2443	Empress Lilly 10th Anniversary	2 - 10
P2444	The American Adventure costume pin	10 - 40
P2586	Goebel New Arrivals	2 - 8
P2587	I Love Walt Disney Films	1 - 5
P2588	WED/MAPO Halloween '85	5 - 25
P2589	Imagineering Open House 1986	3 - 15
P2595	One Stop Poster Made in USA series, each	1 - 2
P2600	One Stop Poster "Wise crack" series, each	.50 - 1
P2614	The Disney Store	1 - 2
P2618	Mickey Mouse Club	1 - 5
P2620	Snow White 50th Anniversary, 3"	2 - 4
P2621	Snow White and the Seven Dwarf set, wood grain boarders (8), each	1 - 2
P2622	McDonald's employee Snow White poster	3 - 12
P2624	6" character buttons (15), each	2 - 3
P2830	Ice Show 86-87, Sport Goofy (2), Wuzzles, Gummi Bears, w/ribbons, Snow White, each	2 - 5
P2854	5th Mouse Club Convention pins (Limited editions of 600 w/gold bags & 400 w/brown bags over Mickey's head — 2 designs.) Sold for $6 each at 1987 convention.	

P3400 PLATES — COLLECTOR'S

P3405	Fantasia, 50's Disneyland souvenir	50 - 200
P3723	Mickey's Greatest Moments miniatures, each	2 - 5
P3724	Walt Disney World 15th Anniversary	20 - 35
P3725	Figment from EPCOT Center	4 - 8
P3726	Walt Disney	Retail price 75
P3730	Disney Classics, Lady and the Tramp, 101 Dalmatians, The Aristocats, The Jungle Book, The Rescuers, and The Fox and the Hound, each	4 - 8
P3739	Snow White 50th Anniversary	15 - 30
P3740	Christmas plates 1986 and 87, each	10 - 25

P6000 POSTCARDS

P6054	Disneyland die-cut, each	5 - 25
P6062	Disneyland 3-D, set of 4, each	4 - 10
P6065	'60's Disneyland scenes	1 - 3
P6066	Disneyland souvenir folders, each	2 - 8
P6067	13 Panorama views	5 - 50

P6067

P6066

P6065

How To Catch a Cold—
Stay out in the rain.

From the film
"HOW TO CATCH A COLD"
by Walt Disney Productions

P6062

P7550

How To Catch a Cold—
Park yourself in a cool stiff breeze.

From the film
"HOW TO CATCH A COLD"
by Walt Disney Productions

P8120

P7550

P6577

P6054

P6073

P6073   Captain EO or Videopolis, bumper sticker
        postcards, each   1 - 2

P6500 POSTERS — OTHERS
P6575   Kite safety poster   20 - 60
P6577   Kleenex industrial film posters, each   15 - 30

P7250 PRINTING SETS
P7261   Pinocchio Art Stamp Picture Set (Fulton)
        large size   28 - 95
P7286   Mickey Mouse Rubber Stamp set   1 - 3

P7300 PRINTS — ART AND FRAMED PICTURES
P7320   Citroen luminous pictures — Mickey, Dopey,
        Doc and Grumpy, each   2 - 12
P7351   The Band (Boyer)   35 - 80
P7353   Tokyo Disneyland (Boyer)   50 - 180

P7550 PUBLICATIONS
    Disney News has been the exclusive publication of the Magic Kingdom Club since 1965. The Disneyana Collector has been published by Grolier since Summer 1982. These publications provide information on the Walt Disney Company and, on occasion, about collecting Disneyana. It is only natural that the publications themselves become collectible. They are only worth about 1-4 now, but worth keeping.

P8000 PUPPETS AND MARIONETTES
P8075   Peter Puppet marionettes, Mickey, Minnie,
        Alice, Dopey, Peter Pan, Wendy and Captain
        Hook, each   10 - 45
P8110   Pocket Puppets, Mickey, Donald, Goofy,
        Pinocchio, each   1 - 8
P8120   Hand puppets, vinyl   1 - 7
P8130   Storytime Puppets (Whitman)   1 - 4

P6575

P7320

P6040

P7286

P7550

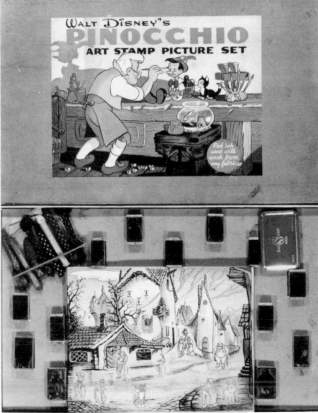

P7261

P8075

P9535

P8110

P8130

P9530

P9631

P9680

P9000 PUZZLES AND PUZZLE SETS

P9206	Marks Brothers picture puzzles, each	10 - 30
P9525	Pinocchio Picture Puzzles (2) boxed (1939) Whitman	12 - 50
P9526	Pinocchio jigsaw Jaymar	4 - 15
P9530	Dumbo puzzle set (3) Ontex	8 - 24
P9532	The Band Concert stand-up puzzle Jaymar	10 - 50
P9535	Flying Donkey jigsaw	5 - 18
P9580	Jaymar tray puzzles (1947) Set of 4	8 - 32
P9610	Cinderella jigsaw	3 - 15
P9631	Peter Pan Picture Puzzles (6) boxed set	18 - 55
P9650	Lady and the Tramp, jigsaw or tray, each	3 - 12
P9660	Mickey Mouse Club, jigsaw or tray, each	3 - 12

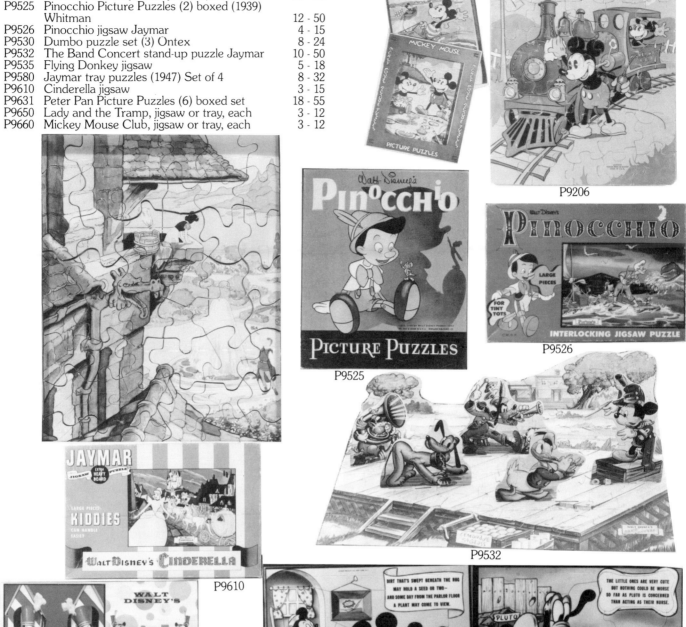

P9206

P9525

P9526

P9532

P9610

P9760

P9580

P9760

R3200   R3023   R3024

| P9680 | Disneyland, jigsaw or tray, each | 3 - 12 |
| P9760 | Other jigsaw or tray, 60's | 2 - 10 |

R3000 RECORDS, PHONOGRAPH

R3014	Pinocchio, illustrated (Victor) 78 rpm album	25 - 100
R3023	Bambi (RCA) 78 rpm	4 - 24
R3024	Snow White (RCA) 78 rpm in album	15 - 65
R3026	Peter and the Wolf (RCA) 78 rpm	3 - 20
R3030	Johnny Appleseed (Decca) 78 or 45 rpm	6 - 30
R3031	Ichabod and Mr. Toad (Decca) 78 or 45 rpm	3 - 20
R3056	The Sorcerer's Apprentice (Capitol) 78 rpm	5 - 25
R3200	Little Golden Records	1 - 7
R3200	Theme park series	1 - 10
R3200	Sleeping Beauty titles	1 - 10
R3549	Wheaties Mickey Mouse Club package back records, each	2 - 8
	Disneyland On Records (See D5140)	
R3550	33 1/3 LP Albums, 50's	1 - 15

P9650

R3030

R3026

See D5140

R4220

R3031

R3056

R3549

R3551

R3557

R3556

R3014

R3200

R3550

R3200

R3600

R3700

R5000 RINGS

R5041 Weather Bird Pinocchio ring   20 - 100
R5043 Sugar Jets series of 8 character rings —
      Mickey, Minnie, Donald, Pluto, Dumbo,
      Snow White, Pinocchio, and Peter Pan, each   3 - 15

R6000 ROCKING HORSES, BOUNCE, SPRING ACTION AND OTHER PLAY EQUIPMENT

R6009 Mickey, riding scooter (Mengel)   75 - 300
R6016 Donald see saw   50 - 200
R6017 Donald shoofly rocker   25 - 175
R6018 Snow White and Prince shoofly rocker   35 - 200

S2300 SCRAPBOOKS AND PHOTO ALBUMS

S2303 Three Pigs scrapbook   10 - 45
S2310 Pinocchio (Whitman) #634   15 - 50
S2313 Comic art scrap books, each   5 - 20
S2315 Mickey Mouse Club (Whitman) #1863   4 - 18

R6009

R6017

S2303

R5041

S2310

R5043

87

S2800 SEWING, NEEDLEWORK, EMBROIDERY, ETC.

S2810	Vogue needlework sets, each	5 - 55
S2843	Peter Pan Sewing Cards, boxed set	4 - 20
S2849	Disneyland Lacing Card Set (1955)	5 - 50

S2313

R6016

Counted cross stitch from S2870

S2315

S2843

S2849

S2810

S3000 EVAN K. SHAW COMPANY

The Evan K. Shaw Company was one of the most prolific manufacturers of ceramic figures in the 40's and 50's. Shaw figures were also sold as the products of American Pottery and Metlox Poppytrail Pottery. American Pottery was licensed two years before Shaw, and dual licenses existed for a few years in the 40's. The reason could be a company name change, Shaw was simply a distributor for several makers, a Shaw buy out of American, a separate business division, or perhaps another reason lost in the records.

A record of the ceramic pieces sold by Shaw, however, is complete. In fact, the workshop inventory of Disney figures was stored when all licensing rights expired. This stock was sold in 1986 and made available to collectors. It included the miniature figures produced near the end of Shaw's license and rarely seen prior to this discovery. A very special "thank you" goes to Bob Molinari for help in providing corrections to Volumes 1 and 3 regarding American Pottery and Evan K. Shaw, as well as background for the expanded list of Shaw figures seen below. The

S3096   S3084   S3086

S3086

S3002

S3005   S3006   S3004 S3007 S3030   S3003

S3008

S3010   S3026

97

S3001

S3055   S3058   S3051   S3054

S3052

S3040

S3044   S3046   S3048   S3041

Shaw figures seen on the color pages are from Bob's collection. Bob Molinari is the owner of *Fantasies Come True*, an exclusively Disneyana shop, 7408 Melrose Ave., Los Angeles, CA 90046. The code numbers have been revised in this section to reflect the additions and corrections made. High end prices are mainly obtainable on the West coast where ceramic collecting is very popular and where earthquake damage has placed a premium on mint specimen originals with tags.

Code	Description	Price
S3001	Snow White and the Seven Dwarfs, 5″ to 8″, set	500 - 1200
S3002	Bambi or Faline (9 versions produced in two general sizes, approximately 7″ and 10″ — see S3061 for miniatures and fourth size figures) large approximate 10″, each	40 - 150
S3003	medium approximate 7″, each	40 - 150
S3004	Thumper or Thumper's girl friend large 4″	20 - 40
S3005	medium 2 1/2″	30 - 60
S3006	Flower, large 4″	20 - 45
S3007	Flower, 2 1/2″	20 - 45
S3008	Mickey or Minnie 7″	60 - 150
S3009	(often marked "Mexico") 4″	30 - 90
S3010	Donald, Jose or Panchito, each	75 - 200
S3014	Dumbo, standing or sitting up, each	40 - 120
S3016	Little Toot	200 - 400
S3017	Large Thumper planter	100 - 250
S3018	Large Flower planter	100 - 250
S3019	Pottie	400 - 1500
S3020	Pinocchio or Jiminy Cricket, each	150 - 400
S3022	Figaro, 2 running, 1 seated, each	50 - 200
S3026	Pluto, 4 different poses, each	20 - 150
S3030	Owl, 2 1/2″	50-150
S3032	Br'er Rabbit planter	100 - 400
S3033	Planters, Bambi, Thumper, or Flower, on log, each	75 - 250
S3034	Planters, Donald in boat or Pluto in doghouse, each	50 - 200
S3036	Large Bambi planter	100 - 250
S3037	Planters, Donald beehive or Minnie w/buggy, each	50 - 200
S3039	Stag (Adult Bambi)	90 - 500
S3040	Cinderella in rags	100 - 400
S3041	Cinderella or Prince dressed for the ball, each	75 - 300
S3044	Bruno, sitting or prone	50 - 150

S3093   S3089   S3092

S3061

S3036   S3033   S3018

S3037   S3034

S3081   S3079

S3077   S3069   S3072

Walt Disney's
The Ballad of
DAVY CROCKETT
...and songs of the period

S3283

Walt Disney's
Lady and the Tramp

S3283

Mary Poppins
SOUVENIR SONG ALBUM

S3311

S3362

S3450   S3450   S3450

S3046	Gus or Jaq, each	35 - 125
S3048	Bluebirds, Mama Mouse or Baby Mouse, each	50 - 150
S3051	Alice In Wonderland (There was a typographical error on this piece in the first edition Volume Three)	75 - 300
S3052	Tweedle Dee or Tweedle Dum, each	50 - 200
S3054	Walrus	50 - 200
S3055	March Hare, White Rabbit or Mad Hatter, each	50 - 200
S3058	Doormouse	50 - 150
S3059	*Fantasia* and *Dumbo* figures from Vernon Kilns molds were sold as American Pottery. The absence of Vernon Kilns marks and glaze on the bottom usually indicates an American Pottery piece. Elephants, Hippos and Dumbo figures have been seen. They are currently selling for 20% to 40% below prices for Vernon Kilns (See V3000).	

In Volume Three there was possible confusion between the medium Shaw figures identified in this volume as S3003, S3005, S3007, S3009, and the miniature series produced in 1955-56. These were made as Poppytrail Pottery figures by Metlox Manufacturing Company, Manhattan Beach, CA. The line was called Walt Disney's World of Enchantment in Ceramics. In addition to the figures listed below, there was a fire plug and ceramic dog house. There were also a few figures produced in a fourth size between the medium and the miniatures.

S3061	Snow White and the Seven Dwarfs, set	200 - 600
S3062	Peter Pan, sitting or standing, each	50 - 150
S3064	Tinker Bell or Mermaid, each	50 - 300
S3066	Wendy, Michael, or Nana, each	40 - 100
S3069	Lady or Tramp, each	20 - 65
S3071	Peg	50 - 100
S3072	Jock, Trusty, Dachshund, or Limey, each	15 - 50
S3076	Si, Am or Scamp Pup, each	50 - 100
S3077	Pup#1, Pup#2 or Pup#3, each	20 - 60
S3078	Bambi with butterfly	30 - 90
S3079	Bambi, standing or prone, each	30 - 80
S3081	Thumper, Flower w/Flower, or Flower w/o Flower, each	20 - 50
S3084	Dumbo or Timothy, each	40 - 150
S3086	Pinocchio, Figaro, or Jiminy Cricket, each	40 - 150
S3089	Mickey or Donald, 2 sizes, each	30 - 80
S3092	Pluto	40 - 120
S3093	Huey, Louie or Dewey, each	20 - 40
S3096	Three Little Pigs (3), each	20 - 40
S3099	Stormy, standing or prone, each	10 - 30

S3100 SHEET MUSIC, FOLIOS AND MUSIC BOOKS

S3224	Mickey Mouse's Birthday Party (1948), Bourne	4 - 10
S3283	Disneyland Music Books (Hansen Publications) 1955 — The Ballad of Davy Crockett, Lady and the Tramp and other titles listed in Volume Three	5 - 12
S3289	Mickey Mouse March (Hansen)	5 - 15
S3311	Mary Poppins Souvenir Song Album	3 - 10

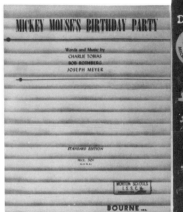

S3224   S3289

S3450

S3315

S7000

15 YEARS

Walt Disney World

S3450

Sam the Olympic Eagle

© 1980 L.A. Olympic Committee

Official Olympic Souvenir Bag

S3450

Tokyo Disneyland

S3450

DISNEYLAND
ALWEG-MONORAIL

World Rights reserved

Schuco

T5000

T5025

MERRY CHRISTMAS
Tokyo Disneyland

Tokyo Disneyland
OPENING, SPRING OF 1983

Family Entertainment

T9047

| S3315 | Jungle Book (Wonderland) | 2 - 8 |
| S3362 | Sherman Brothers Bicentennial song | 1 - 5 |

S3450 SHOPPING BAGS

Disneyland and Walt Disney World used the same colorful plastic shopping bags for several years. A special one was used for America on Parade and there have been several design changes since. All in all, they make a colorful display. Value 1-4 each.

S7000 STICKERS AND STICKER BOOKS

More Panini stickers and albums are being sold in the U.S. The Aristocats, 101 Dalmatians, and Snow White were marketed during 1986-87. These, however, were abbreviated versions of the same titles sold in Canada and Europe. Value 15-35 for complete sets and albums.

T5000 TOKYO DISNEYLAND

Tokyo Disneyland has continued to develop (See Disney Time Line) and the merchandise has been extremely well done, but well beyond the scope of this book. U.S. collecting interest has been buttons, and there have been many. A sample is shown. Souvenir maps are also now being issued.

T5025	Character souvenir buttons, each	2 - 10
T5026	Special promotion buttons, each	4 - 20
T5028	Press or employee buttons, each	10 - 70
T5031	Cinderella Castle Magic Mystery Tour opening day holograph key ring	5 - 15

Tokyo Disneyland merchandise may be obtained from Tokyo Disneyland Mail Order Service c/o Merchandise Division 1-1, Maihama, Urayasu-shi, Chiba-ken, 270-01 Japan.

T9000 TRAINS AND HANDCARS

The second version of the Schuco Disneyland Alweg monorail has been identified. It is blue with one less car. The color of the monorail train is red in the larger set. These sets, licensed and produced in Germany, were imported and sold at Disneyland in 1962-63 for around $30. Pride Lines did a great train for the 50th Anniversary of Snow White.

| T9047 | Blue monorail set (Schuco) | 200 - 400 |
| T9048 | Red monorail set (Schuco) | 250 - 500 |

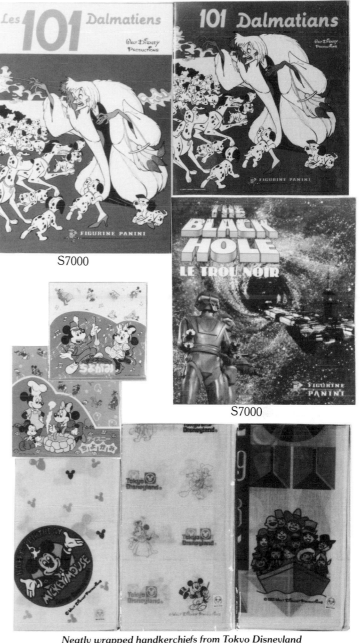

S7000

S7000

T5026   T5026

Neatly wrapped handkerchiefs from Tokyo Disneyland

T5000

V1526

V1527　　　　　V1527

T9222

V1526　　　　　V1527　　　　　V1526

U6004

V1529

V3032　　V3033　　V3034　　　V3029　　V3027　　　V3025

V3028

T9200 TRAYS

T9221	Disneyland map tray	5 - 20
T9222	Swift and Company Disneyland tray	5 - 25
T9250	Trays, 70's or 80's	1 - 6

U6000 UMBRELLAS

U6004	Borgfeldt Mickey design	45 - 120

V1500 VALENTINES

V1525	Snow White or Pinocchio regular Valentines, each	1 - 10
V1526	Snow White or Pinocchio small mechanical	2 - 10
V1527	Snow White or Pinocchio large mechanical	5 - 30
V1528	Main characters, regular	2 - 12
V1529	Main characters, mechanical	3 - 20
V1535	Mechanical set (1957), each	1 - 6

V3000 VERNON KILNS CERAMICS

Vernon Potteries, Ltd. (LA) was a Disney licensee from Oct 10, 1940 to July 22, 1942 when they assigned all rights, inventory and molds to American Pottery Company. In that short time the company distinguished itself as a major contributor to Disneyana. Thirty-six of the forty-two figurines, all eight bowls and vases, plus all the company's Disney china patterns were based on *Fantasia*. The figures are museum quality art. Each figure has a number incised in the unglazed cavity, plus ink markings — "Disney Copyright 1940 (or 41) Vernon Kilns U.S.A." The last digit(s) in the Tomart number is (are) identical to the number incised on Vernon Kilns figures, bowls and vases. Photos are from the collection of Bob Molinari.

V3001-		
V3006	Satyrs, 4-1/2", each different	35 - 100
V3007-		
V3012	Sprites, standing, each different	45 - 120
V3008	Reclining Sprite	40 - 160
V3013	Unicorn, black with yellow horn	70 - 165
V3014	Sitting Unicorn, 5"	100 - 220
V3015	Rearing Unicorn, 6"	100 - 230
V3016	Donkey Unicorn, 5-1/2"	125 - 270
V3017	Reclining Centaurette, 5-1/2"	110 - 240
V3018	Centaurette, 7-1/2"	150 - 300
V3019	Baby Pegasus, black, 4-1/2	60 - 175

T9221

V1535

V3038

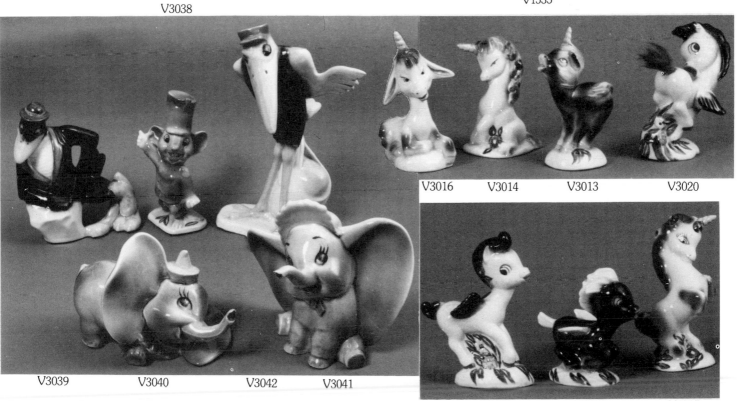

V3039   V3040   V3042   V3041

V3016   V3014   V3013   V3020

V3021   V3019   V3015

105

V3024   V3018   V3031   V3017   V3022   V3023

V3001-V3006   V3007-V3012   V3008

W1923

W1923

W1923

W1916   W2031   W1952

V3020	White Pegasus, head turned, 5"	60 - 175
V3021	White Pegasus, 5-1/2"	60 - 175
V3022	Centaurette, 7-1/2"	125 - 350
V3023	Nubian Centaurette, 8"	150 - 375
V3024	Nubian Centaurette, 7-1/2"	150 - 375
V3025	Elephant, 5"	140 - 245
V3026	Elephant, trunk raised	150 - 280
V3027	Elephant, dancing, 5-1/2"	150 - 260
V3028	Ostrich, 6"	175 - 350
V3029	Ostrich, 8"	175 - 350
V3030	Ostrich, 9"	195 - 400
V3031	Centaur, 10"	450 - 650
V3032	Hippo, arm outstretched, 5-1/2"	140 - 245
V3033	Hippo	100 - 225
V3034	Hippo, 5"	100 - 225
V3035-36	Hop Low mushroom salt and pepper set	75 - 100
V3037	Baby Weems	110 - 300
V3038	Timothy Mouse	75 - 125
V3039	Crow	175 - 350
V3040	Dumbo, falling on his ear	20 - 50
V3041	Dumbo, standing	45 - 85
V3042	Mr. Stork	175 - 450

(Higher values on bowls and vases are for hand painted rather than solid colors)

V3120	Mushroom bowl	35 - 125
V3121	Goldfish bowl	70 - 200
V3122	Winged Nymph bowl	45 - 150
V3123	Winged Nymph vase	100 - 185
V3124	Satyr bowl	75 - 135
V3125	Sprite bowl	90 - 155
V3126	Goddess vase	100 - 210
V3127	Pegasus vase	110 - 225

There were two basic designs to Vernon Kilns china dinnerware plate patterns — a border and a full plate design. The teapot, cream and sugar and salt and pepper are particularly attractive pieces in the set. Asking prices on dinnerware are 30-50 per large plate up to several hundred for a teapot, cream and sugar set in the most sought after patterns. The author has first hand knowledge of only one dinnerware sale — four dinner plates for 30 each and a complete service for 8 for 1500.

V3123   V3124   V3127   V3120   V3121

W1900 WALT DISNEY WORLD

Walt Disney World's Magic Kingdom has been slow to expand since the opening of *EPCOT Center*. Special events have been the main focus. The 15th year celebration was the main event covered by this volume. The Gift Giver promotion was moved from Disneyland and the 15-year logo was merchandised throughout the park.

W1914	Liberty Square Declaration of Independence given to children who join fife and drum corps for Liberty ceremony	5 - 25
W1916	Haunted Mansion souvenir tombstone	3 - 12
W1923	Hotel newspapers, 1985-87, each	1 - 3
W1951	Operating supplies, 15th year, each	.50 - 3
W1952	Illustrated Dixie Crystal sugar bags, each	1 - 2
W1953	Fun Meal box	.50 - 1
W1980	Pirates of the Caribbean purse	2 - 4
W2030	15th year history book	5 - 15
W2031	I'm a winner sticker	1 - 2

W1980

W2030

W1953

W1914

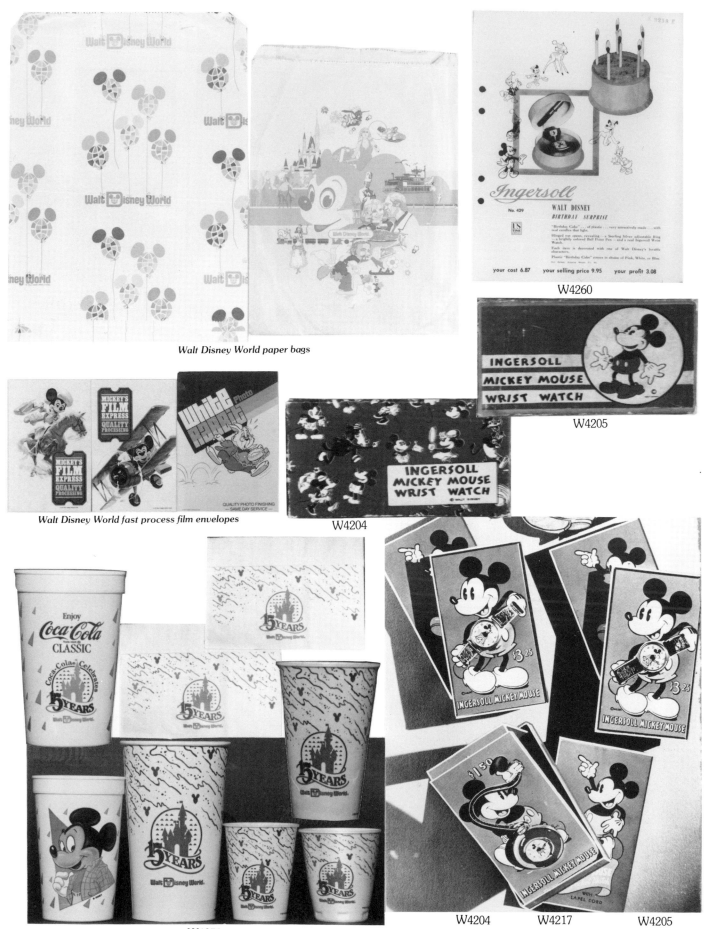

Walt Disney World paper bags

W4260

W4205

Walt Disney World fast process film envelopes

W4204

W1951

W4204   W4217   W4205

W4200 WATCHES

There have been well over 300 Disney character and theme park watches produced . . . many in very limited editions for use as awards or special events. The variety of watches produced accelerated rapidly in 1971. Specialized collecting interest grew with the variety of time pieces. Still, the older watches maintain the greatest value. There were over 6 million of the first Mickey Mouse wrist watches made. You'll find one for sale at any good size antique toy or advertising show. Every collector wants one because it was the first. Yet few are willing to spend much on a limited edition theme park watch that is much rarer. The price guidelines listed in this section are for values identified.

W4203

W4203   W4205

Ingersoll-Waterbury Company (W4203-W4230)

W4203	Mickey Mouse pocket watch	80 - 200
W4204	Mickey Mouse wrist watch — metal band	65 - 175
W4205	Mickey wrist watch — leather band with metal Mickeys	75-185
W4207	Sterling Advertising fob	50 - 250
W4210	Three Pigs and Wolf pocket watch and fob	150 - 400
W4211	Three Pigs and Wolf wrist watch	75 - 200
W4217	Mickey lapel watch with decal on back	100 - 250
W4218	Same as W4217, Donald is main figure	150 - 350
W4224	Rectangular Mickey wrist watch with revolving Mickey second hand	100 - 200
W4225	Same as W4224, but deluxe version with Mickey and Donald charms on band	150 - 250
W4226	Same as W4224, but regular second hand	50 - 135
W4230	Donald Duck pocket watch with Mickey decal on reverse	100 - 250

Ingersoll/U.S. Time (W4240-W4299)

W4240	Mickey, rectangular pupil eyes (1946)	35 - 95
W4241	Donald, rectangular (1946)	60 - 150
W4242	Snow White or Daisy, rectangular	100 - 175
W4243	Little Pig or Louie, rectangular	100 - 200
W4245	Mickey, head only (Kelton/U.S. Time)	75 - 150
W4246	Mickey, round, two sizes (1947)	20 - 80
W4248	Donald round, adult (1947)	30 - 90
W4249	In 1948 Ingersoll offered 10 different character watches with luminous hand dials. This 20th birthday watch promotion featured Mickey, Donald, Daisy, Pluto, Bongo, Pinocchio, Jiminy Cricket, Dopey, Joe Carioca and Bambi, each	20 - 85
W4260	Mickey's 20th birthday watch in cake box	100 - 200
W4261	In 1949 the same series was reoffered in special boxes that included a ball point pen with Mickey or Donald decal, boxed, each	55 - 125
W4270	Danny (1949)	50 - 175
W4275	Cinderella wrist watch, came in silver slipper box	15 - 55
W4280	Davy Crockett wrist watch	15 - 55
W4282	Zorro wrist watch (Name only), hat box	10 - 40
W4285	Cinderella, Snow White and Alice in Wonderland wrist watches with ceramic statuettes of namesake, with name only on watch dial, each	20 - 55
W4288	Same as W4285, except figures are plastic and image appears on each watch	10 - 30

W4246

W4261

INGERSOLL
THREE LITTLE PIGS ALARM CLOCK

The Big Bad Wolf's hungry jaws open and close in rhythm to the clock tick. It's a great clock and a sure-fire seller. The dial and case are bright red. The display carton in which the clock is packed has original Walt Disney drawings on it. You'll sell a lot of these clocks. $1.50 retail. $1.05 trade.

FREE display card for the 3 Little Pigs Watch. The pigs and wolf drawn by Walt Disney himself. A sure "stopper" for your window.

Ingersoll Three Little Pigs Watch and Fob

The wolf's evil eye is winking. The 3 Little Pigs are right there on the red dial. It's a great watch and you ought to sell a pile of 'em! The back makes the watch a good luck token because it has a personal message from Walt Disney: "May the big bad wolf never come to your door"... But loads of customers will come into your door if you display the watch in your window. $1.50 retail. $1.05 trade.

NEW MICKEY MOUSE
Alarm Clock

On the dial is an animated Mickey Mouse head wagging, hands pointing the time. Choice of red or green case. Packed in a self-display carton which makes selling easy. $1.50 retail, $1.05 trade.

MICKEY MOUSE DISPLAY

—a sure attention-getter for your windows. Also valuable as a counter sales-card. Places on it for 3 pocket watches and 2 wrist watches. FREE DISPLAY.

INGERSOLL MICKEY MOUSE POCKET WATCH AND FOB—

complete in a colorful gift box. Mickey's own hands point the time, getting into comical positions doing so. It's the watch sensation of the decade and a wonderful value at $1.50 retail. $1.05 trade.

INGERSOLL MICKEY MOUSE WRIST WATCH—

with Mickey's hands telling the time. A million have already been sold—more millions will be. Leather band or metal Mickey Mouse strap. $3.75 retail. $2.50 trade.

W4299 Mickey Mouse or Donald Duck wrist watch,
no image, name only   10 - 25
W4300 Mickey Mouse Timex Electric (1970)   150 - 300

Elgin National Industries/Bradley Time (W4325-W4600)

Elgin and Bradley Time continued innovative packaging and added a lot of product excitement by reintroducing pocket watches, pendant and lapel watches, animated and digital wrist watches, plus special edition watches. The number of different watches produced since 1972 far exceed the number of Ingersoll/ U.S. Time/Timex watches produced from 1933-1971. These are categorized rather than identified by individual watch.

W4325 Child's character wrist watch, regular	15 - 40
W4350 Special event wrist watch	20 - 60
W4375 Regular and Railroad pocket watches, each	15 - 75
W4390 Special event pocket watches, each	25 - 100
W4400 Numbered special editions, each	20 - 75
W4425 Same as W4400, but precious metal, each	50 - 350
W4426 Golf Classic gift watches	?
W4500 Animated children's wrist watches, each	20 - 50
W4600 Children's plastic play watches, each	1 - 4

The next section provides a detailed list of post-1971 watches priced in the above categories. The values given fairly well cover the entire list of Disney models produced from 1971 through 1985. The major exception is the 1972 Goofy "backwards" watch valued at 75-400. Lorus division of Seiko became the licensee in 1986, and shows 52 different character watches in their 1987 retail catalog.

1960's Round dial, 1″ in diameter, Mickey is holding a hat (Seiko), plastic case

1967-69 Round dial, 1' in diameter with sweep second hand, labeled "Disneyland" above figure. Made in Japan by Hamilton (Vantage) and sold only at Disneyland. There was also an electric version, and one with a clear plastic back. The first 500 had white gloves on Mickey

1968-71 Round dial, 1' in diameter, labeled "Ingersoll/ c. WDP" Black numbers, Numeral 5 on foot, some versions do not have the Ingersoll name, #160101

Winnie the Pooh and honey pot (1969)

1969-71 Round dial, 17 jewel, made by Windert for sale at Disneyland, "Disneyland" above figure. Also two versions with 3/4″ dial, one with yellow point at end of its second hand (#10035/1762)

Snow White and Dopey (1970) heads only

Cinderella bust with castle (1970)

Alice in Wonderland, head in pink flowers (1970)

Walt Disney World Open (1971), Helbros (limited edition), #408 Electric

Skindiver, standing Mickey (1971) Bradley, #6418

Pinocchio (1971)

Minnie Mouse, wearing hat, facing right (1971) Timex, 1″ and 3/4″ version

Winnie the Pooh and balloon, Winnie the Pooh with honey

Mickey small size wrist watch, numeral 6 on foot (1972), Bradley #6801

Mickey small size wrist watch, smaller Mickey figure (1972), Bradley, #6811

Mickey walking, old style, shoe touches numeral 7 (1972), Bradley

Mickey calendar (date), Helbros (1972)

Mickey calendar (day-date), Helbros (1972)

Mickey calendar (date), self-winding, Helbros (1972)

Mickey calendar (day-date), self-winding (1972), Helbros, #1-633/65392

Mickey pendant (1972), Bradley, #6826

Mickey 17 jewel (1972), Helbros

Mickey electric calendar, Helbros (1972)

Walt Disney World Open (1972) with Mickey, Elgin (limited edition)

Skindiver, standing Mickey, silver face (1972), Bradley, #6824

Minnie Mouse (1972) facing left, Bradley #6809

Minnie Mouse (1972) wearing bow, facing right, Bradley #6822

Minnie Mouse (1972) pendant watch, Bradley

Donald Duck (1972) Bradley #6825

Cinderella (1972) Bradley #6810

Alice in Wonderland (1972) Bradley #6818

Goofy (1972) Bradley

W4225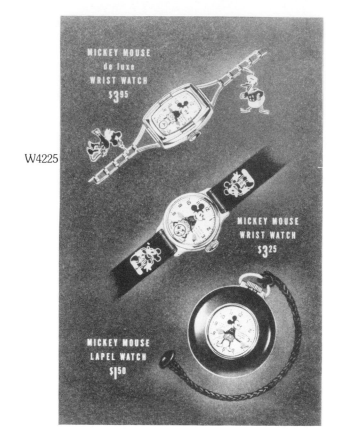

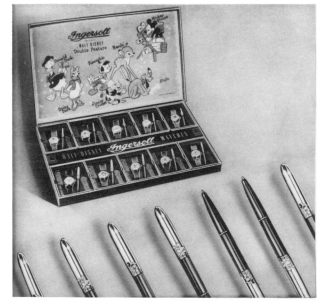
W4261

W4275

Goofy (1972) Bradley, counterclockwise numerals
Winnie the Pooh (1972) Bradley #6806
Minnie Mouse (1972) 17 jewel, Helbros
Mickey skindiver, walking old-style Mickey (1973)
Mickey digital, rectangular face, #6848 (1973)
Old-style Mickey walking, shoe does not touch numeral 7, stem
   adjacent to 4, #6990 (1973)
Old-style Mickey walking, shoe does not touch numeral 7, stem
   adjacent to 3, #6808 (1973)
Mickey bubble case #6870, Mickey bubble pendant, #6870 (1973)
Mickey Walt Disney World Open (1973), Elgin (limited edition)
Mickey Disney 50th Anniversary (1973), individually numbered,
   #6868
Mary Poppins (1973) Bradley #6880
Walt Disney World Open 1974, Helbros (limited edition),
   #3101/67931-S
Mickey Mouse Time Teacher (blue dial, small MM head) 1974
Mickey Mouse digital, round face, 1974
Winnie the Pooh (1974) digital
Winnie the Pooh Time Teacher (1974) Bradley
Robin Hood (1974) Bradley #6931
Walt Disney World Golf Classic, Elgin (limited edition) 1975
Mickey Mouse Club, (1975) #6646
Bicentennial, labelled "July 4, 1776" (1975) Mickey in Colonial
   garb, #6642

W4350

W4241

W4240

W4200

Bicentennial pocket watch (1975)
Oval watch, old-style Mickey, (1975) #6691
Walt Disney World Golf Classic (1976), Elgin (limited edition)
   #6641GC
Mickey Accutron (1976), Bulova, #6001/T1113417
Redesigned Mickey from 1972 watch, larger figure (1976), men's
   (#6305), ladies' (#6307)
Minnie Mouse (1976) wearing bow, facing right, no polka dots on
   skirt, Bradley #6303
Minnie Mouse (1976) Golf Classic wrist watch, Elgin
Winnie the Pooh (1976) Sears, 7-Jewel, revised design Pooh
   w/honey
Walt Disney World Golf Classic (1977), three versions (limited
   edition)
Elliott the Dragon (1977), Bradley
Penny (1977), Bradley, #6676
Mickey baseball (1978) #6699
Mickey football (1978) #6701

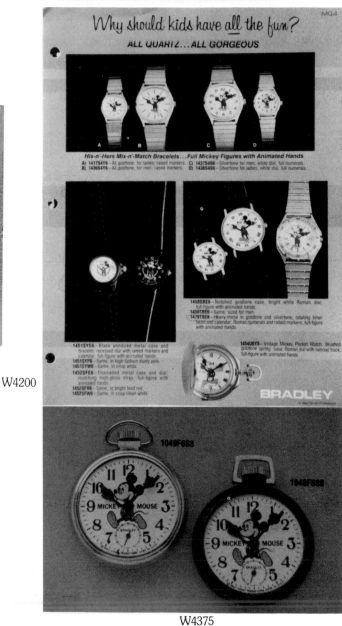

W4375

W4325

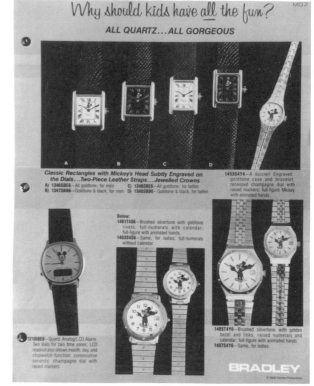

W4200

W4600

1473SBE6—Ladies' Goldtone Coin. Charcoal dial with raised golden markers. Raised and engraved goldtone Mickey with animated hands.
1474TBE6—Same, for men.

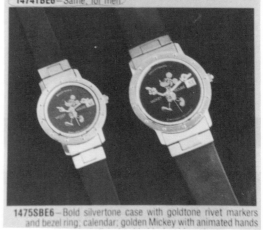

1475SBE6—Bold silvertone case with goldtone rivet markers and bezel ring; calendar; golden Mickey with animated hands

W4200

Mickey tennis (1978) #6700
Mickey basketball (1978) #6702
Mickey watch same as 1976, but with clear lucite case (1978), #6317
Mickey watch same as 1976, but 7 jewels (1978), #6695
Walking old-style Mickey, 7 jewels1 1/4" face, silver bkgd. (1978)
Mickey, moving head (1978)
Mickey's 50th Birthday, 1" face, round, old-style Mickey (1978), #6506
Mickey's 50th Birthday, 7/8" face, round, old-style Mickey (1978), #6507
Mickey's 50th Birthday, rectangular face, old-style Mickey (1978), #6505
Mickey and Minnie (1978), Bradley #6504
Mickey and Minnie Tennis (1978), Bradley #6957
WDW Golf Classic, '78 National Team Championship
Winnie the Pooh (1978) Sears
WDW Golf Classic, '79 National Team Championship
Animated eyes, stopwatch/counter functions, day/date display (1980) Alba quartz (Japan), #Y728-4000 42
Mickey Mouse jogger, rotating Mickey (1980), Bradley #1255DFE4
"Supersize" Mickey (1980), Bradley #1137CFR3, also available in small dial size and tank shape
Mickey LCD quartz, 1" face (1980), #1094ZFE4, Bradley
Mickey Mouse soccer, moving foot (1980), Bradley, #1168DFE2
Mickey and Minnie disco, moving heads and rim, black face (1980), Bradley #1073DFW5
Mickey oval bangle, silver (1980), Bradley #1029F4S4, also available in round version
Mickey square bangle, silver (1980), Bradley, #1120F4SF
WDW Golf Classic, '80 National Team Championship, Elgin
WDW Golf Classic, 1980 Pro-Am, Elgin
Mickey tank watch (1980), #1138EFE2, Bradley
1980-81 digital Mickey with blinking eyes, day/date, #Y744-5080, Alba
Disneyland 25th Anniversary (1980), Elgin #6207
Minnie Mouse (1980) moving head, 3/4" face, Bradley (rare — only 334 made) #1570BFR4
Herbie Goes Bananas (1980) Lucerne
Fox and the Hound (1980) Bradley
Mickey gold figure in relief, 7 jewels, stars for numbers (1981), #0185-10300, Bradley
WDW Golf Classic, '81 National Team Championship, Elgin
WDW Golf Classic Tencennial (1981), Elgin
William Tell Mickey (Alba), alarm, Mickey shoots arrows at falling apples game, digital Mickey and Minnie digital, musical alarm (Alba, model #Y758-5000) plays theme from "Mickey Mouse Club," Minnie's eyes wink (1981)
Mickey and Minnie "Valentine" digital, musical alarm, Alba, model #Y755-5000, Mickey throws kisses to Minnie, plays "Holidaya" and "Cuckoo Waltz" (1981)
Mickey and Minnie Tennis digital, musical alarm and game, Alba, model #Y757-5010, plays "Jambalaya" and "De Camptown Race" (1981)
WDW Tencennial watch, Accutron (Bulova, 1981) #92154/10610 (limited edition), women's pendant version, (very limited edition)
Snow White digital (1981) Alba, musical alarm, plays "It's a Small World"
Chip & Dale digital (1981) Alba
Chip & Dale (1981) Alba, green face

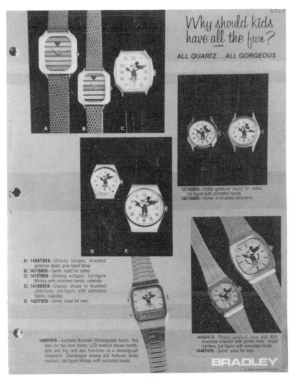

1477SBE6 — Goldtone wide-bezel case with engraved numerals; golden Mickey with animated hands against rich black dial.
1478TBE6 — Same, for men.

W4200

W4200

WDW Golf Classic (1982), Elgin, quartz
Mickey Mouse LCD, quartz 7/8″ face (1982), Bradley #1192XFE4 (Mickey is "holding" the display)
Western Mickey, twirling lariat, western-tooled plastic band (1982), Bradley #1233DFD4
Mickey and Pluto LCD, quartz, 1″ face, MM is holding the display (1982), Bradley #1191YFE4
Mickey and Pluto, standard movement, 7/8″ face, MM is holding a bone, Pluto has a "wagging" head (1982), Bradley #1078DFE4 (1982)
TRON (1982), Bradley
WDW Pro-Am 1982 Golf Classic, Elgin, quartz, EPCOT symbol
WDW Pro-Am 1982 Golf Classic, Elgin, quartz, EPCOT symbol, women's
Minnie Mouse LCD quartz (1982), Bradley #1581XFR4
Sport Goofy Tennis (1982), Bradley #1844DFE4
Sport Goofy Golf (1982), Bradley #18430DFE4
Sport Goofy Soccer (1982), Bradley #1845DFE4
EPCOT Center/Figment (1982), Bradley, digital LCD, 5 function quartz, white or black band
EPCOT Center/Figment with rainbow (1982), Bradley #1396BFW4, white or black band
EPCOT Center (1982), Elgin, rectangular black face, gold logo and lettering, quartz movement, black leather band, #1373SB
EPCOT Center (1982), Elgin, same as above, women's, #1372SB
EPCOT Center (1982), Elgin, round brushed gold 1″ face, with black logo and lettering, stainless steel link band with gold trim, quartz movement, #1378S4Y6
EPCOT Center (1982), Elgin, same as above, 3/4″ face, women's, #1377S4Y4
EPCOT Center (1982), Bradley, quartz, round gold face w/silver Spaceship Earth, gold monorail and planters (1 1/4″ face), silver link band with gold trim, #1384S4Y6
EPCOT Center (1982), Bradley, 15/16″ face, same as above, women's, #1383S4Y6
EPCOT Center (1982), Accutron, quartz movement, gold 1 1/8″ round face w/gold raised EPCOT Center logo, black leather band
EPCOT Center (1982), Accutron, same as above, 3/4″ face, women's
50th Anniversary/MM watch, old-style Mickey, 7/8″ face, gold face (1983), Bradley, men's or ladies' version, "50 Years of Time with Mickey" inscribed on back
WDW Golf Classic (1983), Elgin, quartz
"The Mickey Mouse Classic Collection" (Japan), gold casing, 1 1/8″ face, calendar/date, brown leather band (limited edition of 2000) (1983)
Disney Channel premium, Mickey as Sorcerer's Apprentice (digital) 1984
Baume & Mercier 14k gold Mickey Mouse watch (Mickey head from cartoon opening), 1 1/8″ face, gold mesh band (1984)
Baume & Mercier 14k gold Mickey Mouse watch, ladies' style (Mickey head from cartoon opening), 5/8″ face, gold mesh band (1984) **Gold watches now run 1500-1800**
WDW Golf Classic, Elgin, quartz (1984)
Mickey runner pop-up LCD, Bradley, square red plastic case, 1 1/8″ face red plastic band, figure of Mickey against yellow circle background, pop-up button on face (1984)
Donald Duck 50th birthday watch, Bradley, 7'8″ round face, inscribed on back: "Birthday Commemorative Edition, Donald Duck (1984)," #1603AFB3
Donald Duck 50th birthday watch, Bradley, 1 1/8″ round gold face, labelled on back: "Birthday Commemorative Edition, Donald Duck (1984)," #1605TBE6
Donald Duck 50th birthday watch, Bradley, quartz, 13/16″ round gold face, ladies', #1604SBE6 (1984)
Disneyland, Seiko, gold relief of Sleeping Beauty Castle on gold face, gold band, 1 1/8″ face, quartz (1984)
Disneyland, Seiko, 7/8″, same as above, ladies' style (1984)
Donald Duck 50th birthday watch, Donald Duck Orange Juice promotion (1984)
Cinderella, Bradley quartz, LCD, 3/4″ white face w/castle and Cinderella picture, light blue plastic band (1984)
Disney Summer Magic 1985, Mickey against NYC skyline (Walt Disney Speciality Products)
Disneyland 30th Anniversary (1985), Bradley, quartz, 1 1/8″ white

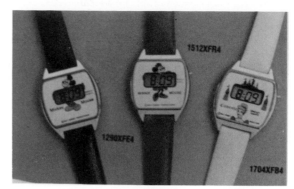

W4200

W4200

W4200

W4325

face with rainbow-colored 30th Anniversary castle logo

Disneyland 30th Anniversary (1985), Bradley, quartz, same as above, ladies', 3/4" face

Disneyland 30th Anniversary (1985), Bradley, quartz, 1 1/8" gold face with embossed Mouse ears logo, "Disneyland Thirty Years, 1955-1985," Gift-Giver machine prize

Disneyland 30th Anniversary (1985), Bradley, quartz, 3/4" face, same as above, ladies' style

Black Cauldron (1985), silver case, black band, premium (Frito-Lay/"Chee-tos"), 1" face

Disneyland 30th Anniversary (1985), Bradley, quartz, gold face with Disneyland castle logo in relief, "Disneyland" (in black letters), "30th year" (in gold relief), 1 1/8" face

Disneyland 30th Anniversary (1985), Bradley, quartz, 3/4" face, same as above, ladies' style

Walt Disney World 15th Anniversary (1986), Lorus, quartz, gold face (1 1/8") with 15th Anniversary logo

Walt Disney World 15th Anniversary (1986), Lorus, quartz, 3/4" face, same as above, ladies' style

Captain EO/The Disney Channel promo watch (TDC promotion) (1986)

Star Tours Inaugural Flight January 1987 Disneyland, Ballanda Corp.

Snow White Golden Anniversary (1987), Lorus

W4200

W7196

W7000 WIND-UP TOYS

W7020 Mickey Mouse drummer c. 1930-31	500-1000
W7115 Composition Donald walker (1938) Borgfeldt	125 - 275
W7118 Dopey walker (1938) Marx	50 - 165
W7119 Ferdinand the Bull (1939) Marx	45 - 100
W7120 Composition Pinocchio walker (1940) Borgfeldt	125 - 275
W7127 Bouncing Dumbo (1941) Marx	50 - 175
W7136 Mickey Mouse Express (1949) Marx	100 - 350
W7196 Stretchy Pluto (Linemar)	50 - 195
W7197 Mickey on roller skates (Linemar)	75 - 350

W7920 WHISTLES

W7923 Wax whistle in box	10 - 50

W7020

W7923

W7120

W7115

Close up of track for T9027 seen in Volume 3

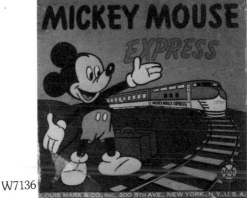

W7136

117

W7928

W8075

Z5097

Z5075

W8300

W8300

Z5013

W7928 Lido plastic slide whistles, Mickey, Donald,
Goofy & Joe Carioca, each   2 - 10

W8000 WORLD WAR II
W8015 Plate, 63rd Signal-BN-Assoc. Reunion   5 - 25
W8075 What is Propaganda? booklet   4 - 20
W8076 Winter Draws On booklet on de-icing featur-
ing Gremlin type "Spandules"   4 - 20
W8300 Dispatch From Disney (Vol 1, No. 1), 1943
Only issue of magazine type booklet created
by the artists left at the studio to those in the
service. Covers people, projects, Walt and
plans for the future   100 - 250

W8076

W8015

Z5000 ZORRO
Z5013 Costume and mask (Ben Cooper)   7 - 18
Z5030 Plastic figures, Zorro on horse (Lido) 3 sizes   8 - 50
Z5034 Large plastic Zorro on horse w/all accessories
(Marx)   35 - 150
Z5035 Tray or jigsaw puzzles (Jaymar), each   4 - 12
Z5036 Bookends, pair   12 - 55
Z5040 Oil painting by numbers (Hassenfeld)   10 - 40
Z5045 Magic paint with water pictures (Whitman),
each   3 - 9
Z5075 Lunchbox with thermos (Aladdin)   6 - 20
Z5090 Coloring and Story books (Whitman), each   2 - 20
Z5097 Pocket flashlight (Unmask Zorro)   4 - 20
Z5100 Zorro game (Whitman)   5 - 35

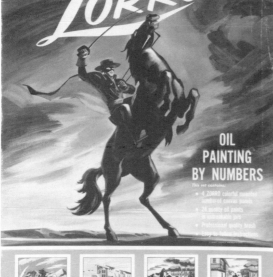

Z5040

Z5036

Z5035

Z5100

Z5045

119

Walt Disney
CHARACTER MERCHANDISE
Licensees

c.1929 to
February 20, 1987

LIST OF DISNEY LICENSEES

The following list includes every licensee on record at the Disney Archives as of February 20, 1987. A few additional companies appear because merchandise has been identified even though no contracts have been found.

This information supersedes data listed at each classification in Volumes 1 thru 3. Accuracy and completeness were the major goals in compiling this material, but errors and omissions are likely to remain. While intended mainly for reference in and dating Disneyana, it can be fun to read the list just to get a basic background on all the different products made over the years. Hidden in this list, for example, are the manufacturers of full size Mickey Mouse cars and yachts; roll-out-gardens; various obscure ceramic figures; and over 25,000 other character merchandise items.

Herein is the wealth of Disneyana knowledge. Use it to help locate the classification in which an item of interest can be found in *Tomart's Illustrated DISNEYANA Catalog and Price Guide.* Use it to gain a better understanding for acquiring and dealing in Disneyana collectibles.

The illustrations used throughout the list are from the 1932 United Artists Campaign Book developed by Kay Kamen. The printing "cuts" were designed to be used on merchandise and in advertising.

MICKEY MOUSE
11—One Col. Drawing
(Mat 05¢; Cut 30¢)

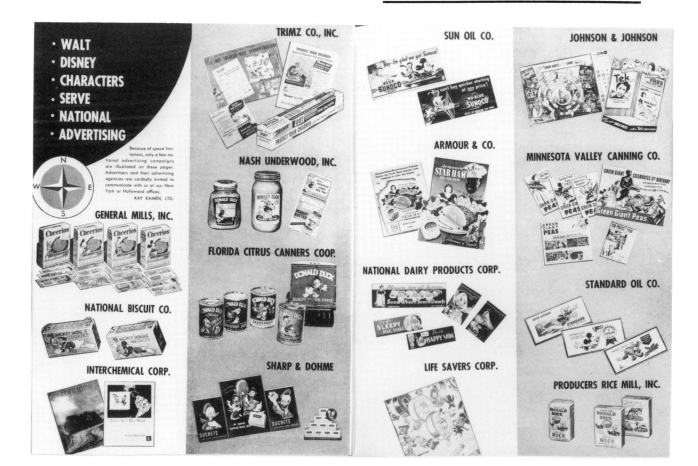

A.E.D. Alexander Ltd. (NYC) 1965-66
Winnie the Pooh dress coats with velvet collars (Sears, Roebuck and Co.)

A.L.S. Industries, Inc. (Torrance, CA) 1984-86
Children, sports toys and accessories

A.P.L. Corp. (see Admiral Plastics Corporation)

Abbeville Press, Inc. (NYC) 1978-87
Disney animation calendar, books

Harry N. Abrams, Inc. (NYC) 1973-87
Art prints, calendars, books

Absorbene Mfg. Co. (St. Louis, MO) 1959-64
Activity kits, consisting of modeling dough and molds known as "Fun-Dough," Annette Wibbler (a new plastic balancing toy), "Flubber" (a "Silly Putty" substance)

Acme Underwear Co. (NYC) 1933-35
Children's pajamas

Action Films Inc. (Mountain View, CA) 1970-74
Hand-operated 8mm viewer and cartridges

Adica Pongo Inc. (Clifton, NJ) 1984
Self-hardening modeling clay sets

Adler Favor & Novelty Co., Inc. (St. Louis) 1938-41
Candy favors and party goods

Kurt S. Adler, Inc. (NYC) 1966, 82-87
Christmas decorations

Admiral Plastics Corp./A.P.L. Corp (Brooklyn, NY) 1968-87
Plastic cups, mugs, bowls, pop moulds, molded children's furniture

Admiral Toy Company (Chicago) 1956-57
Wooden paddle ball, yo-yo, baseball and golf cards, kaleidoscope, jacks, wooden tops, kites

Adtrix Corporation (NYC) 1959-61
Wiggle pictures for a Cheerios premium among other uses

Ad-Vance Trailer Corp. (NYC) 1931
Trailers

Ahoskie Mfg. Co. (Ahoskie, NC) 1965-66
Winnie the Pooh coats (Sears, Roebuck & Co.)

Aime Des Biens (Monterey Park, CA) 1944-45
Flocked wood toys

Air Baby, Inc. (Englewood Cliffs, NJ) 1967-68
Children's slippers (Sears, Roebuck & Co.)

Aladdin Industries, Inc. (Nashville, TN) 1956-87
School lunch kits (metal and vinyl) with vacuum bottle, notebooks

Alagold Products (Montgomery, AL) 1982-83
Foam-cushioned vinyl resting mat, lap desk

Joel Alan, Inc. (NYC) 1968-69
Winnie the Pooh Nehru sportcoat (Sears, Roebuck and Co.)

Alco (Miami Springs, FL) 1975
Electronic Calculator

Alco Products, Inc. (Miami, FL) 1985
Sports, gym, athletic, school, beach and tote bags, school supplies

Alexander Doll Co. (NYC) 1933-1939, 51-53, 59, 68-70
Dolls and marionettes

Alfred-Leon, Inc. (NYC) 1955-56
Sun suits

Alladin Plastics, Inc. (LA) 1949-51
Plastic charms

C.S. Allen Corporation (Brooklyn, NY) 1935-37
Toffee

S.L. Allen & Co., Inc. (Philadelphia) 1935-40
Sleds

Allied Associate (NYC) 1941-42
Statuettes, toy banks, salt and pepper shakers

Allied Chemical Corporation (NYC) 1968, 71-72
Melamine dinnerware

Allied Manufacturing Company (Portland, OR) 1952-58
Electric Clocks

Allied Plastics Co., Inc. (LA) 1949-53
Plastic tumblers

Allison Manufacturing Co. (NYC) 1976-87
Children's' and adult's knit pajamas, shirts and sweatshirts, T-shirts, jogging shorts, boys' knit pajamas warm-up suits

All Styles Hanger Company, Inc. (NYC) 1945-47
Clothes hangers

Almar Rainwear Corporation (NYC) 1967
Girls' raincoat, umbrella, kerchief set (Sears, Roebuck & Co.)

Alpha-Craft (NYC) 1946-47
Costume jewelry

Aluminum Speciality Co. (Manitowoc, WI/NYC/St.Louis/Chicago/San Francisco) 1935-40
Aluminum cooking utensils, cookie cutters, tea sets, dishes

Alyssa Originals (NYC) 1964-71
Assorted style dresses

Amcor Group, LTD. (NYC) 1982-83
Hand showers and shower heads

American Advertising and Research Corp (Chicago) 1968-69
Promotional items

American Can Co. (NYC) 1968-69
Disposable meal service items, including plates, bowls, cups, forks, spoons, napkins, and placemats

American Candy Manufacturing Co. (Selma, AL) 1976-87
Hard candies, lollipops

American Characters International (LA) 1980-87
Children's and adult's sweaters, sweatshirts (retail $15 or more), running shorts, satin, down, and leather jackets, vests, skirts and other miscellaneous sportswear with ornamentation, costume jewelry with light, voice and holograph

American Creative Toys, Inc. — sub of Rotadraw, Ltd. (NYC) 1975
Drawing sets

American Dental Association (Chicago) 1940-55
Rubber molds, good teeth award certificates

American Hard Rubber Co. (NYC) 1935-37
Pocket combs

American Latex Corporation (NYC) 1936-39
Rubber pants

American Lighting Specialities (Torrance, CA) 1981-83
Roller skates and ice skates

American Lithographic Co. (NYC) 1931
School tablets

American Manufacturing Concern (NYC) 1939-41
Toy blackboards

American Merri-Lei Corp. (NYC) 1934-35
Snapping mottoes, dressed noisemakers, special party goods, etc.

American Metalcrafts Company (Attleboro, MA) 1947-49
Children's silverware

American Mills, Inc. (Griffen, GA) 1969-72
Winnie the Pooh layette and gift set

American Mirror Works (Bronx, NY) 1957-58
Magic flasher, heliograph signaler, Mickey fun house, weekly reminder, fold-up mirror, mirrored toy furniture

American Needle and Novelty Co. (Chicago) 1965-71
Winnie the Pooh corduroy Eton cap

American Playground Device Co. (Anderson, IN) 1958-60
Outdoor playground equipment, swimming pool accessories

American Pottery Company, Inc. (LA) 1943-55
Ceramic figurines and dinnerware sets

American Pre-school (Holyoke, MA) 1962
Wooden educational toys

American Publishing Corp. (Watertown, MA) 1979-87
Posters, jointed cardboard figures, puzzle notes, rub-on transfers, "Stick 'n lift"

American Sponge and Chamois Co., Inc. (Long Island, NY) 1970-71
Compressed diecut sponge character sheets with printed scene including diecut shaped characters

American Syrup and Sorghum Company (St. Louis) 1949-50
Corn syrup products

American Telecard Corp. (San Pedro, CA) 1964
Audio-visual greeting cards (produced by Columbia Records, Hollywood)

American Telecommunications Corp. (El Monte, CA) 1976-84
Telephones

American Toy and Furniture Co., Inc. (Chicago) 1956-57, 81-87
Wood burning sets, wooden step chair, tool sets, toy chests, peg desk, clothes rack, easels, night table, indoor play gym

American Toy Works (NYC) 1938-41
Games

American Tree and Wreath, div. of American Technical Ind. (NYC) 1981
Christmas tree themes, decorated trees and wreath ornaments, tree tops

Americana Sweets & Novelty Corporation (Elizabeth, NJ) 1975-76
Stickers with taffy

Ameritex div of United Merchants and Manufacturers, Inc. 1973-74

MINNIE MOUSE

Fabric, piece goods (See U. M. & M.)

The Amloid Company (Lodi 36-39/Rochelle Park 40-41 NJ) 1936-41
Celluloid baby bottles and novelties

Amsco Corporation (NYC) 1965-68
Toon-a-vision, sponge bath toys

AMSCO Industries, Inc. div of Milton Bradley 1965-66, 72
Toon-a-vision, Winnie the Pooh wristwatch, Snow White yarn plaques, toy cleaning sets, decorative assembly game, toy luggage

Anchor Hocking Corporation (Lancaster, OH) 1986-87
Glass bowls, plates and drinking glasses

O. B. Andrews Company (Chattanooga, TN/NYC) 1933-35
Playhouses

Anson Incorporated (Providence, RI) 1985
Silver and gold filled costume jewelry

Animals Plus Inc./Animal Toys Plus Inc. (Brooklyn, NY) 1976-83
Banks (Name changed to Animal Toys Plus Inc. in 1977)

Antioch Bookplate Company (Yellow Springs, OH/NYC/Chicago IL) 1946-50
Bookmarks and bookplates

Apco Mfg. Co. (Chicago) 1968-69
Winnie the Pooh "Pooh for President" sweatshirt (Sears, Roebuck and Co.)

Apon Novelty Company (Philadelphia) 1938-39
Novelties

Applause, div of Wallace Berrie & Co., Inc. (Woodland Hills, CA) 1985-87
Plush rag dolls and PVC figures

Apsco Products Inc. (LA) 1960-64
Pencil sharpeners

Arco Industries Ltd. (Westbury, NY) 1983-87
Sprinkler toy, crib rail rocker, "Peg 'n Play" boards and "Cartwheel" action toys, rack and novelty toys (also see - Sharose Consultants, Inc.)

Arden Farms, Inc. (LA) 1940-41
Printed or lithographed advertising material

Arden Jewelry Mfg. Co. (Providence, RI) 1963-64
Pendants, bracelets, earring and pin sets, necklaces

Aristocrat Leather Products, Inc. (NYC) 1955-63
Mickey Mouse and Davy Crockett wallets, key cases, vinyl plastic placemats, hair brushes, leather and plastic toilet cases

Armour & Co. (Chicago) 1938-39, 47-48, 57
Snow White and the Seven Dwarfs ham wrapper quality meats

Arrow Handicraft Corp. (Chicago) 1976-81
Wooden paint sets, shrink art sets, decoupage sets, craft activity sets

Arrow Products, Inc. (Lake Geneva, WI) 1961-62
Babes in Toyland shoe boxes (Sears, Roebuck & Co.)

Artco Infant Products, Inc. (NYC) 1972-73
WTP pram suit, bunting

Artcraft Paper Products (Cincinnati, OH) 1955-56
"Magicpaint" with water pictures

Artex (Overland Park, KS) 1987
Men's big and tall knit tops, sweatshirts and pants, jackets, jerseys, shorts, tank tops

Artisto, Inc. (NYC) 1938-39
Framed pictures

Arton Studios (Philadelphia) 1940
Pinocchio lamps

Artvogue of California (San Francisco/LA/NYC/Chicago/Seattle WA) 1945-48.

Boys' shirts

Alexander Asquine, Inc. (Pittsburgh) 1986
Wooden hangers, wooden valets

Atari Incorporated (Sunnyvale, CA) 1983-84
Home video game cartridges

Athletic Shoe Company (Chicago/NYC/San Francisco) 1934-37
Sheepskin moccasins

Athol Plastics Corp. (NYC) 1970-71
Grooming sets

Atlantic Syrup Refining Corp. (Philadelphia) 1949-54
Corn syrup products

Atlas Development Co., Ltd. (Richmond, CA) 1934-35
Children's furniture

Auburn Rubber Co., Inc. (Auburn, IN) 1958-62
Swim accessories, wheeled toys of flexible rubber or plastic, clay pictures by number sets, clay modeling sets

Aurora Products Corp. (West Hempstead, NY) 1975
Multi-faced dolls and playsets

Authentics, Inc. (NYC) 1941-42
Costume jewelry

Auto Shade, Inc. (Van Nuys, CA) 1987
Auto shade covers, autoshade cover clips, mirrors for visors, steering wheel covers, bobbing characters, litterbags (molded plastic), magnetized dashboard figures

Automatic Recording Safe Co. (Chicago) 1935-37
Savings banks, money boxes

Automatic Retailer of America, Inc. (Philadelphia) 1964-66
Blow-molded toys molded in and dispensed through coin-operated machines

Automatic Toy Company (Staten Island, NY) 1952-53
Toy T.V. set

Aviva Enterprises, Inc. (San Francisco) 1970-71
Trophyettes

Avon Products, Inc. (NYC) 1970-71
Toiletries, soaps, bubble bath, shampoo, cosmetics

Azrak-Hamway (NYC) 1975-80
Toy car, power pack car, toy sewing machine, boat, motorcycle vehicle and road race set, Fun Mobile, articulated figures, Mouse Power

B & S Mfg. Company (Philadelphia) 1969-70
Boys' corduroy sportcoat

Babcock Phillips div of Dart Industries (Richmond, VA) 1974-80
Bean bag chair, pouf, building blocks, hassocks, floor pillows

Baby Bathinette Corp. (Canandaigua, NY) 1966-67
Baby bathinettes

Baby Togs, Inc. (NYC) 1976-79
Boys' coordinated playwear

Bachmann Brothers, Inc. (Philadelphia) 1935-36, 57-58
Sun glasses, goggles, pocket magnifiers, plastic toys, party favors

Bacon Mfg. Co. (NYC — before 1983/Swonnanoa, NC) 1939-40, 75-84
Crib blankets, blankets

Charles H. Bacon Co. (NYC) 1968
Winnie the Pooh fancy knit tight (Sears)

George S. Bailey Hat Co., Inc. (LA) 1955-58
Mickey Mouse and Davy Crockett felt hats, cowboy hats

Balantyne Supply Company (Chicago) 1944-45
Wood toys, carved figures

Ballantine Books (NYC) 1979
Paperback books

Bamberger-Reinthal Company (Cleveland, OH) 1972-74
Knitted scarfs and hats

Banner Brothers, Inc. (NYC) 1937-38
"Kiddie Kit" water proof bag

Banner Curtain Co., Inc. (NYC) 1963
Curtains for children's rooms, cotton bedspread & curtain ensemble

Banner Plastics Corporation (Paterson, NJ) 1955-56
Alice in Wonderland tea set, plastic and lithographed metal picture blocks, Davy Crockett molded plastic covered wagon

Bantam-Lite Inc. (NYC) 1955-59
Novelty flashlights

Barmon Brothers Company (Buffalo, NY) 1933-34
Ladies' smocks and wash dresses

H. Barnard Stamp & Stencil Co., Ltd. (Canada) 1949-50
Printing sets

Barnett Mirror Corp. div American Mirror Works (Bronx, NY) 1957-58
Mirrors, mirror toys, mirror furniture

MICKEY MOUSE

Baron Buckles & Leather Craft Supplies, Inc. (LA) 1982-84
Solid brass, lead or zinc belt buckles, paperweights, automobile license plates, frames, motorcycle license plate frames

Barricks Manufacturing Company (Chicago IL/NYC/Atlanta GA) 1944-49
Blackboards

Bert B. Barry (Chicago) 1939-41, 48-49
Hand made wood figures (imported)

Barton's Candy Corporation (Brooklyn, NY) 1979-81
Milk chocolate and other candy

Bassett Mirror Company (Bassett, VA) 1965-68, 77-79
Framed character wall mirror, infants and children's mirrors

Bata Shoe Co. (Belcamp, MD) 1970
Jeepers shoes

Bates Art Industries (Chicago) 1934-35
Framed pictures

Bates Fabrics, Inc./Bates Nitewear Co., Inc. (NYC) 1955-56, 79-83
Fabrics by yard, bedspreads & drapes, girls' night gowns, pajamas and robes, children's underwear

H. Bates Co., Inc. (NYC) 1960-61
Schiffli embroidered piece goods for sale by the

yard or piece in retail stores and through mail order catalogs

Bates Mfg. Co. (Lewiston, ME) 1955-56
Cotton bedspreads and draperies

Baxter Co. Inc. (Cincinnati, OH) 1955
Disneyland space ship control panel

Bayshore Industries, Inc. (Elkton, MD) 1952-62
Foam rubber, "Bend-me" toys, thumb puppet, toy muscle builder kit, grip exerciser and chest expander, foam rubber pillows and back rests, rigid foam plastic bathtub toy

Beach Products, Inc. (Kalamazoo, Michigan) 1955-87
Paper napkins, table cloths, party sets, Davy Crockett and Mickey Mouse napkins party goods (paper napkins, tablecloths, plates, cups, streamers, placemats), candy cake decorations, nut cups, party invitations

Beacon Mfg. Co. (NYC) 1939-40, 65-72, 75-84
Crib blankets (Montgomery Ward Co.)

Beatrix Jewelry Co. (Pawtucket, RI) 1967-69
Pins

The Becker Corporation (Baltimore, MD) 1973-85
Store displays and decorations

L. Bedell Inc. (NYC) 1965-66
White acetate umbrellas

Behrend & Rothschild (NYC) 1938-40
Banks

Arthur Beir & Company, Inc. (NYC/Providence, RI) 1938-39
Cotton print fabrics, novelty jewelry

Belding Sports (LA) 1987
Golf bags, straps, fuzzy head covers, golf shirts, windbreakers, rainsuits

Benay-Albee Novelty Company (Maspeth, NY) 1956-87
Novelty hats, buttons, modeling dough, bubble toys, play wallets and money sets, jump ropes

Mike Benet Formals (Pittsburgh, TX) 1987
Formal evening gowns

Bennington Brush Co., Inc. (Bennington, VT) ???
Girls' comb, brush and mirror, boys' military brushes and combs (sold individually and in sets)

Bergenicht Brothers (NYC) 1952
Children's dresses

Louis Bergnes (NYC) 1949-50
Towels, robes

Irving Berlin, Inc./Bourne (NYC) 1933-87
Sheet music, orchestrations

Earl Bernard Co., Inc. (NYC) 1955-56
Mickey Mouse scarfs, stoles, collars, belts, Eton caps, fabric handbags

Edward Bernard Co., Inc. (Chicago) 1955
Planters, automatic candy dispensers, candy refills, plastic parakeet toys, figurines

Berner Co. (Coral Gables, FL) 1972-73
Donald Duck cufflinks (Citrus World only), 1,000 pairs

Bernstein Sons Shirt Corp. (NYC) 1938-41
Boys' blouses and shirts

Russ Berrie & Co. (Oakland, NJ) 1975-76
Novelty wall mirrors, pens, leather wrist bands

Berst-Forster-Dixfield Company (NYC) 1938-39
Paper napkins, plates, dishes, towels, Cleaning tissue, Waxed paper, wooden Hors d'oeuvres sticks, spoons, forks, clothespins

Best Plastics Corporation (Brooklyn, NY) 1955-57
Rigid plastic party favors

Bestlyne Company (NYC) 1939-40
Latex Bathing Suits

Bettye Babs Novelty Togs (LA) 1940-41

Children's Wear

The Bibb Company (NYC) 1982-84
Bedspread, comforters, pillow shams, valances, draperies, curtains, dust ruffles, bed canopies and textile wall hangings

Bibo-Lang, Inc. (NYC) 1930-32
Mickey Mouse book, music publishers of Mickey Mouse song

Biederlack Gmbh and Co. Kg. (NYC) 1986-87
Adult blankets and cuddle wraps

Binky Baby Products (NYC) 1970-72
Winnie the Pooh training cup (Sears)

Binney & Smith, Inc. div Creative Activities (Easton, PA) 1979-83
Educational card games (Formerly Ed-U-Cards)

Birge Wallcoverings (Buffalo, NY) 1980
Vinyl wallpaper

Black Leaf Products (Elgin, IL) 1972-80
Outdoor fun showers

Blackett-Sample-Hummert, Inc. (Janesville, WI) 1941-42
Agency for Parker Pen Co. and Quick ink — use of Dumbo in promotional materials and advertising

H & J Block (NYC) 1938-39, 50-51
Girls' coats

Blowout Creations, Inc. (LA) 1987
Sportswear (jumpsuits, overalls, blouses, shorts, fashion woven tops, woven shirts, dresses, skirts) ladies' and men's

Blue Bell, Inc. (Greensboro, NC) 1955-56
Mickey Mouse & Davy Crockett shirts, jackets pants; boys' and girls' cotton & corduroy pants, shorts, shirts for outerwear

Blue Jeans Corp. (NYC) 1951-53
Blue jeans

Blue Ribbon Books, Inc. (NYC) 1933-34
Waddle and Pop-Up story books.

Blue Ridge Manufacturers, Inc. sub of Boy-Tone Shirt Co., Inc. (Baltimore, MD) 1958-59
Children's & boys' overalls, jeans, dungarees, trousers, dress & sport shirts

Blue Star Knitting Inc. (Milwaukee) 1965-66
Nylon stretch pants for Sears

Blum's (San Francisco) 1949-50
Blum's Candy

Bo Peep Mfg. Co., Inc. (NYC) 1952
Dresses, sun suits & dresses, pinafores, brother & sister sets, play togs, aprons & slacks

Body Glove (Hermosa Beach, CA) 1987
Wet suits, neoprene croakies, neoprene sunglass case, neoprene head gasket visor

The Bonneau Co. (Dallas) 1985-87
Adult, junior and children's sunglasses

Bonny Products, Inc. (Lynbrook, NY) 1970-87
Metal children's flatware, ice cream scoopers

Bonnytex Co., Inc. (NYC) 1956-57
Nursery items

Bontempi (Edison, NJ) 1987
Musical instruments

Borden — see Sunworthy Wall Covering

Borgenicht Brothers, Inc. (NYC) 1952-53
Children's dresses

George Borgfeldt & Company (NYC) 1930-50
Toys, dolls of several manufacturers (including Dean Rag Book, Schoenhut, & Steiff), games, novelties, bisque and wood figures, Schuco wind-up toys, ceramic tea sets, composition wind-ups, celluloid figures & wind-ups, tops, wooden toys

Bosell and Jacobs, Inc. (Omaha, NE) 1938-39
Snow White and the Seven Dwarfs advertising materials for client not named

Boston Underwear Mfg. Co. (NYC) 1939-40
Ladies' and Misses' blouses

Bostonian Process Co. (Hackensack, NJ) 1955-56
Silkscreened Mickey Mouse Club emblems/insignias

Bourne, Inc. (NYC) 1947-87
Music publishers

Bow-Age Togs, Inc. (NYC) 1944-45, 48-49
Children's clothes

Bowman Apple Products Co., Inc. (Mt. Jackson, VA) 1948-54
Apple sauce, apple butter & apple juice

Bradford Novelty Co., Inc. (Cambridge, MA) 1955-56
Mickey Mouse wall plaques, Mouseketeer insignias, do-it-yourself Easter and Christmas decorations, 3-dimensional character assembly kits

Milton Bradley Co. (Springfield, MA/NYC) 1931-42, 72-79, 87
Games, skill-action 3-D board games, bendable characters, brick model sets

Bradley Time, div Elgin National Industries, Inc. (NYC) 1972-85
Watches, clocks and talking alarm clocks.

Brandle & Smith Co. (Philadelphia, PA) 1932-34
Mickey Mouse candy

Brayton's Laguna Pottery (Laguna Beach, CA) 1938-40
Ceramic pottery figures

George M. Brazil Plumbing Co., Inc. (San Pedro, CA) 1964
Audio-vision greeting cards

Dan Brechner & Co., Inc., (NYC) 1961-63
Ceramic cookie, candy and lollypop jars, salt & pepper shakers, book ends, mugs, pitchers, etc. Flashlights, ceramic-base night-lights, ice cream scoops, metal litho rings, whistles, compasses, badges, buttons, paper mache nodders

Brier Mfg. Company (Providence, RI) 1935-42, 55
Wood-like and metal jewelry (pins, rings, bracelets, necklaces, charms, barrettes)

Bright Of America, Inc. (Summerville, NY) 1982-87
Placemats, plastic laminated

Bristol Myers Co. (NYC) 1957-58
Triple R western tie & slide (1957) Ipana contest (1958) Snow White characters

Broadcast Music (NYC) 1942-53
Sheetmusic

Brookfield/Hyde Athletic (Peabody, MA) 1987
Roller skates, scooterboard, skateboard, ice skates

The W.A. Brophey Co., Ltd. (Canada) 1949-54
Umbrellas

Brown & Bigelow (St. Paul, MN) 1936-39
Calenders

Bryant Electric Co. (Bridgeport, CT) 1934-41, 61-62
Children's dishes and tea sets made of "Beetleware," an early Bakelite type plastic

Bucks County Frozen Products, Inc. (Doylestown, PA) 1949-51
Frozen foods

Buddy L Corporation (NYC) 1979-80
Novelty banks

Buckley Dement & Co. (Chicago) 1940
Pinocchio IGA poster stamps and album

Bunny Bear, Inc. (Everett, MA) 1959-63
Crib bumpers, mattresses, etc.

Burlington Basket Co. (Burlington, IA) 1969-72
Winnie the Pooh valet folding dressing table (Sears)

Burlington Luggage Co., Inc. (Seattle, WA)

1945-48
Children's luggage

Leo Burnett Co., Inc. (Chicago) 1941
Advertising and promotional materials

Charles D. Burnes Co., Inc.
(Newton Centre, MA) 1987
Photo frames, photo magnets

Butler Enterprises, Inc. (Winston-Salem, NC)
1945-46
Lithographed wood blocks

Butterfly Originals (Cherry Hill, NJ) 1976-77
Luggage

Buzza-Cardozo (Anaheim, CA) 1969-71
Greeting cards, calendars, wrapping paper,
inflatable greeting cards

CBS Toys div of CBS, Inc. (NYC) 1979-85
Busy infant toys, roly-polys, trapeze toys,
puppets, tricky walkers, Pop-O-Matic games,
squeeze toys, musical Jack-in-box, pop pals,
Tricky Trikes, action novelty toys, infant and pre-
school toys

Cadillac Toy Mfg, Co. (Bronx, NY) 1953-54
Color Craft numbered painting sets, Hobby Craft
set

Irving Caesar (NYC) 1932-33
Music publisher

Cal Fiber Company-see California Stuffed Toys

Calhoun's Collector's Society
(St. Paul, MN/Minn. MN) 1975-1976
Pewter figures of Presidents

Cali-Fame Hat Co. (LA) 1945-48
Children's caps

California Headwear Inc. (LA) 1982-83
Baseball styled caps, adjustable size

California International Apparel, Inc.
(Gardena, CA) 1975-76
Boys' jackets, shorts, jeans, coveralls and bib
overalls

California Metalware Corp. (El Segundo, CA)
1955-58
Litho metal trays with or without stand

California Originals (Torrance, CA) 1979
Ceramic mugs, cookie jars

California Stuffed Toys, div of Cal Fiber Co. (LA)
1972-74, 87
Stuffed characters from 9½ inch cuddle to 40 inch
tall Mickey Mouse, bean bags, hand puppets, and
wooden kokeshi pendants.

Cameo Doll Products Co. (Port Allegany, PA) 1942
Wood dolls

Capitol Cravat Company (NYC) 1938-39
Neckwear

Capitol Records (Hollywood, CA) 1947-55
Record albums

Caproni Galleries, Inc. (Boston) 1938-39
Sculptured figures made of plaster

Carbide & Carbon Chemicals Corp. (NYC) 1938
Posters used on "Pyrofax Gas Distributors"
trucks

Cardinal Products div of Josten's Business
Products, Inc. (Minn., MN) 1983-84
Vinyl binders, portfolios, pad holders/clipboards

Carlton Plastics, Inc. (Philadelphia) 1957-66,
(Bristol, PA) 1968
Plastic aprons and panties, bibs

Carnival Toy Inc., div of Lorraine Industries
(Bridgeport, CT) 1973-82,
(Overland Park, KS) 1983-87
Metal litho Jack-in-the-box, plastic ukulele, banjo,
guitar, mouse guitar, ring toss game, rhythm
band, musical toys

Carolace Embroidery Company (Edgewater, NJ)

1961-62
Schiffli emblems

Carolina Enterprises, Inc./Empire of Carolina,
Inc. (Tarboro, NC/NYC) 1973-87
Electric Christmas decorations, jumbo bat and
golf game, ride-on and ride-in toys, desks, chairs,
doctor and nurse kits (77-81), lawnmower and toy
tool sets (80-81), table and chair sets, wall plaque
decorations

Carrousel Party Favors, Inc. (North Hollywood,
CA) 1979-82, (Las Vegas, NV) 1983-87
Party goods: paper hats, blowouts, horns, bags,
invitations, name tags, signs & games, candles,
lunch bags

Carson Manufacturing Company (Chicago)
1940-41
Clocks

The William Carter Company
(Needham Hts., MA) 1967-71
Slippers, night shirts, pajamas

Cartier, Inc. (NYC) 1937-42, 81-87
Jewelry, precious metal jewelry

Cartoon Characters of America (LA) 1980
Children's and adults' t-shirts (retail $12 or more),
denim trousers, vests, shorts, skirts and jackets

Catalina Mfg. (LA) 1987
Swimwear, accessories, bikeshorts

Catton Brothers (NYC) 1975-87
Infants newborn diaper gift sets, booties, toddler
jacquard sweaters, sport uniforms

Cazenovia Abroad, Inc. (Cazenovia, NY) 1982-85
Sterling silver, silver plated and 14 carat gold
Christmas ornaments

Ce De Candy (Union, NJ) 1984-86
Candy watch

Celeste Inc. (Wilton, CT) 1964-65
Paper place mats, wash-away cloth

Centra Leather Goods Corporation (NYC)
1948-49
Wallets and purses

Century Mills, Inc., sub of Kayser-Roth Corp.
(NYC) 1976-77
Girls' panties and undershirts

Century Products (Cleveland) 1966-67, 71-72
Infants vinyl dressing tables, inflatable chairs

Rudy Cervantes Neckwear, Inc./Cervantes
Neckwear, Inc. (LA) 1972-87
Men's neckties, belts, ladies' scarves

Chalk Line (Anniston, AL) 1987
Jackets (award, polar fleece, coaches and
windbreakers

Hugh Chalmers Jr., Pontiac Spring and Bumper
Co. (Detroit, MI) 1937-40
Bouncing toy

Chambers Belt Co., Inc. (Phoenix, AZ) 1984-86
Belts (infants through adults), children's western
kerchief, leather stools

Champion Products, Inc. (Rochester, NY)
1983, 87
T-shirts, sweatshirts and warm-up suits for
schools through grade 12

Chanal Plastics Corp. (Rego Park, NY) 1958-59
Vacuum-formed plastic pieces to assemble dolls

Character Art Manufacturing Co., Inc.
(Brooklyn, NY) 1935-37
Thermometers

Character Novelty Company (South Norwalk,
Connecticut) 1940-47
Stuffed toys

Charlotte Charles, Inc. (Chicago) 1976-77
Jelly and ice cream topping gift sets

Charlsam Footwear Corporation (Brooklyn, NY)
1939-40

Slippers

The Charmore Company (NYC) 1946-47
Jewelry, ballpoint pens

Chatham Manufacturing Company
(Elkin, NC/NYC) 1950-52, 86-87
Woven crib blankets

J. Chein and Co., Inc./Chein Industries, Inc.
(Newark, NJ/Burlington, NJ/NYC) 1953-55, 68-85
Lithographed metal toys, sand pails, serving
trays, wastebaskets, canister sets, cookie jars,
spinning tops, paper towel holder, metal containers, Bi-centennial sparklers

Chemtoy Corporation (Chicago) 1970-81
Modeling dough, bubble toys, play wallets and
money sets, jump robes, play putty, Easter coloring sets, jack and ball sets

Chesapeake & Ohio Railway Company
(Cleveland) 1946-50
Right to decorate 3 family coaches with Disney
characters, including playroom & theater

Chester Mfg. Co. (Henderson, TN) 1968-73
Jeans and shorts

Chicago Art Needle Works Co. (Chicago) 1938-39
Needlework kits

Chicago Printed String Co. (Chicago) 1939-42
Gift wrappings

Chicago Superior Mirror Works
(Chicago) 1944-46
Wall plaques

Chicopee Mills, Inc. (NYC) 1955-62
Flat and fitted youth bed sheets, diaper pads,
diaper holders, disposable diapers

Childcraft Coat Company Inc. (NYC) 1964-65
Mary Poppins coats, coat and hat sets

Child Guidance Toys, Inc. (Bronx, NY) 1964-73
Magnetic puzzles, Mick-A-Matic camera

Child Life Wallpaper Company, Inc.
(Kingston, NY) 1953-55
Wallpaper

Childhood Interests, Inc. (Roselle Park, NJ)
1955-57
Lady and the Tramp, Davy Crockett jointed figures and puppets, Davy Crockett tom-tom

Childstar, Ltd. (NYC) 1974
Rings and barrettes, silver and woodgrain table
radios

Chocolate International, div of Confections by
Sandra (Canoga Park, CA) 1987
Fine Chocolates

Kay Christy of California (LA) 1937-39
Mickey Mouse and Silly Symphony fabric made
into garments, table linen, draperies, etc. (not to
be sold to the public as fabric)

The Cincinnati Galvanizing Co. (Cincinnati, OH)
1962-64
Metal stamped & formed waste paper baskets,
table & chair sets, hampers

Cinderella Foods (Dawson, GA) 1947-50
Peanut Butter

Cinderella Hat Co., Inc. (NYC) 1960-61
Girls' hats

Henry A. Citroen (NYC) 1944-46
Luminous pictures

Citrus World, Inc. (Lake Wales, FL) 1977-86
Fruit juices, fruit salads, canned, frozen, and fresh
fruit

Joseph H. Clark (NYC) 1932
Women's silk hosiery

Clarson Dairy Co. (Richland Center, WI) 1953
Ice cream and sherberts

Clayton div of Kellwood Corp. (NYC) 1971-72
Dresses

Cleo Wrap Corporation, div of Gibson Greeting

Cards, Inc. (Memphis, TN) 1968,1970-72, (NYC) 1976-87
Gift wrap, gift wrap package with bows and ribbon, Santa sacks

Clevelite Products, Inc. (Cleveland, OH) 1946-48
Table and wall lamps

Clopay Corp. (Cincinnati, OH) 1936-39
Stuffed dolls, window shades, place mats, etc.

Clover Embroidered Trimmings, Inc. (NYC) 1975-83, 85
Embroidered patches, iron ons

Cohan, Roth, and Stiffson (NYC) 1946-47
Neckties, T-shirts

Victor Cohen Inc. (NYC) 1964-65
Mary Poppins hats

T. Cohn Inc. (Brooklyn, NY) 1956-60
Record players, records, games, metal lithos

Cohn and Rosenberger (NYC) 1931-36, 41-42
Children's novelty jewelry

Cohn-Hall-Marx (NYC) 1938-41, 59-69
Printed cottons, "Con-Tact" (vinyl wall covering)

Colcombet-Werk, Inc. (NYC) 1937-39
Silk printed fabrics

Coleco Industries (Hartford, CN) 1972-73, 76-77
Children's snow shovel, shorty skis, sand box, snow-cone maker, doll carriages

Colgate-Palmolive-Peet Co. (Jersey City, NJ/NYC) 1937-40, 53, 68
8 pictures of Snow White and Seven Dwarfs given away with the purchase of Super Suds (37-40), Peter Pan soap and map (53), "Soaky" liquid bubble bath, "Soaky" soap bar dispenser, picture and bars

Collegiate Pacific (Gardena, CA) 1976-86
T-shirts and sweatshirts for schools

Collins-Kirk, Inc. (Chicago) 1932
"Sticker Tots" (Paper cut-outs)

Collund Manufacturing Corp. (LA) 1947
Toy motion picture projectors

Colorama, Inc. (LA) 1947-48
Chenille bedspreads

Colores International, Inc. (Bellevue, WA) 1987
Windsock™ banners

Colorforms (Norwood/Ramsey, NJ) 1959-87
Vinyl stick-on activity sets, rubber stamp sets, print putty, Peg-Pals, dress-up toys, gardening sets, rub-ons, sewing cards

Colourpicture Publishers (Boston) 1979-86
Boxed Valentines, punch-out Valentine books, decorated gift boxes, wall plaques

The Colson Company (Elyria, OH/NYC) 1933-35
Tricycles

Columbia Products Corporation (Brooklyn, NY) 1937-38
Waterproof bag made of suedine, suitable for carrying toys books, etc. — known as "Kiddie Kit," beach and knitting bags

Columbia Records (NYC) 1955
Story-telling albums, Davy Crockett records

Comdial Corporation (NYC) 1985
Telephones, phonelamps and accessories

Comet Candy (Brooklyn, NY) 1946-49
Candy bars, etc.

Come Play Products Company (Worcester, MA) 1975-76
Corrugated walk-in playhouse

Comfort Slipper Company (Long Island, NY) 1932
Slippers

Commonwealth Toy and Novelty Co. (NYC) 1938-40, 70-72
Autograph toy with pen, curler bags and caddies

Comptone Company, Limited (NYC) 1955-62, 68
Sunglasses

Concept 2000/Intoport Development Company (NYC/Miami, FL) 1972-81
Fold-away Disney Playworld game, transistor radios, table radios, take-apart clock, intercom set, "Walkie-talkie" set, bicycle horn, 3-dimensional figures, powdered soap dispenser, calculator, tape recorder, talking card player (See also: Mattel Toys)

Cone Expert and Commission Co. (NYC) 1938-40
Fabrics

Congoleum-Nair, Inc. (Kearny, NJ) 1961-63
Rugs, yard goods

Milton B. Conhaim Retail Reporting Bureau (NYC) 1941-42
Use of Donald & nephews in advertising materials

Connecticut Leather Co. (Hartford, CT) 1955-56
Moccasin and handbag kits, leathercraft kits

Connor Toys (Wausau, WI) 1971-72
Wood inlay puzzle

Consolidated Biscuit Co. (Chicago) 1938-40
Suckers

Container Corporation of America (Chicago/NYC) 1944-46, 48-50
"Slotties," "Joinies" and advertising premiums

Continella Industries Corp. (NYC) 1970-71
Printed fabric of knit or woven construction

Continental Cushion Spring Co. (Chicago) 1938-40
Children's leatherette hassocks and chairs

Continental Hosiery Corp. (NYC) 1947-56
Children's hosiery (anklets and socks)

Continental Paper Box Company (Philadelphia) 1970-73
Framed character wall plaques

Continental Undergarment Co., Inc. (Brooklyn, NY) 1938-39
Panties, bloomers and slips

Converse Rubber Company (Malden, MA/NYC/Chicago/St. Paul, MN) 1933-44
Shoes and rubber boots (shoes were canvas), storm boots, rubber shoes

Ben Cooper, Inc. (NYC/Brooklyn) 1943-87
Costumes, masks, play outfits, Christmas wall plaques, tree skirts, fun ponchos

Floyd L. Cooper (Huntington, CA) 1933-34
Wooden jewelry

Michael Cooper (NYC) 1933
Children's bath and lounging robes

Gertrude Cornell (Blairstown, NJ) 1954-56
Disney costumes for promotional use

Corning Glass Works (Corning, NY) 1974
Christmas ball ornaments

Coro, Inc., aka Eastern Jewelry Mfg. Co. (NYC) 1948-53, 56
Costume Jewelry (except rings)

Cosmopolitan Doll and Toy Corp. (Jackson Heights, NY) 1955-57
Dolls

Cosrich (Perth Amboy, NJ) 1987
Toiletries

Courvoisier Galleries (San Francisco/NYC) 1938-46
Framed cels and pictures

Guthrie Courvoisier (San Francisco) 1946
Framed pictures having a three-dimensional effect

Wm. E. Coutts, Ltd. (Canada) 1949-50
Greeting cards

Covington Fabrics Corp. (NYC) 1955-56
Mickey Mouse and Davy Crockett curtains, drapes and bedspreads

Cowden Mfg. Co. (Lexington, KY) 1968
Jeans, shorts

Craftool Company (Wood Ridge, NJ) 1972-73
Craft kits

Craftsman's Guild (LA) 1943-49
Kodachrome Slides and Viewers

Cragstan Corporation (NYC) 1967-71
Pull toys, tip toe dancing toys, slush molded vehicle toys, rock and roll toys, injection molded pull toys

Cramer-Tobias-Meyer, Inc. (NYC) 1938-1941
Promotional specialties, printed specialties

Crawford Furniture Mfg. Co. (LA/Shreveport, LA/Waco, TX/St. Charles, IL) 1934-35
Pillows, tents, chairs, stools

Creations for Children (Chicago) 1945-46
Children's furniture and hassocks

Creative Merchandisers Co. (Chicago) 1957-59
Series of 8 Snow White and the Seven Dwarfs wall plaques

H.S. Crocker (San Bruno, CA) 1979-87
Postcards

Crown Novelty Company., Inc. (Philadelphia) 1936-37
Curtains and draperies

The Crown Overall Mfg. Co. (Cincinnati, OH) 1935-38
Clothing, playsuits

Crown Toy Mfg. Co., Inc. (Brooklyn, NY) 1937-41
Banks and dolls

Crunden-Martin Mfg. Co. (St. Louis) 1964-66
Paper kites

The Cudahy Packing Company (???) 1940-41
Pinocchio Hats for boys and girls given away with purchase of 2 pounds of Sunlight Butter

Curtiss Candy Co. (Chicago) 1938
Candy

H. H. Cutler & Company, Inc. (Grand Rapids, MI) 1979-87
Infants' play and sleepwear, combination receiving blanket, bib and sleepwear, boys' and girls' coordinated playwear

Cypress Novelty Corporation (Brooklyn, NY) 1936-38
Birthday cake candles and holders

Thomas D'Agostino (Philadelphia) 1958-59
Zorro buttons

Daffy of California (LA) 1986-87
Junior and misses swimwear and cover-ups

Daisy Manufacturing Company (Plymouth, MI/NYC) 1955-59
Mickey Mouse and Davy Crockett pistol and holder sets, pop guns, pistols, powder horns, plastic canteens, target games, safety belt, toy rifles

R. Dakin and Company (San Francisco) 1972-73
Articulated vinyl figures

Danal Jewelry Company (Providence, RI) 1970-71
Costume jewelry

Danara Products, Inc./Danara International, Ltd. (South Hackensack, NJ) 1975-87
Pacifiers, teethers, diaper pins, training cups, food warmer, hot dish, training toothbrush, training hair brush, musical bells toy, "Klatter Balls" toy, lace locks, safety scissors

Danny Dare, Inc./Little Squire (Kansas City, MO) 1965-66, 68-73
Little Eton suit, vest, jacket, sports coat, blazers & coats (Sears)

Danoca Industries, Inc. (NYC) 1966-73
Winnie the Pooh knit skirts and dresses (Sears)

Dapol Plastics, div of Plascor, Inc. (Worcester, MA) 1957-60, 71-72

Outdoor garden figurines (lawn decorations)

Dasco Manufacturing Co., Inc., sub. of Pak-Well Corp. (Oakland, CA) 1973-74
Composition books, looseleaf paper, binders, memo books, activity kits (see also: Pak-Well)

David Aircraft Products, Inc. (Northport, L.I., NY) 1963
Auto seat belts

Davis and Holly, Inc. (NYC) 1932
Stationery

The Dayton Toy and Specialty Co. (Dayton, OH) 1935-36
Wheel toys: steel wagons, scooters, buttons

Debway Corporation (NYC) 1952-53
Children's handbags

**Decca Distributing Corporation/
Decca Records, Inc.** (NYC) 1947-55
Record albums (also Davy Crockett)

Decoplaque, Inc., sub. of American Technical Industries (NYC) 1980
Christmas wall plaques

Deka Plastics, Inc. (Elizabeth, NJ) 1984-86
Toy box, table and chair set, Sport Goofy plastic dinnerware

Dell Publishing Company, Inc. (NYC) 1938-42, 47-63
Newsstand editions and Walt Disney Comics, Davy Crockett comics

Delman Inc. (NYC) 1950
Cinderella slippers for advertising, exploitation, and publicity

Delmonico Foods, Inc. (Louisville, KY) 1948-50
Macaroni, Spaghetti, etc.

MICKEY MOUSE

Delta Jewelry and Casting Co. (LA) 1945-48
Jewelry

Deluxe Game Corporation (Wilkes Barre, PA/NYC) 1968
Blackboards, toy chests

Deluxe Premium Corp. (NYC) 1955-56
Snow White rubber doll (clothed), 7 Dwarfs rubber figurines

Denis Crib, Inc. (Holyoke, MA) 1961
Wooden doll cribs & beds, educational toys

Dennison Mfg. Co. (Farmington, MA/NYC) 1933-36, 62-65
Party supplies (printed crepe papers, napkins, table covers, doilies and decorations

DEP Corporation (LA) 1974-77
Children's hair and skin care products, bubble bath

Derby Sportswear, Inc. (NYC) 1955
Girls' shirts, blouses, play suits (Lady and the Tramp only)

Designcraft (NYC) 1986-87
14K gold, sterling silver and vermeil jewelry

Determined Productions, Inc. (San Francisco) 1970-73
Throw pillows, paperweights, oversized coloring books, bookends

Detroit Creamery Co. (Detroit) 1938
Advertising materials

De-Ward Novelty (Angola, NY) 1939-41
Ring toss game

Dewl Plastic-Toy Corp. (Newport, Long Island, NY) 1957-58
Link kits, plastic bracelets, sparkle art, spelling game, fire safety toy

Dexter Manufacturing Company (Providence, RI) 1952-84
Charm bracelets (Mickey Mouse, Lady and the Tramp, Davy Crockett), necklaces, lockets, pin, cuff links, tie bars, tie tacks, costume jewelry, souvenir teaspoons

Diablo Products Corp., sub of General sales Corp. (Concord, CA) 1982-85
Musical light switch

Diamond Crystal Shaker Salt (???) 1940-41
Pinocchio balloon given away with each package of salt. Also salt sold through newspaper ad depicting Pinocchio

Theodore Diamond, Inc. (NYC) 1937-37
Mirrors

Diener Industries, Inc. (Van Nuys, CA) 1968, 1970-72
Itty Bittys, erasers, "Jigglers" (bendable figures), finger puppets and erasers

Joseph Dixon Crucible Co. (Jersey City, NJ) 1931-42
Pencils and Pencil Boxes

Charles William Doepke Mfg. Co., Inc. (Rossmayne, OH) 1955
Mickey Mouse Club express, outdoor train, Disneyland copter

Dolls by Jerri (Charlotte, NC) 1982-85
Porcelain dolls with accessories

Dolly Toy Co. (Dayton/Tipp City, OH) 1934-35, 51-55, 59, 68, 70-87
Animated Mickey Mouse toys, paper-board wall plaques (Multi-piece pin-ups), lamps, crib mobiles, switch plates and blocks

Donald Art Co., Inc. (Mamaroneck, NY) 1950-51
School tablet covers

David D. Doniger, and Co. (NYC) 1933-34
Sweaters

The Donruss Co. (Memphis, TN) 1965
Gum trading cards - Disneyland 10th anniversary series

Doris Lamp Shades, Inc. (NYC) 1938-39
Lamp Shades

Doubleday & Co., Inc. (NYC) 1964-65
Emil & the Detectives books

Doughboy Industries, Inc. (New Richmond, WI) 1948-49, 58
Inflatable plastic toys

Dover Handbags Co. (NYC) 1987
Hug-A-Pet knapsacks, handbags (part bag—part plush)

Draper-Maynard Company (Plymouth, NH) 1933-34
Sporting goods

Dream Girl (Columbia, TN) 1970-72
Robes

Dri-Mark Products, Inc. (Mt. Vernon, NY) 1968-70
Felt tip markers, markers with coloring book

Jack Dubin Mfg. Corp. (NYC) 1936-37
Ladies' hats

Duchess Doll Corp. (Jackson Heights, NY) 1952-54
Dolls (Peter Pan and Tinkerbell)

Helen Hughes Dulany (Chicago) 1933-35
Trays

Donald F. Duncan, Inc. (Evanston, IL) 1962-65
Spinning tops, paddle balls, plastic kites, yo-yo return tops

Dundee Mills Inc. (NYC) 1987
Infant bedding

DuPont de Nemours (NYC) 1940-41, 55-58
Pinocchio ads depicting DuPont enamel paint (40-41), hand and nail brushes, tooth brushes, tooth brush holders, combs and comb cases, soap and powder containers

Durand Mfg. Co. (Chicago) 1964-65
Autograph books, photo albums, scrap books, diaries, pencil caddies, telephone and address books, blotter pads for desks banks, waste baskets

Durham Industries (NYC) 1972-1983
Wind-up walking toys, battery operated trains, plastic figures, water guns

Dynamic Merchandising Inc. (Minneapolis, MN) 1976
Placemats, adult target game, bathtub appliques, door knob hangers

Dynamic Toy, Inc. (Brooklyn, NY) 1962
Decal skin transfers

E-Z Mills, Inc. (NYC) 1953-73
Mickey Mouse and Davy Crockett sweat shirts, knitted cotton underwear, knitted cotton sleepwear with feet

Eagle Affiliates div. of Admiral Plastics Corp. (Brooklyn, NY) 1972-84
Plastic cups, mugs, bowls, pop moulds, molded children's furniture

Eagle Knitting Mills (Milwaukee) 1970-73
Scarf/hockey cap set

Eagle Rubber Co., Inc. (Ashland, OH) 1949-55
Rubber balls and balloons

Eastern Jewelry Mfg., Inc. (NYC) 1949-50, 52
Costume jewelry

Ebeling and Reuss (Philadelphia) 1955-???
Importers of Disney Goebel figures

Eckhardt, Max, and Sons (NYC) 1968
Christmas ornaments

Eckmar Corp. (Oakbrook, IL) 1967-68
Christmas decorations

Econolite Corporation (LA) 1954-57
Lamps, silk screen pictures

Economy Blouse Company div. of Kelvyn May Co., Inc. (NYC) 1955
Blouses (Lady and the Tramp only)

Economy Products Corp. (Chicago) 1961-62
Babes In Toyland comforters

L. M. Eddy Mfg. Co., Inc. (Framingham, MA) 1955-57
Mickey Mouse, Disneyland, and Frontierland play outfits, Davy Crockett outfits (hats, holsters, pistols, etc.)

Edgewood Knitwear Company (Hempstead, NY) 1965-66
Winnie the Pooh sweaters (Sears)

Ed-U-Card (Commack, NY) 1968-78
Educational card games, children's craft kits (see also: Binney and Smith, Inc.)

Effanbee Doll Corporation (NYC) 1985-86
Dressed vinyl character dolls

Finson-Freeman Company (Long Island, NY) 1933-34, 39
Paper masks

Einson-Freeman Publishing Corp. (NYC) 1935-36
Electric Game (Funny Facts)

Eisendrath Glove Company (Chicago) 1933-36
Gloves and mittens for boys, girls, children

Howard Eldon, Ltd. (Van Nuys, CA) 1972-84
Cloisonne and cast jewelry, costume lacquer box

Eldon Manufacturing Company (LA) 1954-60
Toy beach and garden sets, jump ropes with plastic handles, Lady and the Tramp pull toys, drinking tumblers

Elegent Heir (E. Norwalk, CT) 1965-70
Sport coats, suits

Elgin National Industries/Time Products Group (NYC) 1972-85
Disney character watches and clocks

Elliot Knitwear Corp./Elliot International, Inc. (NYC) 1959-63, 71-83
Knitted slipper sock, Children's handbags, wallets, coin purses, key holders

Elrene Manufacturing Corporation (NYC) 1952-55
Plastic aprons, raincapes, novelty hats, Davy Crockett hat (synthetic fur) daughter and doll vinyl apron sets

Ely and Walker Dry Goods Co. (St. Louis, MO) 1933-34
Girls dresses, etc.

Emenee Industries, Inc. (NYC) 1955-58, 64-67
Musical instruments

Emerson Radio and Phonograph Corp. (NYC) 1933-40
Radios and portable phonographs

Emery Industries, Inc. (Cincinnati, OH) 1957-58
Printed dry cleaning bags

Empire/Empire of Carolina (see Carolina Enterprises, Inc.)

Empire Pencil Company, div. of Hasbro Ind., Inc. (Shelbyville, TN) 1968-71
Pencil cases

Empire Products Corporation (Two Rivers, MI/NYC/San Francisco/Chicago) 1935-37
Pop corn popper

Empire Shield Company, Inc. (Brooklyn, NY) 1968-84
Infants' stretch garments, diaper bags, waterproof baby pants

Empire State Woven Label Co., Inc. (NYC) 1955-56
Mickey Mouse and Mouseketeer woven labels

Enesco Imports, Inc. (Chicago) 1968-72
Ceramics, cookie jars, banks, mugs, planters, pencil caddy with sharpener

Englander Co., Inc. (St. Paul, MN) 1973-???
Mattresses, bunk and trundle beds, adult bedding

Cliff Engle Associates (Carlstadt, NJ) 1985-87
Boys' and men's jaquered sweaters

Entex Industries, Inc. (Compton, CA) 1982-83
Loc Blocs construction sets

E.P.I.C., Inc. (Philadelphia) 1965-71
Framed pictures

J.H. Erbrich Products Co. (Indianapolis) 1948-51
Household bleach and ammonia, mustard

Erie County Milk Association (Erie, PA) 1940
Cups

Ero Industries (Chicago) 1982-87
Slumber bags, life vests

E.S.G. Industries, Inc. (Elgin, IL) 1970-71

Waste baskets

Etched Products Corp. (Long Island, NY) 1933-34
Match box holders, book marks

Ethelle (LA) 1939-40
Dresses and sportwear

Ettelbrick Shoe Company (Greenup, IL) 1968-69
Girls' patent stretch boots

David Ettelson (Chicago) 1955-57
Cameras and camera cases, flash attachments, tripods

Evans-Aristocrat Industries, Inc. (NYC) 1972-???
Teens' and women's leather goods, hair dryer hoods, curler bags, tape measures, cosmetic bags, watch bands, belts

Evenflo Juvenile Products Co., div of Questor Corporation (Ravenna, OH) 1984-87
Infant nursers

Everett Pulp and Paper Co. (Everett, WA) 1938-40
Writing and pencil tablets, notebooks, composition books, and loose leaf fillers

Ever Ready Label Corp. (NYC) 1955-56
Paper stickers with MMC emblems

Allen D. Everitt Knitting Co. (Milwaukee) 1969-70
Hockey cap, stocking caps, knit scarfs (Sears)

Ewing-Von Allmen Dairy Co. (Louisville, KY) 1940
Cups

ExCell Plastics (NYC) 1952-53
Plastic drapes

Excello Paper Products (Cincinnati, OH) 1955-56
Picture cards

F. & M. Shoe Shine Kits (Hollywood, CA) 1954-55
Shoe shine kits

F. & V. Manufacturing Co., Inc. (E. Providence, RI) 1945-47
Bracelets

Faber-Castell Corporation (Newark, NJ) 1975-87
Pens, pencils, markers, erasers, liquid paints, glue, colored pencils

Fabil Manufacturing Co. (NYC) 1976-80
Boys' and girls' rainwear and jackets

Fabrovin Co. div of Dart Industries (Paterson, NJ) 1971
Vinyl wall covering

Falcon Plastic Products Mfg. Co. (Culver City, CA) 1953-55
Plastic piggy bank, switch plates

Fallani & Cohn, Inc, (NYC) 1936-37
Table runners and cloths

Famous Character Promotions, Inc (NYC) 1963-64
Games or contests

Famous Raincoat (Flushing, NY) 1987
Girls' and boys' raincoats, ponchos, rainjackets

Famus Corporation (Brooklyn, NY) 1984-87
Carded small toy kits

Farm Crest Bakeries, Inc. (Detroit) 1936-37
Biscuits, cookies, crackers, and cakes

Farmington Industries (St. Louis) 1971-72
WTP washable infants shoes

Farragut Company (NYC) 1952-53
Girls' bathing suits, play clothes

Fashion Footwear Co., Inc. (Rutherford, NJ) 1969-70
Children's slippers

Fashion-Rite Girl Coat Co., Inc. (NYC) 1966
Girl's double breasted wool coat with velveteen collar

Federal Glass Company (???) 1975
Ceramic figurines, wall plaques, assorted gift items, glassware

Federal Glass Company of Ohio (???, OH) 1955
Supplied glass tumblers to Canada Packers Ltd. for York Peanut butter

Feldco Loose Leaf Corp. (Chicago) 1949-50
Binders, tablets, etc.

James Feldman (Brooklyn, NY) 1939-41
Washing compound

Ferry-Morse Seed Co., Inc. (Mtn. View, CA) 1965-67
Pre-planted planters

Fidelity Packaging (Oakland, CA) 1987
Decorative boxes

Fine Art Pillow and Specialties Corp. (NYC) 1948-51
Chair pads, playpen pads, crib bumpers, etc.

Fine Arts Pictures (NYC) 1937-39
Cut-out figures and wall plaques

Fine Industries, Inc. (Deerfield Beach, FL) 1985-86
Soap sponge toiletry items

Fine Infants Dress Co., Inc. (NYC) 1938-39
Children's dresses

Fiorentini Imports (NYC) 1987
Ladies' designer denims without ornamentation

Fisch and Co., Inc. (LA) 1931-33
Pants, caps and emblems, Mickey Mouse felt pennants, banners, caps

A. S. Fishbach, Inc. (NYC) 1938-42
Costumes

Fisher Price Toys, div. Quaker Oats Co. (East Aurora, NY/NYC) 1935-59, 63-64, 75-87
Toys (wooden pull type), Mickey Mouse choo choo, MM puddle jumper, Donald Duck cart, hand operated 8mm viewer and cartridge, Table top 8mm projector and cartridge

H. Fishlove and Company (Chicago) 1939-41
Miniature live turtles with character decals on shellback

Fleischman Manufacturing Co. (NYC) 1944-46
Shoo-flys, table and chair sets, toy chests

Walter Fleisher Co. — see Selandria Designs

Flexo Products (Chicago) 1940-41
Lamps and shades

Flexton Corporation (NYC) 1952-53
Vinyl yard goods

Flights of Fancy (Santa Monica, CA) 1982-83
Soft-sculptured ceramic jewelry

Florida Citrus Canners Cooperative (Tampa/Lake Wales, FL) 1941-87
Canned citrus, juices (frozen)

Foremost Dairies (Jacksonville, FL) 1946-47
Orange juice

Foremost Dairies (San Francisco) 1967-68
Snow White milkshake mix

Forest Lamps & Gifts, Inc. (Brooklyn, NY) 1985-87
Capodimonte fine porcelain figurines

Fort, Inc. (E. Providence, RI) 1980-85
Character collectable spoons (silverplate and pewter) dinner bells and miniature plates

Fortune Toys (Jackson Heights, NJ) 1955-57
Character dolls (Mickey Mouse, Davy Crockett, Lady and the Tramp)

Foster Grant Co. (Leominster, MA) 1962-64
Donald Duck fun shower and lawn sprinkler

Fotoplak Co. (NYC) 1942-43
Plaques

Fox Sportswear, Inc. (San Marcos, CA) 1982
Nylon wallets, bags, checkbooks, key cases, eyeglass cases, wallet and calculator set

Franco Manufacturing Co., Inc. (NYC) 1976-87
Beach towels, kitchen ensembles, bath towels, embroidered fingertip towels

H. Frankenstein Company (LA) 1948-50
Boys' and juniors' woven textile shirts

Franklin Mint Corporation (Franklin Center, PA) 1982

Limited edition 26mm gold on silver "Winnie the Pooh" pendant commemorating 100th anniversary of A.A. Milne's birth

Franklin Tru-Fit Glove Company (Chicago/NYC) 1946-59
Gloves and mittens, scarf set

Frankonia Products, Inc. (NYC) 1966-69
Mickey Mouse top, touring bus, mechanical Pluto, Mickey, Donald handcar, Melody Train

W. N. Fraser and Co. (St. Louis, MO) 1955-56
"Frontierland" decals

Freeman-Toor Corp. (NYC) 1967
Boys' & infant corduroy Chukka boots, infant corduroy Bluchers

G.H. and E. Freyburg, Inc. (NYC) 1933-34,72
Stamped materials (33-34), dresses (72)

Friedberger-Aaron Mfg. Co. (Philadelphia) 1933-34
Wash cloths, dish cloths

Fruit Products Corporation (NYC) 1951-57
Wrappers for frozen confections

Fuld and Company, div. of Metropolitan Greetings, Inc. (Rockaway, NJ/Cambridge, MA) 1968-79
Valentine cards, punch out Valentine, boxed Christmas cards

Fulton Specialty Co. (NYC/Elizabeth, NJ) 1933-42
Rubber stamping sets and games

Fun Frills (NYC) 1965-73
Aprons, dresses, shifts, pants sets

Fundimensions div. of CPG Products Corp. (Mt. Clemens, MI) 1981-84
Juvenile craft kits (see also: Lionel of Fundimensions)

G.A.F. Corp./Sawyer, Tru-Vue and View-Master are subs. (Portland, OR/NYC) 1970-81
3-D film cards, viewers, color reels, and projectors, scramble game, camera, Showbeam projector, Tru-Vue and View-Master products

G.S.I. Distributors (Houston) 1985-86
Fine stainless steel children and infant flatware sets

Samuel Gabriel Sons and Co., Inc./Gabriel Industries (NYC) 1955-62, 66-82
Cardboard blocks, paper dolls, games, trapeze toys, puppets, tricky walkers, pull toys, Pop-O-Matic games, squeeze toys, musical Jack-in-the-box, pop pals, busy infant toys, roly polys, tricky trikes, Gabriel action novelty toys, child guidance infant and preschool toys, bubble pipes, target sets, toy TV sets, plastic pill puzzle, scissors, water guns, game wheel, (see also: CBS Toys, Gabriel Industries, div. of CBS, Inc.)

Galax Mirror Co. (Galax, VA) 1938-39
Mirrors

Garan, Inc. (NYC) 1983
Children's and adults' sweaters

Gardner and Company (Chicago) 1955-60
Basketball game, bean bag bucket game, Casey Jr. game, Davy Crockett adventure play set

Gare, Inc. (Haverhill, MA) 1975-1978
Molds, plaster castings remained available until 1986

Gaston Manufacturing Company (Cincinnati, OH) 1953-55
Wooden block puzzles, changeable story puzzles

Gay Belle Mfg. Co., Inc. (NYC) 1961-62
Babes In Toyland aprons

Gay-Craft (NYC) 1947-48
Schoolbags and novelties

Geisha Robe Company, Inc. (NYC) 1955-71
Boys' and girls' robes, pajamas, nightgowns and sleeping bags

Wendy Gell Jewelry, Inc. (NYC) 1987

Costume jewelry, gloves, handbags, belts, denim jackets all hand encrusted with jewels, sequins, feathers and ornamentation of the like

Gelmart Knitting Mills, Inc. (Great Neck, Long Island, NY) 1967-68
Stretch knit gloves (Sears)

Gem Color Company, Inc. (NYC) 1958
Rocks, minerals, jewelry and craft kits

General Beverages, Inc. (Chattanooga, TN) 1952-55
Donald Duck Cola, Donald Duck soft drinks

General Electric Company, Radio Receiver department/Northern Lights Concourse (Utica/Syracuse, NY) 1970-75
"Show 'n Tell" phono-viewers, Picturesound programs, clock-radios, phonographs

General Electric Company, Wiring Device department (Providence/Warwick, RI) 1968-87
Nite Guide Lights, switch plates

General Foods Corp. (NYC) 1933-42, 58-59, 82
Post Toasties cereal box cut-outs featuring Mickey Mouse and friends, Silly Symphonies, Ferdinand the Bull, Snow White and Pinocchio, use in ads

General Ice Cream Corp. (Schenectady, NY) 1940
Cones

General Mills, Inc. (Minn., MN) 1947-48, 50-51, 53-59, 63-65
"Cheerios" cereal, Wheaties, etc.

General Mills Fun Group, Inc. (Mt. Clemens, MI) 1972-74
Toy train sets

General Molds and Plastics Corp. (Pittsburgh) 1956-57
Remote controlled electric toy irons

General Products of Chicago (Chicago) 1956-57
Photo and activity albums

General Ribbon Mills, Inc. (NYC) 1933-36, 38-43
Ribbons

Herbert George Co. (Chicago) 1946-48
Cameras and dresser sets

Germain Seed and Plant Company (LA) 1937-40
Flower seeds

Gersten Brothers, Inc. (NYC) 1953-54
Fibre board toy chest

Geuder, Paeschke and Frey Co. (Milwaukee, WI) 1935-37
Lunch kit

Geyer, Cornell and Vewell, Inc. (NYC) 1942
Promotional materials

Gibson Art Company/Gibson Greeting Cards (Cincinnati, OH) 1956-59, 85-87
Greeting cards, bridge tallies, calendars, candles, gift wrap, ribbons, bows, tags, packaged cards, party papers (also see: Cleo Wrap)

Gilberg Brothers (Philadelphia) 1968-69
Dresses

Gilbert and Ryan, Inc. (Canton, MI) 1976-77
Leg stools

A.C. Gilbert Co. (New Haven, CT) 1963-64
Scrubble Bubble

Gildex Corporation (NYC) 1950-53
Towel, wash cloth set, beach robes

Gillette Safety Razor Company (Boston) 1939-41
Pinocchio masks are offered as give-aways to promote sales of Gillette Blue Blades

I. Ginzkey-Maffersdorf, Inc. (NYC) 1931-32
Baby blankets

Glaser-Crandell Co. (Chicago) 1934-36
Jam (jars could be used as banks)

Glass, Henry, and Co., Inc. (NYC) 1952-53, 87
Cotton yard goods, cut-outs

Glenco Infants Items, Inc. (Dumont/Northvale, NJ) 1968-86
Bibs, crib pads, knitted diapers, training pants, sun suits (also see: Playskool Mfg. Company)

Glenn Confections, Inc. (Buffalo) 1937-39
Chewing gum

Glensder Textile Company (NYC) 1939-40, 45-55
Scarfs and ascots (women's and children's)

The Ernest Glick Company (Chicago) 1966-67
Boys' tie and pocket square set

Glitter Products Company (Denver) 1955-56
"Glitter" decorating set (Davy Crockett and Lady and the Tramp), "pixie dust"

Globe Lighting Products, Inc. (Brooklyn, NY) 1947-49
Electric lighting fixtures

Globe-Union Inc. (Milwaukee, WI) 1957-59
Roller skates

E.R. Godfrey and Sons, Inc. (Milwaukee, WI) 1953
Frozen fruits and vegetables

Goebel (W. Germany) 1981-87
(Park licensee) Plates, figurines (see also: Ebeling and Reuss Co.)

Goebel United States (Pennington, NJ) 1986-87
Small World ceramic and wood figurines and dolls, standard character figurines, Baby Mickey program assorted items, miniatures

Gold Bond Ice Cream Company (Green Bay, WI) 1975-86
Mouseketeer Bars, frozen ice sticks, snow cones, ice cream cones

Gold Key Comics (NYC) 1968
Comic magazines and digests

Gold Medal, Inc. (Racine, WI) 1984-85
Children's and adults' director chairs

Gold Seal Rubber Company (Boston, MA) 1973-77
Sneakers, rain and snow footwear

Golden Eagle Enterprises, Inc. (Selma, AL) 1984-85
Children's prescription eyeglass frames

Golden Press, div. of Western Publishing Co., Inc. (NYC) 1948-87
Golden books, toy books

B.J. Goldenberg, Inc. (NYC) 1943
Ladies millinery

The Gong Bell Mfg. Co. (E. Hampton, CT) 1956-60
Toy telephone, push chimes, rocking horse and rider toys, toy bus, blocks, music box

Good Housekeeping Magazine (NYC) 1938-42
Monthly comic or cartoon illustrations

H. Goodman and Sons, Inc. (???) 1939-41
Barrettes

L.A. Goodman Co. (Chicago) 1966-67
Nursery decorator kits

B. Gordon Press (NYC) 1944-46
Tattoos

Gordy International Inc. (E. Brunswick, NJ) 1980-81
Battery-operated toys, water target game

Gort Girls' Frocks (NYC) 1962-63
Dresses and sportswear for children

Gotham Pressed Steel Corporation (NYC) 1938-40
Toy cleaning sets

Gottfried Oppenheimer, Inc. (NYC) 1950-52
Children's playclothes, sweaters, beach coats, and bathing suits

Goyer Company (Greenville, MI) 1948-50
Coffee

Graber Company (Middleton, WI) 1973-76
Decorated window shades

Graham Mfg. Co. (Holyoke, MA) 1938-39
Gift wrappings

The Grant Mfg. Co., Inc. (Oklahoma City) 1951-53
Plastic cookie cutters

Great American Design Center (LA) 1987
Bags of all types made of nylon, canvas, vinyl, fleece or denim with or without fabric, leather patches or trim

Great American Novelty Co./Great American Plastics Co. (Leominster, MA) 1940-43, 48-51, 56-57
Baby toys, Christmas ornaments, dolls, etc.

Great American Plastics Co. (Fitchburg, MA/ Nashua, NH) 1949-51, 56-57
Toys, banks, crayons, polyethylene nursing bottles, toys

Great Lakes Press Corp. aka Rendoll Paper Corp. (Rochester, NY) 1950-55
Gift wrappings, party kits, paper napkins

Green America (Norwood, NJ) 1977
Gardening sets

Green Duck Company (Chicago) 1957, 63-66, 68-69
Buttons

Green Way Mfg. Co. (Dallas) 1939-40
Play clothes, slack suits, pajamas, and night-gowns for children

W H Greene, Co. (Chicago) 1943-45
Cardboard toy

E. Greenwald and Co. (NYC) 1953-56
Children's rayon panties

Grolier Enterprises Inc. (Danbury, CT) 1970's-87
Mail order sales of books, The Disneyana Collector newsletter, collectible porcelain bisque figures, plates, music boxes, ceramic plates, stained glass, dolls, Christmas ornaments and other commemorative merchandise

Grossett and Dunlap, Inc. (NYC) 1937-50, 66-71
Books, children's books

Grotta and Co., Inc. (NYC) 1941-42
Women's and girls' neckwear

Guild Lingerie of California (LA) 1962-63, 65-66
Sleepwear (Sears, Roebuck & Co.)

Antonio Guiseppe (LA) 1976-77
Men's and women's jackets (retail $400)

Gulf and Western Corporation (Bronx, NY) 1972
Mirrors, picture frames, wall organizers

Gum, Inc. (Philadelphia) 1933-37
Penny chewing gum

Gund Mfg. Co. (NYC/Chicago/San Francisco/ LA/Seattle) 1947-71
Stuffed toys, puppets, dolls, plush sleeping bags, plush carry-all bags

Carl Gutmann and Co., Inc. (NYC) 1946-51
Children's sportswear

H-G Toys, Inc. (Long Beach, NY) 1982-87
Cowboy sets, Jr. sports equipment, gardening sets, stickhorses, jump ropes, play gas pump and car tools, board items, rubber stamps, sand and beach toys, Jr. housekeeping

H.P. Incorporated (Ramona, CA) 1984-86
Ceiling fans

Hagen-Renaker Potteries (LA) 1955-61
Ceramic figures

Hales Pictures, Inc. (NYC) 1937-38
Poster pictures

Hall Bros., Inc. — also see: **Hallmark Cards, Inc.** (Kansas City/NYC) 1931-55
Greeting cards, bridge sets, card favors, "Hall-mark" greeting cards

Virginia Hall, Inc. (Macon, GA) 1953-54
Rubber bath sponges

Hallmark Cards, Inc. (Kansas City, MO) 1972-84
Greeting cards, holders, felt-tipped and ball point pens, postage stickers, bookmarks, switch plates, posters, party goods, plastic eating utensils, craft kits, stationery, posters, plaquettes, party favors, album, seals, pop-up books, cardboard cutouts, name tags, candles, party sets, plastic straws

Hallmark Homecraft Corporation (E. Natick, MA) 1970-71
Model-casting kits, "Knit-Wit Kits," "Pom Poms"

Halsam Products Co., later div. of Playskool Mfg. Co. in 68 (Chicago/NYC) 1934-43, 54-62, 68
Wooden alphabet and picture blocks, Davy Crockett Frontierland wooden construction kits

Hamilton Enterprises, Inc. (Kansas City, MO) 1938-41
Candy vendor

Hamilton Metal Products Co. (Hamilton, OH) 1935-36
Tools and tool boxes, fishing kits

Hamilton Watch Company (Long Island, NY) 1970
Clocks

Hampden Specialty Products, Inc. (Easthampton, MA) 1956-57
Metal folding table and chair set

The Hand Printers, Inc. (NYC) 1966
Mary Poppins sheets and cases

Victor B. Handal and Bro., Inc. (NYC) 1983-87
Gloves, mittens, ear muffs, leg warmers

Handi-Pac, Inc. (St. Louis, MO) 1961-63
Games and toys

Hanes Knitwear, Inc., div. of Consolidated Foods Corp. (Winston-Salem, NC) 1983-87
Boys' underwear

Hankscraft Company (Reedsburg, WI) 1957-72
Night lights, bottle warmers, feeding sets

Happyknit Inc. (NYC) 1968-70
Winnie the Pooh sweaters (Sears, Roebuck & Co.)

Harlyn Products Inc. (LA) 1970-72
Jewelry, keychains, Tie-tacs, etc. (Sears)

Harmony Books (NYC) 1979
Poster books, pop-up books

Harn Corp. (Chicago) 1962-63
Crib bumpers, play yard pads (Sears)

Haroco (Skokie, IL) 1980
Ceramic cookie jars and mugs

Harper and Bros. (NYC) 1938
Books

Harrell Brothers Canning Co. (Eastman, GA) 1948-50
Canned field peas, chowder, peas, pimentos

Harrich, Inc. Keepers of California (LA) 1972-74
Men's and youth hosiery

Harwood Company (Farmingdale, NJ) 1970
Plastic pails with shovels and Halloween novelty pails

Harwood Manufacturing Corp. (NYC) 1955-57
Mickey Mouse and Davy Crockett woven paja-mas, sleepwear, shorts

Hasbro Industries, Inc./Hasbro Bradley, Inc. sub of Playskool (Pawtucket, RI/Northvale, NJ) 1968, 1970-87
Coloring activities, talking telephones, rub-ons, sewing sets, Mickey Mouse gum ball machines, toy clock, marching Mickey, MM club playset, Dancing Donald and acrylic paint-by-number sets, Magic Kingdom playset, pencil box, Lite-brite, finger paints, plush toys, infant bibs and aprons, washcloths, hooded towels, trainer cups, infant feeder set

Hasko Trays, Inc. (Indianapolis) 1954-56
Serving trays

Hassenfeld Bros., Inc., later div. of Empire Pencil Co. in 68, div. of Hasboro, Inc. in 71 (Pawtucket, RI) 1949-69
Pencils, pencil kits, pouches, boxes, plus stationery sets, toy doctor and nurse kits, sewing kits, makeup kits, numbered coloring sets, talking Mickey Mouse coloring activities, Stardust, talking telephones, rub-ons

Haugh's Products Limited (???) 1949-50
Inflatable plastic toys, etc., and rainwear

Hawthorne House, Inc. (Bloomington, IL) 1972-73
Soap making set

Hazel-Atlas Glass Company (Wheeling, WV) 1955, 59
Mugs, cereal dishes and saucers (for sale to Ogilvie Flour Mills Co. Ltd. of Canada) tumblers of Sleeping Beauty for Proctor and Gamble

D.C. Heath and Company (Boston) 1939-51
Story readers, educational books

L.S. Heath and Sons, Inc. (Robinson IL) 1975-80
Milk chocolate bars

Hedstrom Company (Bedford, PA) 1976-77
Strollers, playpens, walkers, infants' swing, high chairs

Heelprint Company, Ltd. (Sebastopol, CA) 1972
Clothes hangers

Henry Heide, Inc. (NYC) 1938-39
Candy

H.J. Heinz Company (Pittsburgh) 1965-68
Happy Soups

Helm Toy Company (NYC) 1979-87
Operational camera, talking toothbrush and hairbrush, doll furniture, and animated quiz toy, bicycle horns, pom poms, dandy bike hand, handlebar grips

Hemmerich Inc. (Denver, PA) 1970-73
Stretch shorts & tops

Herbert Hosiery Mills, Inc. (NYC) 1938-39
Children's hosiery

The Herrmann Handkerchief Co., Inc. (NYC) 1932-51
Handkerchiefs, purses (children's)

Herz and Kory (NYC) 1931-33
Children's pocketbooks

Herz Manufacturing Corporation (NYC) 1947-68
Drinking straws

Hettrick Manufacturing Company (Toledo, OH/ Statesville, NC) 1955-59
Mickey Mouse and Davy Crockett tents, chest hassock, covered wagon (pedal wagon) with rifle and powder horn, tricycle with rifle and powder horn, chaise lounge, toy chest, dinette set, T.V. chair

Hickok Belt Co. (Rochester, NY) 1932-39, 70-71
Belts

A. Stein-Hickory, and Co. (NYC/Chicago) 1934
Clothing and accessories

Hi-Flier Manufacturing Company, Inc. (Penrose, CO/Decatur, IL) 1975-84
Kites

Hi Line Company Inc. (NYC) 1964
Children's vest & slacks sets

Highland Art Embroidery Co. (Pasadena) 1953-55
Toy embroidery sets

Highpoint Knitting (NYC) 1987
Socks, legwarmers, pantyhose, infant to adult

N. N. Hill Brass Co. (E. Hampton, CT) 1933-42
Metal pull and bell toys

Himalayan Pak Co., Inc. (Monterey, CA) 1957-59
Child's chair

His Nibs Shirt Corporation (NYC) 1955
Boy's woven shirts (Lady and the Tramp)

H-K Corporation (Atlanta) 1970-71
Men's, youths' and boys' pants

Hobby Stationers (Kansas City, MO) 1945-47
Children's stationery

Holiday Products, Inc. (West Warwick, RI) 1977-86
Christmas stockings and tree skirts

Holiday Publishing Company (Park Ridge, IL) 1969-72
Gift wrap and cards

Holland Hall Products, Inc. (Stamford, CT) 1963-68
Squeeze toys, baby bottle holder

F. Hollander and Son, Inc. (NYC) 1968-83
Umbrellas, rainwear

Hollywood Accessories (Compton, CA) 1979-83
Automobile convenience products

Hollywood Film Enterprises (Hollywood) 1932-50
16mm and 8mm film, color slides

Hollywood Luggage Co. (LA) 1947-48
Children's luggage

Hollywood Toycraft, Inc. (Glendale, CA) 1947-49
Metal construction sets

Hollywood Uniform Company, Inc. (LA) 1955
Hair cloths (for barber shops)

Home Foundry Mfg. Co. (Chicago) 1935-37
Caster sets and molds

Home Front Publishing Co. (NYC) 1943-44
"Mickey Mouse on the Home Front" — house organ

Homemaker Industries, div. of Beatrice Foods Co. (Chicago/Shawnee Mission, KS) 1976-80
Sleeping and slumber bags

Mickey & Co. by J. G. Hook, Inc. (NYC) 1985-87
Women's and men's sportswear and accessories

Hal Horne, Inc. (NYC) 1935-36
Mickey Mouse Magazine

Horsman Dolls, Inc. (NYC) 1964-84
Dolls, toy umbrellas, doll carrying case with toy umbrella, Mouseketeer doll and accessories, Mickey Mouse doll, laughing/talking Mickey Mouse doll

Host Apparel (NYC) 1987
Men's sleepwear and robes

House Beautiful Curtains, Inc. (NYC) 1965-66
Curtains, draperies, and bedspreads

The House of Perfection (NYC) 1966-67
Skirts

Hudson Electronics Corporation (Mt. Vernon, NY) 1952-53
Phonographs

Hudson Universal Ltd. (Englewood, NJ) 1984
Children's sunglasses

Hughes-Autograf Brush Co., Inc. (NYC) 1934-41
Brushes (hair and tooth)

Henry L. Hughes Company, Inc. (NYC) 1934-37
Toothbrushes and toilet sets

Hummel (see Ebeling and Reuss)

Hummelwerk, sub of Goebel Art (Elmsford, NY) 1984-85
Earthenware figurines, chess sets

Hungerford Plastics Corp. (Rockaway, NJ) 1955-57
Dolls (from 5-24 inches)

Hutzler Manufacturing Company (Long Island, NY) 1947-49
Napkin rings and holders

Hyde Athletic — see Brookfield

Hydrox Corp. (Chicago) 1940
Cups

Hygiene Shower Curtain Mfg. Co. (NYC) 1942-43
Shower curtains

I.S.I. Special Graphics Products, Inc. (Hicksville, NY) 1983
Rub-downs and rub-down notecard, stationery and postcard kits

ITT Continental Baking Co., Inc. (Rye, NY) 1973-80
Bread, cakes

Ice Cream Novelties, Inc. (NYC) 1948-53
Bags and wrappers for frozen confections

Ideal Aeroplane and Supply Co., Inc. (NYC) 1935-38
Toy Aeroplanes, construction sets, etc.

Ideal Novelty & Toy Co. (NYC) 1937-43
Dolls, plastic toy tea sets

Ideal Toy Corp. (Hollis, NY/NYC) 1952-53, 56-58, 68-82
Inflatable toy figures, pool and swim toys, 3-D games, inflatable furniture, shaker maker craft kits, move-a-picture vinyl carry-all books, spray paint kits, puncheo's, "Magic Ship," musical TV toy with reticulated screen, Yakkers

Illfelder Toy Co., Inc./Illco Intl. Ltd./Illco Toy Co. USA Ltd. (NYC) 1973-87
Pre-school, infant and juvenile toys

Imaginings 3 (Niles, IL) 1986-87
School bags, backpacks, purses, wallets

Impact Florida Inc. (Longwood, FL) 1982-87
Unframed and/or framed photo prints, photo-print calendars

The Imperial Knife Co. (Providence, RI/NYC) 1936-38, 55-59
Pocket knives, Davy Crockett pocket knives and novelty combination children's cutlery

Independent Grocers' Alliance (???) 1940-41
Series of 32 colorful Walt Disney Pinocchio poster stamps and albums

Independent Products Co. (West Point, PA) 1987
Hangers

Indiana Rayon Corp. (Greenfield, IN) 1965-69
Winnie the Pooh shirts (Sears)

Industrial Tape Corporation (New Brunswick, NJ) 1944-50
Gift tape and transfers

Infantseat Co. (Eldora, IA) 1971-72
Jump Up

Ingersoll-Waterbury Company (Waterbury, CT/Chicago/NYC/San Francisco) 1933-44
Watches and clocks (see also: United States Time Corp., Timex)

Inkograph Company, Inc. (NYC) 1935-38
Fountain pens

Interchemical Corporation (???) 1947-48
Fabric finishes

Intercontinent Toy Corp. (NYC) 1945-47
Tricycles, bicycles

Inter-Governmental Philatelic Corp. (NYC) 1979-87
Stamps, stamp albums, first-day covers, coins

Intermatic/Intermatic Electronics Corp. (Spring Grove, IL) 1986-87
Musical light switch

International Design Corp. 1972-74 (Chicago) 1972-74
Store displays, Christmas decoration

International Games (Joliet, IL) 1981-83
Rubber stamp machine

International Latex Corp. (NYC) 1936-42
Baby pants, bathing suits, sheeting

International Molded Plastics (Cleveland, OH) 1955-60

Plastic dinnerware

International Outerwear Inc. (NYC) 1965-66
Children's duffel coats

International Rotex, Inc. (Reno, NV) 1982-94
Hand-held embossing tool, vinyl label-maker tape

International Shoe Company (St. Louis, MO) 1957
Hardy Boys rings (mfg. by Specialty Advertising Services, Inc.), offered with shoes

International Silver Co. — also see: William Rogers and Son (Meriden, CT) 1931-41
Children's silverware, cups, plates, etc.

Interstate Industries (Mundelein, IL) 1976-82
Electric phonographs and radios

Intex Recreation Corporation/Intex International Corporation d/b/a **Zee Toys, Inc.** (Long Beach, CA) 1985-87
Summer inflatable toys, vinyl tents

Irresistible, Inc. (NYC) 1937
Advertising material

Irwin Corporation (Fitchburg, MA/NYC) 1949-51
Plastic toys and novelties

Alfred Israel Co. (Chicago) 1965-66
Winnie the Pooh six quarter crown stitched brim roller (Sears)

J and J Manufacturing Company (NYC) 1981-82, 87
Girls' trousers

JFD Electronics (Oxford, NC) 1975-77
Indoor TV antennas

Jacmar Mfg. Co., Inc. (NYC) 1953-61
Electronic question and answer game, printing set (also Davy Crockett 1955)

H. Jacob and Sons, Inc. (Brooklyn, NY) 1938-39
Slippers and shoes

Jackson (Yonkers, NY) 1987
Shower curtains, soapdishes, bathroom accessories

James Industries, Inc. (Hollidaysburg, PA) 1968
Slotted, compressed sponge toys

Walter J. Jamieson, Corporation (NYC) 1955-59
Lady and the Tramp children's bath sets, Mickey Mouse molded cosmetic soap

J'attoo Inc. (LA) 1987
Fashion skin jewels

Sharon Jay Togs (NYC) 1987
Woven separates and sets — girls' and boys'

Jay Zee Inc. (St. Louis) 1965-73
Skirts, slacks

Jaymar Specialty Co. (NYC) 1943-87
Jigsaw puzzles, games, pipe cleaner activity toy kit, piano books, musical jewelry boxes, toy organ, kazoos, string piano & puppet theater, toy piano, toy float, face maker activity game

Jebaily-Lonschein Co. (NYC) 1955
Women's negligees, robes, housecoats, brunch-coats, dusters

Jenkintown Metal Products (Jenkintown, PA) 1972-73
Infant swings and walkers, hampers, valets, playpens, sand boxes

Jewel Togs, Inc. (NYC) 1952-53
Snow suits, flannel lined estron jackets

Johnson and Johnson (???) 1938-39, 47-48
Snow White and Seven Dwarf game offered with the sale of every Tek toothbrush

Johnson Service Company (Chicago) 1940-41
Advertising materials

Joanna Western Mills (Chicago) 1985-86
Rollup shades, blinds

Jolly Blinker Company, Inc. (NYC) 1955-58

Mickey Mouse see-through straws and water-filled toys, other toys

Ralph H. Jones Co., Inc. (Cincinnati) 1940-41
Advertising materials

Tom Jones Sportswear, Inc. (Miami, FL) 1975-76
Men's, boys' and juvenile swim trunks

W.C. Jones Publishing Company (LA) 1968-71
Stereo-dimensional pictures

Jordan, Brown, and Co. (El Monte, CA) 1972-74
Patio chairs

Jorges Carpet Mills, Inc. (Rossville, GA) 1976-80
Carpets featuring children's games

Josie Accessories, Inc. (NYC) 1952-55
Peter Pan novelty hat, aprons, raincoats

Joy Carpets (Ft. Oglethorpe, GA) 1982
Tufted broadloom carpeting, featuring the Race to the Magic Kingdom game

The Judy Company (Minneapolis, MN) 1944-50
Inlay puzzles (wooden)

Judy Crib Sheet Company (Long Beach, CA) 1953-54
Crib sheets, juvenile sheets, pillow cases

M. Julian Co. (LA) 1987
Leather jackets, suede jackets, coordinating pants and skirts

Junal, Inc. (Paterson, NJ) 1962-63
Lady and the Tramp amplifier for transistor type radios

Just 4 Kids, div of Victor B. Handel & Bro., Inc. (NYC) 1985-87
Hats and accessories, boys' swimwear

Justin Products, Inc. (NYC) 1984-87
Children's radios, calculators, kiddie electronics

K.K. Publications, Inc. (NYC/Poughkeepsie, NY) 1938-49
Mickey Mouse magazine, "Walt Disney Comics" and newstand editions

Kay Kamen, Ltd. (NYC) 1936-41
Promotional items

MICKEY MOUSE

Kamen Soap Products Co., Inc. (Long Island, NY) 1961-62
Games

Kannapolis Mfg. Co., Inc. (Kannapolis, NC) 1955-57
Lady and the Tramp terry cloth kimono, terry cloth play pen set

Max Kasnowitz and Sons (NYC) 1938-39
Children's purses and pocketbooks

Ira G. Katz (NYC) 1938-39
Hats

Julius Katz & Son (NYC) 1964-65
Winnie the Pooh charms and pins

Kaye Novelty Co., Inc. (Brooklyn, NY) 1951-52
Plastic pinwheels, place mats

The Kaynee Company (NYC/Cleveland, OH) 1932-35
Clothing

Kayser-Roth Hosiery Company, Inc. (NYC) 1953-61
Socks, stretch tights

Robert Kayton (NYC) 1938-39
Miniature garden kit

Keepers Industries, formerly Harrich, Inc. (Woodland Hills, CA) 1975-84
Men's/youth hosiery

Ben E. Keith Company (Ft. Worth, TX) 1953
Frozen fruits and vegetables

J.H. Kellman Company (NYC) 1965-73
Boys' coats

Kellwood Company (NYC) 1969-73
Childrens' coats

Kelvinator div Nash-Kelvinator Corp. (Detroit) 1951-53
Advertising materials

Kemper-Thomas Co. (Cincinnati, OH) 1943-44
Ach trays, lapel pins, stationery, plaques

Kenilworth Press, Inc. (NYC) 1933-34
Games

Kenner Products Co. (Cincinnati, Ohio) 1958-74
Mobiles, plastic wall-walker, juke box, electric tooth brush

Kennington, Limited (LA) 1970-77
Shirts of cotton and/or blended yarn for men and women, ties and scarves, polo shirts, tennis shirts, sweaters

Percy Kent Bag Company, Inc. (Kansas City, MO) 1953
Flour feed bags

Kerk Guild, Inc. (NYC) 1936-39, 45-51
Wall plaques, molded soaps, soap figures and closet accessories

Kestral Corporation (Springfield, MA) 1953-55
Children's plastic wallets, inflatable vinyl toys, pools, Lady and the Tramp inflatable, Davy Crockett peace pipe with whistle

Ketterlinus Lithographic Mfg. Co. (Philadelphia) 1940-42
12 paintings for use in calendars

Kewaunee Equipment Co., Inc. (Kewaunee, WI) 1970-71
Hunny Tree-hanger up

Keystone Mfg. Company (Boston/NYC) 1934-37
Movie projectors

Kidco, Inc. (Elk Grove Village, IL) 1981-82
"Spin-a-bout" tops

Kids Stuff Creations (Ft. Worth, TX) 1974-???
Diaper stackers, infant's shoe bags and handy bags, children's plastic hangers

Kiki International (NYC) 1987
Ladies' underpants, camisoles and tank tops

Kilgore Mfg. Co. (Westerville, OH) 1935-1937
Toys, bubble-buster guns

Kimberly-Clark Corp. (Neenah, WI) 1986
Disposable baby diapers (also see - Lion Brothers)

King Features Syndicate, Inc. (NYC) 1930-87
Comic strips

King Innovations, Inc. (NYC) 1934-36
Purses

King Kole Inc. (Miami) 1970-71
Boys' cabana sets

King, Larson and McMahon (Chicago) 1944-46

"Hingees" cardboard figures

Martin King & Son (Chicago) 1944-46
Building block games, "Hingees"

Kinnerton Confectionery Co., Inc. (Long Island City, NY) 1983-85
Assorted chocolates and soft candies

Samuel Kirk and Sons (Baltimore, MD) 1973-74
Silver collector's plates and medals

D. Klein & Son, Inc. (NYC) 1960-61
Umbrellas

Kleinert Mfg. Co. (NYC) 1970-71
Suits, pant sets

Knapp Electric (Indianapolis, IN) 1939-40
Toys, "Krazy Ikes," "Electric Questioner"

Knickerbocker Plastic Co., Inc. (N. Hollywood) 1955-59
Plastic water pistols, toys, figurines, plastic and metal toy bells

Knickerbocker Toy Co., Inc. (NYC/Middlesex, NJ) 1934-42, 76-83
Stuffed and composition dolls and animals (34-42), plush toys, soft puzzle blocks, vehicles with rag dolls, dolls, bathtub toys (76-83)

Knitrite Mills Inc. (Brooklyn, NY) 1965-73
Winnie the Pooh sweaters (Sears)

Kohn-Goldschmidt, Inc. (NYC) 1941-42
Doilies and mats

Kohner (NYC/E. Patterson, NJ) 1952-56, 67-74
Press action toys, Mickey Mouse Club ears headband, trapeze toys, push button puppets, Spinikins, string puppets, Tricky walkers, Jump-kins, mini puppets

Kolcraft Products (Chicago) 1966-67
Crib and youth mattresses, youth beds, seat covers for nursery chairs

Kraft-Phoenix Cheese Co. (???) 1938-39
Snow White and Seven Dwarf Tumblers sent for 8 lids from Parkay Margarine

Kramer Bros., Inc. (NYC) 1966-67
Crochet stretch tights

Kranz-Nectow, Inc. (Boston) 1966-67
Printed duck material for sneakers

Clyde A. Krasne (LA) 1946
Cards and/or boxes

Kreiss & Company (LA) 1955-56
Porcelain & earthenware figurines, planters, banks, salt & pepper shakers

Kroehler Manufacturing Co. (see Atlas Development Co.)
Mickey Mouse

Richard G. Krueger, Inc. (NYC) 1931-41
Children's chinaware, bath sets, toothbrushes, hot water bottles, celluloid and rubber novelties, bathroom accessories, dolls and animals, baby gifts

K-2 Corporation (Seattle) 1987
Adult and junior snow skis

Kurlash Co. (Rochester, NY) 1937-39
Scissors

Kusan, Inc., div. of Bethlehem Steel Corp. (Nashville, TN) 1961-62, 73-???
Roller skates, ice skates, picture-frame play sets, table and chair sets

Kushins, Inc. (Santa Rosa, CA) 1946-47
Slippers, shoes

Kute Kiddie Coats, Inc. (NYC) 1970-71
Dress coats

L.J.N. Toys, Ltd. (NYC) 1975-82
Toy typewriter, toy piano, Toss 'n Pop Game, intercom set, tic toc pop game, flip chip game, super draw, Dial-a-song, Pitch 'n Pop game, Spin-a-bout tops

Philip Labe (NYC) 1935-37
Pillow tops, table covers, etc.

Ladd Industries (High Point, NC) 1982
Juvenile furniture and ensembles

Nathan Lagin Co. (NYC) 1940-41
Lamps

Lakeside Industries, Inc., div of Leisure Dynamics (Minneapolis, MN) 1968-82
Mini- and Super-flex toys, toy watch, electric Mickey Mouse drawing set, Jack-in-the-box, drawing sets, nested blocks, Bendi-faces, 3-D board game, miniature activity games

Lakeside Plastics & Engraving Co. (Minn., MN) 1962-66
Electric drawing desk w/ lamp

Lambert Pharmacal Co. (St. Louis) 1950-51
Plastic figures to sell with Listerine toothpaste

LaMode Studios, Inc. (NYC) 1938-39
Lamps

The Lance Corporation (Hudson, MA) 1985-87
Pewter figurines

Lanco Handbag Co., Inc. (NYC) 1984
Purses, totes, diaper bags, wallets, coin purses and key holders

The Lander Company, Inc. (NYC) 1938-40
Perfume

Sam Landorf and Co. (NYC) 1956
Girls' cotton dresses

Langer Knitting Mills, Inc. (North Bergen, NJ/NYC) 1935-36
Sweaters, pull-overs

Lapin-Kurley Kew, Inc. (NYC) 1938-40
Hair Ornaments

Larami Corporation (Philadelphia) 1970-72
Harmonicas, flashlights, xylophones, pipe cleaners, binoculars, beginners' roller skates, T.V. Viewers, jack 'n balls

Lasting Impressions (Framingham, MA) 1982-83
Shoelaces

Layettes, (Cohes, NY) 1969-72
Sacque

Lea Industries, div. of S and H Furniture Co., Inc. (High Point, NC) 1981
Juvenile furniture and ensembles

Leadworks, Inc. (Beachwood, OH) 1982-83
Transparent adhesive tape; character dispensers sold only with character tape

Leaf Brands, Inc. (Chicago) 1947-53
Gum and candy

Leavens Mfg. Co. (Attleboro, MA) 1957
Metal rings and whistles

Lee Belt (NYC) 1987
Belts, suspenders

Susie Lee, Ltd. (Herne Bay, Kent, CT) 1987
Better handknitted sweaters, vests, cardigans, hats and scarves for children - adults

Leeds China Co. (Chicago) 1944-54
Ceramic tableware, etc., figurines, pottery

Leeds Music Corp. (NYC) 1946-51
Music books

Lee-Tex Rubber Products Corporation (Chicago) 1946-49
Rubber balloons

Lehn and Fink Products Corporation (Bloomfield, NJ) 1958-59
Bubble bath

Leisuramics, Inc. (Haverhill, MA) 1972-79
Hobby craft kits (ceramics)

Leisure Dynamics, Inc. (Minneapolis, MN) 1972-74
Mini-flex and super-flex toys, toy watch, electric Mickey Mouse drawing set (see also: Lakeside Industries)

Leslie-Henry Co., Inc. (Wilkes-Barre, PA) 1962-65
Toys

Lesney Products Corporation (NYC/Moonachie, NJ) 1971-72, 79-82
Wind-up mechanical vehicles, die-cast vehicles and accessories

G.R. L'Esperance (???) 1949-50
Wrist watches

Lever Brothers Co., Inc. (NYC) 1970-86
Toothbrushes

L. Lewis and Son (NYC) 1939-41
Children's hats

Libbey Glass Company, division of Owens-Illinois Glass Co. (Toledo, OH) 1938-41, 55, 77-80
Glass and metal containers, tumblers, glassware, mugs, and stemware

Libby, McNeil & Libby (Chicago) 1939-40
Promotional materials

Liberman Distributing Company (St. Paul, MN) 1969-70
Sleeping Beauty flashing magic wands

Liberty National Corporation (NYC) 1954-56
Lunch kits (Mickey Mouse and Davy Crockett) and tool kits

Lido Toy Company (NYC) 1954-64
Target game, stencil set, tracing set, plastic bubble pipes, key chain, toy T.V. set, miniature musical instruments

Life Savers Corporation (???) 1947-48
"Life Savers"

Lightfoot-Schultz Co. (NYC) 1934-42
Toilet soap (molded)

Lilly-Tulip Cup Corp. (NYC) 1938
Lids for ice cream containers

Lily, division of Owen-Illinois (Toledo, OH) 1975
Paper cups

O.E. Linck Co., Inc. (Clifton, NJ) 1960-61
Glitter Magic

Lin-Mac Hat Co. (NYC) 1965-66
Hats

Lion Brothers (Owings Mills, MD) 1967-68
Patches for Kimberly-Clark Corp.

The Lionel Corp. (Irvington, NJ/NYC) 1934-38, 62-63, 72-80
Toy trains and handcars

Little America Wood Products, Inc. (Mansfield, OH) 1982-83
Dollhouses (app. $500 to $1,200 retail), Handmade wooden ride-on toys (retail over $50)

Little Craft Co. (NYC) 1965-70
Winnie the Pooh pant sets, shag tops, jumpers, blouses, skirts (Sears)

Little Falls Felt Shoe Company (St. Johnsville, NY) 1965-67
Children's slippers

The Little Prince Company (NYC) 1965-73
Coats and jackets (Sears)

Little Star Dress Co., Inc. (NYC) 1968-69
Dresses (Sears)

Little Toppers Headwear Co., Inc. (NYC) 1968
Hats (sears)

Logo 7, Inc. (Indianapolis, IN) 1981-85
Men's knit shirts, warm-up suits

Loma Plastics, Inc. (Ft. Worth, TX) 1948-53
Plastic cookie cutters, plastic novelties

The Longacre Press, Inc. (NYC) 1939
Printed materials, bottle hangers for National Dairy Products

Loomtogs, Inc. (NYC) 1933-34
Jersey suits, robes

Lorraine Novelty Mfg. Co., Inc. (NYC) 1933-34
Children's purses and pocketbooks

Lorus Products (Paramus, NJ) 1987
Watches, clocks

Joseph Love, Inc. (NYC) 1938-41, 55, 60-68
Children's dresses

M. Lowenstein and Sons, Inc./M. Lowenstein Corp. (NYC) 1942-46, 68-86
Novelty curtains, draperies (see also: Lyman Curtain Corp., Wamsutta Mills, Inc.)

Ludford Fruit Products Company (Hollywood) 1932-35
Ginger ale, fruit drinks

Lyman Curtain Company, div of M. Lowenstein and Sons, Inc. (NYC) 1970-72
Novelty curtains, draperies

Lysander Tufted Products, division of Eli L. Sandler and Co. (NYC) 1968-72
Scatter rugs, textile wall hangings

George Lytle, Inc. (St. Louis, MO) 1953
Frozen fruits, and vegetables

M & M Mars Candy Co. (Chicago) 1970
Clocks

A.P. McAuley Co. (NYC) 1950-55, 65-66
Rugs, towels

McCall Company (NYC) 1932-45, 54-59, 63-67
Paper patterns

McCann-Erickson, Inc. (San Francisco) 1939-40
Advertising materials

McCurrach Organization (NYC) 1938-39
Ties

David McKay Publishing Co, (Philadelphia) 1930-39
Illustrated story books (Mickey Mouse)

McKen Sales Corp. (NYC) 1966-73
Sweaters (Sears)

McKesson & Robbins, Inc. (???) 1940-41
Calox antiseptic mouthwash is promoted with the Walt Disney Pinocchio safedge glasses as give-aways

McLarens Limited (Canada) 1949-50
Peanut butter

A. McLean & Son, Inc. (Chicago) 1937-39
"Penny Rolls" taffy candy kisses

McMaster Pottery Limited (???) 1949-50
Ceramic figurines

McQuiddy Printing Company (Nashville, TN) 1939, 41
Calendars

Magill-Weinsheimer Co. (Chicago) 1938
Poster stamps (Snow White?)

Magnus Organ Corp., sub. of Illustrated World Encyc. Inc. (Woodbury, NY) 1974-75
Organ with song book

Magran Industries, Inc. (Vernon, CA) 1977
Craft kits, wooden slotted figures, Magic Art Finger Paint set, Pendoodler, Vibration Activated Drawing Toy

The Malloy Company (Philadelphia) 1970-71
Polyurethane die-cut sponges and bath mats

J. Manes Company Inc, (NYC) 1965
Mary Poppins piece goods (J.C. Penney Co.)

Manhattan Soap Company (NYC) 1932-35
Soap

Manhattan Wax Candle Co., Inc. (NYC) 1939-41
Candles

Mann Mfg., Inc. (El Paso, TX) 1965-66
Jackets, shorts, slacks (Sears)

Manton Cork Company (Merrick, Long Island, NY) 1972-74
Cork bulletin boards, chalk boards

Mantua Metal Products Co., Inc. (Woodbury Hts., NJ) 1965-66
Train sets

Mar-Kel Lighting, Inc. (Paris, TN) 1986
Ceramic figurine nightlights

Marilyn Baby Bonnets (NYC) 1965-66, 71-72
Baby bonnets (Sears)

Marilyn Sandal Corp. (Stoneham, MA) 1940
Slippers

Marinette Knitting Mills (Chicago) 1948-49
Sweaters

Marks Brothers Co. (Boston/NYC) 1934-41, 46-48
Paint, crayon and sewing sets, toys, puzzles, games, novelty acrobat toys

Marlin Toy Products, Inc. (NYC) 1971-73
Musical steam boat

Maro Industries, Inc./Maro Hosiery Co., Inc. (NYC) 1970-87
Socks, hosiery, tights, booties, leotards, headbands, wristbands

Marshallan Manufacturing Company (Cleveland, OH) 1961-62, 79-83
Metal lap or bed trays with folding legs, tray tables, metal room shelving units

Martine Jewelry Company (NYC) 1970-71
Jewelry

Mart-Ray Manufacturing Company (Brooklyn, NY) 1972-86
Children's slippers, moccasins, sandals, slipper sox, infants' shoes

Louis Marx and Co., Inc. (NYC) 1936-61, 68-80
Mechanical wind up toys (metal and plastic), Linemar toys, ride 'em toys, battery operated toys, toy watches and clocks with transparent features, battery operated Little Big Wheel, nodding head figures, megozoo, Disneykins miniature plastic figures, Disneyland Express, party Pluto and Donald, toy TV playhouse and characters, molded plastic figures, tabletop mechanical car, Lady and the Tramp 3-D molded plastic figures, wind-up roadster, whirling tail toys, friction motor toys, wind-up hand car, Davy Crockett plastic pistols, playsets

Maryland Paper Box Company (Baltimore, MD) 1987
Gift bags and printed tissue

Maryland Paper Products Company, Inc., div of Maryland Cup Corp. (Owings Mills, MD) 1968
Paper drinking straws

Masco Corporation (Chicago) 1946-48
Magnetic novelties

Mastercraft Toy Co., Inc. (NYC) 1946-48
Toy projector (zoetrope)

Mattel Inc. / Mattel Toys (LA/Hawthorne, CA) 1955-60, 67-83
Toy acetate laminated recordings, Davy Crockett and Mickey Mouse "Ge-tars," talking "patter" pillows, See 'n Say, Skediddles, handcraft musical toys, "Clear World" figures and light tables, Little treasures figures, chatter chums talking figures, tape recorder from Concept 2000 div (81)

Mavco, Incorporated (NYC) 1947-51
Plastic candle holders, toys and Christmas tree ornaments, plastic toys.

May Fair Togs, Inc. (NYC) 1938-39
Snow Suits

May Hosiery Mills (Nashville, TN) 1932-36
Hosiery for boys, girls, children

May Knitting Co., Inc. (NYC) 1937-39, 75-79
Sweaters, girls' swimwear

Mayflower Dress Co., Inc. (NYC) 1947-48
Dresses, blouses, play clothes

Mazaltov's Inc. (Amityville, NY) 1975-79
Needlepoint kits

Mead Containers (Cincinnati, OH/Louisville, KY) 1972-82
Storage chest and room divider

Meadowbrook Sportswear, Inc. (NYC) 1939-40
Junior and misses play clothes, beachwear, sports dresses, blouses and evening pajamas

Mechanical Man, Inc. (NYC) 1940
Mechanical window and interior displays for Sun oil Co., A & P Stores, Sears, Montgomery Ward, Standard Oil of California

Mechanical Mirror Works, Inc. (NYC) 1977-81
Photo frames, shadow boxes, glass greeting cards, framed glass wall decorations

Mego Corp. (NYC) 1977-81
Magnanimals, action figures, playsets, vehicles, electronic toys, calculators, rack toys, communication devices, weapons (1979) stretch figures

Melton Industries (El Segundo, CA) 1953-56
Toy film viewers (additional films available)

The Mengel Company (St. Louis, MO) 1935-39
Playthings

Merry Mfg. Co. (Cincinnati, OH) 1963-64
Licensed use not known

The Metal Ware Corporation (Two Rivers, WI/NYC/Chicago) 1936-37
Toy stoves, etc.

Metalcrafters (Chicago) 1946-47
Toy sail boats

Metaltex Inc. (Bayonne, NJ) 1966-67
Winnie the Pooh trinket box, mirror, dresser set, perfume tray, and tissue box

Metco Mfg. Inc. (Detroit) 1950-51
Metal doll coaches (Cinderella?)

Metro Industries (Philadelphia) 1952-53
Juvenile place mats

Meyer Both Company (NYC/Chicago) 1939-41
Promotional materials (newspaper mat service for retailers using Disney products in ads)

The Meyercord Company (Chicago) 1938-41
Decalcomania transfers

Micro-Lite Company, Inc. (NYC) 1938-40
"Kiddy-Lites"

Midsummer Nights Dream, Inc. (NYC) 1939-42
Scenery & backgrounds for a play "Midsummer Nights Dream"

Milbee Products Corp. (NYC) 1977
Children's and girls' loungewear and sleepwear

Milko Cone and Baking Co., Inc. (NYC) 1938-41
Cones

Miller and Company (Denver, CO) 1955-56
Western shirts, pants and skirts, boleros, chaps and vests

Miller Corsets, Inc. (NYC) 1938-39
Foundation garments

Samuel Miller & Co., Inc. (Chicago) 1959-62
Pants and trousers

Miller Studios, Inc. (New Philadelphia, OH) 1975-76
Wall hooks, toothbrush holders

Milo Products, Inc. (Brooklyn, NY) 1966-69
Plastic coloring table cloths

Milton Bradley Company (E. Longmeadow, MA) 1987
Board and VCR Games

Alexander Miner Mfg. Co. (NYC) 1955-56
Vinyl plastic toy school bag

Miner Industries, Inc. (NYC) 1970-77, 81-82
Playpacks, dominoes, roly-polys, Colorola, checker set, doctor set, organ, sports kits, math game (see also: Multiple Products Corporation)

Minnesota Mining & Manufacturing Company (St. Paul, MN) 1955
Scotch tape dispenser

Minnesota Valley Canning Company (???) 1947-48
Canned vegetables

Miracle Girl Coat House, Inc. (NYC) 1939-1941
Outer garments, such as girls' coats, suits, etc.

Miracle Recreation Equipment Co. (Grinnell, IA) 1973-?
Backyard play equipment

Mishawaka Rubber Company (Mishawaka, IN) 1966-70
Shoes

Mitey Miss, Inc. (NYC) 1970-71
Girls' pants

Mo' Money Associates (Pensacola, FL) 1987
Sun visors

Model-Craft, Inc. (Chicago) 1944-55
Modeling sets

Model Products Company, div. of General Mills Gun Group, Inc. (Mt. Clements, MI) 1972-75, 79
Model assembly kits

Modern Kitchen Bureau (???) 1940-41
Electric water heaters

The Modern Pillow Co. (NYC) 1963-66
Pillows

Modern Record Albums (College Point, NY) 1949-50
String puppets of wood and plastic

Modern Woodworking Company (Burbank, CA) 1957
Redwood wastepaper baskets with DL Art Corner decals

Moebius Printing Co. (Milwaukee) 1963
Wall murals

John F. Moloney Co., Inc. (LA) 1949-50
Children's nightwear

Monarch Manufacturing Company (Milwaukee, WI) 1955-56
Mickey Mouse and Davy Crockett suede, wool jackets and leather

Monarch Overall Mfg. Co., Ltd. (Canada) 1949-51
Children's outerwear and sportswear

Monogram Products, Inc. (Largo, FL) 1972-87
Mickey Mouse bike name plates, good conduct ribbons, light switch plates, memento statuettes, key chains, necklaces, Goofy scissors, rack toys, slide ruler, personalized name plates

Monogram Soap Co. (Hollywood/Culver City, CA) 1942-53
Decorated soaps, bubble bath

Monroe Luggage Co., Inc. (NYC) 1938-39
Luggage

Monsanto Company (St. Louis) 1969-70
Indoor/outdoor playground equipment, school furniture & equipment, multi-use convertible furniture

Mon-ta-gue for California (Van Nuys, CA) 1984-85
T-shirts, sweatshirts decorated with self-adhesive ornaments

Montron Corp. (Mountain View, CA) 1975-77
8mm viewer, projector, cartridges, tabletop 8mm projector and cartridges

Jacques Moret (NYC) 1986-87
Girls' and juniors' aerobicwear

Morgan Adhesives Co. (Stow, OH) 1970-74
Self-adhesive wall covering material, safety-tread die-cuts

Morning Milk Co. (Salt Lake City, UT) 1940-42
Canned evaporated milk

Morris Belt & Suspender Co., Inc. (NYC) 1958-61

Belts, head scarfs, sport tops

Morse Shoe, Inc. (Canton, MA) 1977-84
Sneakers, sandals, outerwear boots/rubbers, infants' footwear

Movie Jector Company, Inc. (NYC) 1935-37
Movie projectors and records, toy projectors, paper film

Moviescope Corporation (NYC) 1932-33
Flip books

Walter W. Moyer Company (Ephrata, PA) 1955-56
Babies' coated pants

Ms. Dee (Mound, MN) 1982
Cast pewter jewelry box with accessories

Mullins Textile Mills, Inc. (Mullins, SC) 1965-66
Velour shirts (Sears)

Multi-Market, Inc. (Atlanta, GA) 1982-83
Poster art kits

Multi Products (Chicago) 1940-42
Figures, etc.

Multiple Products Corp., div of Miner Indust. Inc. (NYC) 1960-68
Pop-a-parts, vehicle toys

The Murray Corp. of America (Detroit) 1937-38
All necessary styling work in connection with the manufacturing of automobile bodies

Murray Hill Products, Inc. (NYC) 1968
Sewing kit assortments

Murray Knitwear Company (Brooklyn, NY) 1933-34
Sweaters

Muskin Corporation (Colton, CA/Wilkes-Barre, PA) 1976-79
Vacuum-formed swim pools

Mutual-Sunset Lamp Mfg. Co. (NYC) 1938-39
Floor, bridge, table & bedroom lamps and smoking stands designed by Sakhnoffsky

L.V. Myles, Inc. (NYC) 1973-87
Girls sleepwear and loungewear

My-Toy Company (Brooklyn, NY) 1965-66, 72-???
Banks

M.R. Nadel Company (NYC) 1970-71
Sunglasses, children's toiletries

Naas Corporation (Portland, IN) 1947-53
Canned and bottled tomato, corn and pumpkin products

Nabisco, Inc. - see National Biscuit Company

Nannette Mfg. Co. (Philadelphia/NYC) 1955, 68-69, 77-79
Infants' and small-size dresses, girls' crib sets, slack sets, bootie sets, dresses, overalls and playwear

Nashua Mfg. Company (???) 1938-39
Sold linens through ads depicting Snow White and Seven Dwarfs

Nash-Underwood, Inc. (???) 1944-47
Peanut butter and mustard

National Advertisers (Kay Kamen use/no contract) 1940-41, 47-50
Campaigns and promotions

National Biscuit Company (NYC) 1935-55, 66-68, 75
Figural "animal" crackers, use in advertising

National Dairy Products (NYC) 1933-48
Ice cream and dairy products sold through ads depicting Snow White and Seven Dwarfs, also used with Pinocchio

National Home Products, Inc. (NYC) 1973-81
Melamine dinnerware

National Knitting Mills (???) 1948-50
Children's sweaters

National Latex Products Co., Inc. (Ashland, OH/NYC) 1968-87
Balloons, balls, punch balls, belt buckles, silver metallic balloons

National Leather Manufacturing Co., Inc. (Brooklyn, NY) 1951-70
School bags and utility bags, lunch bags

The National Match Co. (NYC) 194?-43
Pepsi-Cola insignia book matches

National Oats Co. (Cedar Rapids, Iowa) 1943-45
Oatmeal

National Paragon Corp. (NYC) 1974-87
Art needlework kits, instruction booklets

National Pen Corp. (San Diego) 1986-87
Rollerball pens

National Plastic Corporation (Rutherford, NJ) 1984
Artisan Dinnerware melamine bowls, plates, mugs and cups

National Plastikwear Fashions, Inc. (NYC) 1952-54
Rainwear

National Porcelain Co., Inc. (Trenton, NJ) 1939-41
China figures

National Woven Label Company (NYC) 1938-41
Woven labels

Natural Science Industries, Ltd. (Far Rockaway, NY) 1979
Vinyl playhouse, toy tunnel and jumpoline

Naylor Corporation (Chicago, IL) 1938-40
Hand-craft sets

Neevel Manufacturing Company (Kansas City, MO) 1949-56
Children's folding tables, chairs, luggage

Saul S. Negreann, Inc. (NYC) 1975-76
Scarves, handkerchiefs

Neher-Whitehead & Co. (St. Louis) 1937, 41-42
Bottle collars

Thomas Nelson & Sons (NYC) 1937
Book

Louis Nessel & Co., Inc. (NYC) 1938-39
Linens

D.H. Neumann Company (NYC) 1931-41
Boys' neckties and belts, boys' furnishings

Nevins Drug Co. (Philadelphia) 1935-37
Toothpaste

New Enterprises/Butler Enterprises, Inc. (Winston Salem, NC) 1945-47
Lithographed wood blocks

New York Graphic Society (NYC/Chicago/LA) 1945-49, 68-70
Lithographed pictures

New York Merchandise Co., Inc. (NYC) 1941-42
Plastic tableware (Baby Weems)

New York Toy Corp. (NYC) 1966-68
Toys

Newark Felt Novelty (Newark, NJ) 1939-41
Children's hats

Newell-Emmett Co., Inc. (NYC) 1940
Advertising materials for Mutual Savings Banks

Newton Manufacturing Corporation (NYC) 1981-85
Boys', girls' and ladies' underwear

Niagara Lithograph Company (Buffalo, NY) 1946
Window and counter displays

Nintendo of America, Inc. (Redmond, WA) 1983-84
LCD electronic games

Nite Kraft Corporation (NYC) 1955-56
Boys' and girls' sleepwear

Nitec Paper Corporation (Niagara Falls, NY) 1980-1981
Facial tissues

Noble & Cooley Company (Granville, MA) 1935-39, 69-83
Rolling hoops, drums, musical instruments, play drums, trap drums, tambourines, drum banks, games, rhythm sticks

Noblitt-Sparks Industries, Inc. (Columbus, IN) 1938-41
Radios

Noma Electric Corporation (NYC) 1935-38
Decorative electric light bulbs (Christmas lights)

Norman Industries, Inc. (LA) 1970-74
Polyester wall decorations, children's standing night light

Norstar Corp. (Bronx, NY) 1968-70
Screen art cartoon-o-graph, magic printing machine games

North American Glass Corp. (NYC) 1947-50
Blown-glass Christmas tree ornaments

Northern Dairy Company (Marquette, MI) 1953
Ice cream and sherberts

Northern Electric Co. (Chicago) 1961-62
Electric blankets (Sears)

Northern Shoe Company (Pulaski, WI) 1966-70
Infants' and children's shoes

Northwest Cone Company, Inc. (Chicago) 1941-43
Cones

Northwestern Products Co. (St. Louis, MO) 1957-59
Bagatelle, pinball, spin games

Norwich Knitting Co. (Norwich, NY/NYC) 1931-41
Sweatshirts, children's knitted underwear and nightwear, polo and sport shirts, cotton pull-overs

Norwich Mills (NYC) 1965-66
Sweat shirts

Notions, Inc. (NYC) 1938-39
???

Al Nyman & Son, Inc. (NYC/Miami FL) 1972-84
School supplies, pencil sharpeners, staplers, rulers, pencil pouches, electronic calculator, school bags, sports & gym bags, beach & tote bags, athletic bags

Oak Rubber Company (Ravenna, OH) 1934-42, 45-68
Rubber balloons, blow-up toys

Obion Company (NYC) 1987
Blanket sleepers, prams and sleeping bags

Oconomowoc Canning Company (Oconomowoc, WI) 1949-50
Canned corn, peas, etc.

Oculens, Ltd. (NYC/Oceanside, NY) 1976-83
Sunglasses, children's toiletries, bubble bath

Odora Company, Inc. (NYC) 1933-40
Toy chests

Ohio Art Company (Bryan, OH/NYC) 1933-42, 44-45, 64-82
Lithographed metal toys (tin tea sets, pails), Etch-A-Sketch Activity Center, Action Pack Assortment, juke box sound center

Ohio Dairy Products Association, Inc. (Columbus, OH) 1944-45
Posters for safety campaign

Okla Homer Smith Furniture Mfg. Co. (Ft. Smith, AR) 1973-79
Nod-A-Way juvenile furniture, mattresses

Old King Cole, Inc. (Canton, OH/NYC) 1935-42
Window display items

Olympia Knitting Mills, Inc. (Olympia, WA) 1931-32
Children's and adults' knitted wear sweaters, bathing suits, etc.

One Stop Posters (Monterey Park, CA) 1987
Posters, buttons

Oneida Ltd. (Oneida, NY) 1940-42
Silverware

Ontario Textiles, Ltd. (Canada) 1949-50
  Games, puzzles, etc.

E. and A. Opler, Inc. (Chicago) 1934-36
  Cocoa malt flavoring

Opto-Specs, Ltd./Oculens, Ltd. (NYC) 1972-75
  Sunglasses, children's toiletries

Oregib Mfg. Co. (Chicago) 1968
  Winnie the Pooh sweaters (Sears)

Orthopter Company (Denver, CO) 1955-56
  "Wing-e" flying machine

Osford Boys Wear (NYC) 1965-66
  Overalls (Sears)

Ostby & Barton Company (Providence, RI) 1947-49
  Children's rings

Ostow & Jacobs, Inc. (NYC) 1962-64
  Bedspreads, rugs

Overland Candy Corporation (Chicago) 1938-42, 48-53
  Candy

Owens-Illinois Can Company (Toledo, OH) 1938-41
  Glass and metal containers

Owens-Illinois Glass Company (Toledo, OH) 1936-43, 49-52, 55-56
  see Libbey Glass

Owens-Illinois Pacific Coast Company (San Francisco) 1936-37
  Glass containers

Paas Dye Company (Newark, NJ) 1936-55
  Easter egg decorations, dyes, decorating kits, and year-round transfer papers with albums

D.A. Pachter Co. (Chicago, IL) 1943-45
  Toy paint sets

Pacific Chenille Craft Co. (LA) 1940-41
  Bed spreads, housecoats, robes, beach toys

Pacific Home Products/Pacific Home Fashions, div. of M. Lowenstein & Sons, Inc. (NYC) 1973-84
  Novelty curtains, draperies, towels, pillow cases, bed spreads, comforters, sheets and other bed linens

Pacific Waxed Paper (Seattle, WA) 1940-41
  ???

Pagoda Trading Co. (Hazelwood, MO) 1986-87
  Dress shoes, casual athletic, boots, beachwear, sandals, slippers and slipper sox

Pak-Well Corp (formerly Dasco) Consumer Products Division (Oakland, CA) 1975-79
  Composition books, looseleaf paper, looseleaf binders/arrangers, memo books, activity kits

A.G. Palmer Supply Co. (NYC) 1938-41
  ???

Palmer Bros. Co. (NYC) 1933-34
  Comforts, spreads and drapes

Palmer-Weller Co. (NYC) 1940-41
  Party decorations

Pancordion, Inc. (NYC) 1953-55
  Plastic coloring plaques, plastic wall plaques

Paper Magic (Boston) 1987
  Valentine and Christmas boxed cards and punch-out card books, Christmas greeting postcards, decorated gift boxes

Paper Novelty Mfg. Co., Inc. (Brooklyn, NY/NYC) 1938-42
  Valentines

Para Mfg. Co., Inc. (Newark, NJ) 1938-39
  Silk shower curtains

Paragon Art and Linen Co., Inc. (Bronx, NY) 1970-71
  Art needlework kits

Parfait, Inc. (Chicago) 1950-52
  Sachets, molded soap figures, bath salts, etc.

Paris Boyswear (NYC) 1939-40
  Boyswear

Paris Neckwear Co., Inc. (NYC) 1938-41
  Boyswear, neckwear

Parker Bros. (NYC/Salem, MA) 1933-87
  Games and puzzles

Pastime, Inc. (NYC) 1982-83
  Juvenile craft activity sets

The C.F. Pease Co. (Chicago) 1940-41
  Advertising materials

The Peerless Smoking Jacket Co., Inc. (NYC) 1938-39
  Men's beach robes and suits

Peirce & Cutler, Inc. (LA) 1948-50
  Chenille robes, bedspreads, rugs

Pencil Specialty Company (Hoboken, NJ) 1966-67
  Codopens

Penn Emblem Company (Philadelphia) 1979-81
  Embroidered patches

J.C. Penney Co. (NYC) 1950
  Printed instructions for making a Walt Disney Cinderella Apron

Pentel of America, Ltd. (Torrance, CA) 1985-87
  Automatic pencils, porter colors, oil pastels, pastel dye sticks

The Pepsodent Co. (???) 1938-39
  Toothpaste and related items sold through ads depicting Disney characters

Percy Kent Bag Co., Inc. (Kansas City, MO) 1949-52
  Flour and feed sacks

Perfect Fit Ind., Inc. (NYC) 1965-69
  Bedspreads, draperies, matching sets, blankets

Perfect Negligee Co. (NYC) 1939-40
  Negligees

Peri-Lusta, Ltd. (Bronx, NY) 1972-73
  Art needlework kits

Patricia Perkins, Inc. (LA) 1939-40
  Ladies evening wear

Peter Pan Fabrics - see Henry Glass Co.

Peter Pan Toys (NYC) 1961-62
  Pajama bags (Sears)

Peter Puppet Playthings, Inc. (Long Island/Brooklyn, NY) 1951-55, 58
  String marionettes, Davy Crockett guitar and musical toys

Petite Cheri (LA) 1969-70
  Swim suits

Pez-Haas, Inc. (NYC/Long Island/Woodside, NY) 1968-87
  Candy dispensers

Philadelphia Badge Co. (Philadelphia) 1931
  Badges and Buckles

Philbert Hat (NYC) 1939-41
  Sports hats

Leo F. Phillips Co., Inc. (NYC) 1937-39

Novelty dress buttons

Phillips Products Corp. (San Francisco) 1949-54
  Preserves and jams

Philson Ind. Inc. aka **Stephen Products Co.,** now **Worcester Toy** (Middletown, CT) 1953-57
  Projector and film strips (projector in form of gun)

Phinney-Walker (W. Germany) 1969
  Clocks (see also: Semca Time Co.)

Phoenicia Trading Co. (NYC) 1968-69
  Handbag and glove set (Sears)

Pictorial Productions, Inc. (Mt. Vernon, NY) 1961-65, 68-69
  Wiggle Pictures, Mickey Mouse rings

Pictorial Products Co. (NYC) 1934
  Toilet soap

Picture That, Inc. (Miami, FL/Melbourne, FL) 1980-84
  Framed foil pictures

Pilgrim Ind., Inc./Pilgrim Sportswear, Inc. (NYC) 1955-66, 70-87
  Knitted polo shirts, sweat shirts with Dimension Weld or V.T.D. printing, sportswear (see also: **Shirtees, Inc.**)

Pindyck Inc. (NYC) 1965-66
  Blanket sleepers (Sears)

Pines of America, Inc. (Ft. Wayne, IN) 1982-83
  Battery-operated train set, battery-operated ride-on train, pedal drive "Pines Mobile"

Piqua Hosiery Company, Inc. (Piqua, OH) 1936-39
  Sport shirts

Pittsburg Knitting Mills (S. Pittsburg, TN) 1966-67
  Argyle knee socks

Plakie Toys, Inc. (Youngstown, OH) 1968-70
  Pictures (Sears)

Plane Facts Company (NYC) 1943-45
  "Fuzzies," "Scrambles" plaques

Plascor Inc. (Worcester, MA) 1971-72
  Outdoor garden figurines (lawn decorations)

Plastic Metal Manufacturing Co. (Chicago) 1957-62
  Plastic tableware, containers, Freez ur pops, etc.

Plastic Molded Arts Company (Long Island, NY) 1953
  Doll package with 3 costumes

Plastic Novelties, Inc. (NYC) 1935-55
  Catalin/pencil sharpeners, salt and pepper sets, napkin rings and thermometers

Plastic Playthings, Inc. (White Plains, NY) 1952-58
  Plastic baby exercisers, rattles, roly poly toy, vinyl baby bottle holders

Plastimatic, Inc. (Norwood, NJ) 1982-84
  Lighted lucite sculptured nightlites

Plastoy Co., Inc. (NYC) 1943-45
  "Scramble" educational pictures, flocked wall plaques

The Platt & Munk Company, Inc. (NYC) 1936-37
  Slate

Play Pal Plastics, Inc. (???) 1981
  Produced plastic character banks for a limited bank promotion giveaway

Playskool Mfg. Company/Tommee Tippee Playskool, Inc., formerly **Glenco Infants Items, Inc.** (Chicago) 1970-87
  Wooden alphabet blocks, play tiles, wood puzzles, brick model set, talking telephone, Poppin' Pals, sandwich shop, music activity box (also see: Halsam Products)

Playtape, Inc. (NYC) 1967-68
  Playtape and cartridges

Plymouth, Inc. (Bellmawr, NJ) 1986-87
  Notebooks, school supplies, post-it notes

Piltoys, Inc. (NYC) 1944-45

Washable stuffed toys

Poly Soft Products Corporation, div. of Sponge Specialties Corp. (E. Rockaway, NY) 1972-???
Polyurethane foam jigsaw puzzles, building blocks, block puzzles, story block, bowling sets, play sets

Pontiac Spring and Bumper Co. (Pontiac, MI) 1938
Spring action toys

Popcorn Sales, Inc. (Carnarvon, Iowa) 1949-50
Packaged corn for popping

Porter Chemical Company (Hagerstown, MD) 1968
Phonographs

Porter House, Ltd. (NYC) 1982-83
Ladies' designer tops

Postamp Publishing Co., Inc. (Hollywood, CA) 1942-44
Insignia stamps for publicity campaign

Powers Paper Company (Springfield, MO) 1931-40
Children's stationery and school supplies

Practi-Cole Products, Inc. (New Haven, CT) 1954-56
Interlocking plastic building block construction sets, including Davy Crockett

Precision Specialties, Inc. (LA) 1945-52
Plastic toys

Premier Gloves, Inc. (Johnstown, NY) 1976
Children's mittens and gloves

Prepac, Inc. (Bronx, NY) 1975-80
Vinyl toy luggage, carrying cases, insulated bags, shoe bags.

J.L Prescott Co., Inc. (Passaic, NJ) 1969
Toys

Pressman Toy Corp. (NYC) 1955-59, 68
Davy Crockett leathercraft kit, Lady and the Tramp clay modeling set, toy periscope, wooden peg table with desk top, wooden duck bowling pins, metal tapping & engraving set, MMC leathercraft kit, (1968) peg chest, blimps, spin-go-spin-tac-toe game

Pre-Vue Dance Frocks Co. (NYC) 1939-40
Misses' and Juniors' evening dresses

Pride Lines Ltd. (Lindenhurst, NY) 1982-87
Collector banks, handcars and trains

Pride Products Inc. (Long Island City, NY) 1956-58
String marionettes

Print Masters (LA) 1971-73
"Color and Send" booklet

Printowel Corporation (NYC) 1938-40
Towels, etc.

Priss Prints, Inc. (Cincinnati, OH & Falls Church, VA) 1975-87
Self-adhesive wall decorations

Private Label Dental Floss, Inc. (Verona, NJ) 1982-83
Dental floss, accessories, & dental floss related products

Pro-Arts (Medina, OH) 1979
Posters

Procter & Gamble (Cincinnati, OH) 1938-39, 59, 75-76
Snow White & 7 Dwarf masks given away with Camay soap (38-39), Jif peanut butter jars and lids (59), Disney Magazine in test markets (75-76)

Producers Syndicate, Inc. (Tampa, FL) 1942-46
Canned or bottled fruits, juices

Product Development, Ltd. (Ames, Iowa) 1975
Vehicle safety flags

Producers Rice Mills, Inc. (Stuttgart, AR) 1947-60
Donald Duck packaged rice

Proll Toys, Inc. (Newark or Bloomfield, NJ) 1973-86

Recorder, musical toy instruments

Protectoseal Co. of America, Inc. (Chicago) 1939-41
Molded figures

Prudential-Feldco Inc. (Glendale, Queens, NY) 1979-85
Composition books, looseleaf paper, binders/arrangers, memo books, drawing pads, notepads, writing tablets with matching envelopes, paper portfolios and arrangers

Pyramid Belt Company (NYC) 1975-83
Children's belts and suspenders

Pyramid Leather Goods Company (NYC) 1938-43, 69-70
Children's handbags

Quaker Oats Co. (Chicago) 1948
Advertising materials

Quality Mills Inc. (Mt. Airy, NC) 1965-73
Turtleneck pullovers

Questor Education Products div of Questor Corp. (Bronx, NY) 1972-77
Magnetic puzzles, Bubble Barge, stacking toys, finger puppets

Quetta Carpet (Sales) Ltd. aka **Rugby Rugs, Inc.** (NYC/London) 1968-69, 76-77
Area rugs

Quincrafts Corp. (Hingham, MA) 1982
Makit & Bakit craft kits

K.J. Quinn & Co., Inc. (Malden, MA) 1954-63
Scuffy shoe polish liquid shoe refinisher

R.C.A. Victor Corporation (Camden, NJ/NYC) 1933-55
Victor records, phonograph records and albums

R & M Industries (San Marcos, CA) 1980-82
Decorator pillows

R.L.W. Embroidery Corp. (Union City, NJ) 1948-49
Embroidered materials

Radio Steel & Manufacturing Co. (Chicago) 1956-59
Coaster wagons

Railley Corporation (Cleveland) 1947-48
Lamps

Rainbow Art Glass - See Studio Design, Inc.

Rainbow Girl Coat Co. (NYC) 1966-73
Girls' coats

W.S. Rainford Products, Inc. (Closter, NJ) 1947-48
Inflatable vinylite toys

S.E. Rains Company, Limited (NYC) 1948-65
Children's handkerchiefs

Rand McNally & Co. (Skokie, Il) 1955-56
World globe and globe games

Random House (NYC) 1939-40
Books

Rapco, Inc. (Chicago) 1971-72
WTP Fun Tunnel

Rapid Cutting Co. (Brooklyn, NY) 1941-43
Static electric toy (box with clear acetate cover-characters below attracted by rubbing)

Rarities Mint (Anaheim, CA) 1987
24K gold coins, 999 silver coins, copper, bronze, aluminum coins

Rayette, Incorporated (St. Paul, MN) 1953-54
Shampoo

Raylite Electric Corp. (Bronx, NY) 1958
Christmas lights and decorations

Raymodes Negligee, Inc. (NYC) 1955
Children's negligees, robes, housecoats, dusters, (2 to 14 years old)

Reading Clothing Mfg. Co. (Reading, PA) 1946-47
Children's playclothes

W.C. Redmon Sons & Co. (Peru, IN) 1968-72

Toy chests, clothes hampers, waste receptacles

Reecie of London, Inc. (Union City, NJ) 1954-55
Magic clay

Reed and Barton (Taunton, MA) 1987
Collectible and baby silverplate items

Reed Holdings, Inc. (Buffalo, NY/Atlanta, GA) 1979-86
Wallpaper, decorative wall coverings

Regal Knitwear Company, Inc. (NYC) 1955-67
Mickey Mouse and Davy Crockett sweaters, bathing suits

Florence Reichman, Inc. (NYC) 1937-39
Ladies' hats

T. Reinsdorf Co., Inc. (NYC) 1939-1940
Children's dresses

Reiss Games, Inc. (NYC) 1981-83
Mechanical action banks, hand puzzles

Philip Reiter, Inc. (NYC) 1933-39
Solid gold, silver, and platinum jewelry

Relaxon Products (Chicago) 1940-41
Children's chairs, etc.

Reliable Knitting Works (Milwaukee, WI) 1946-49, 55-57, 65-71, 77-85
Knitted caps, infants knitted headwear, scarves, knit dickey

Reliance Gauge Column Co. (Cleveland, OH) 1940
Advertising materials

Reliance Molded Plastics, Inc. (Woonsocket, RI) 1966-74
Infant training seats, diaper pins, rattles

Reliance Picture Frame Co. (Chicago) 1934-35
Framed pictures

Remco Industries, Inc. (Harrison, NJ) 1973
Candy making game, toy airplanes, shoe shine kit

Rendoll Paper Corp., aka **Great Lakes Press Corp.** (Rochester, NY) 1951-55
Gift wrappings, party kits, paper napkins

Renselaar Corporation, aka **Poster Prints** (Conshohocken, PA) 1969-71
Posters and kites

Republic Shoe Company (Nashville, TN) 1968-69
Boys' shoes

Resort Casuals, Inc. (Miami, FL) 1977-80
Men's and boys' swim trunks and cabana sets

Revell, Inc. (Venice, CA) 1956-62, 70-71, 74-???
Plastic model kits, "fabric art"

Reyburn Mfg. Co. (Philadelphia) 1941-44
Window and store display materials

Reynolds Metal Company (Louisville, KY) 1958
Wall plaques (supplied by Creative Merchandisers Co.), small comic books

Rhine Undergarments Co., Inc. (NYC) 1955-56
Children's petticoats and panties made of nylon

Rhythm Band, Inc. (Fort Worth, TX) 1977-79
Elementary musical instruments

Ribbon Finance Corp. (Miami, FL) 1975-77
String and wire art kits

Irvin W. Rice (NYC) 1932
Mickey Mouse soap statuettes (Rice is an importer through D. Harris & Co., London)

The Richmond School Furniture Co. (Muncie, IN) 1934-35
Blackboards

Ben Rickert Inc. (Wayne, NJ) 1980-84
Soap and toiletries

Rieck-McJnukin Dairy Co. (Pittsburgh) 1940
Cups

Riegel Textile Corp. (Johnston, SC) 1981-83
Crib sheets, blankets, pads, infant apparel, infants' layette products

Riegel Textile Sales Co. (NYC) 1968-69
Piece goods

Stephen Riley Co. (LA) 1952-59
Bubble bath

Ripon Knitting Works (Ripon, WI) 1949-60
Loafer sox with leather soles

James River Corporation of Virginia (Dixie Northern) (Norwalk, CT) 1986-87
Dixie cups

Roanna Togs, Inc. (NYC) 1974-77
Girls' dresses, slack sets, short sets, sizzler sets, panty sets and skirt sets

The Robbins Co. (Attleboro, MA) 1940
Official Jiminy Cricket Conscience medal

Robe-Tex, Inc. (NYC) 1959-60
Bathrobes, dressing gowns

Rock Run Mills, Inc., aka Snuggle Rug Co. (Goshen, Indiana) 1932
Infants' and children's bags of the Snuggle Rug or Bunting types and crib cover

The Rockmore Company, Inc. (NYC) 1949-50
Caps and hats

Roff Knitting Mills (Cohoes, NY/NYC) 1933-35
Clothing

Rollic Inc. (Patchogue, NY) 1970-73
Zip jackets

Rosalind Sportswear Co., Inc. (NYC) 1948-49
Children's sportswear

Rose Art Industries, Inc. (NYC) 1981-84
Cork boards, Color Me Mug, magnetic boards, bulletin boards, chalk boards, Play Dough, hardening clay activity kits, non-hardening clay, Color Your Own Mug, counting frame

Rosecraft (Attleboro Falls, MA) 1987
Children's costume jewelry and hair accessories

George H. Rosen Shoe Mfg. Co. (Boston) 1961-62
Children's slippers

Rosenau Brothers, Inc. (NYC/Philadelphia) 1939-41, 49-50, 55, 70-71
Girls' dresses and play clothes, dresses and sportswear

Rosenblatt & Kahn, Inc. (NYC) 1960-61
Girls' coats

Ross and Ross (Oakland, CA) 1933-35
Dolls

Ross Products, Inc. (NYC) 1964-66
Candles, chimes

J.D. Roszell Co. (Peoria, IL) 1939-40
Ice cream cups

Chester H. Roth Co., Inc. (NYC) 1952-56
Children's anklets

Royal American Corporation (Chicago) 1947-48
Electric scissors and binoculars

Royal Mfg. Co., Inc. (Allentown, PA) 1969-70
Jogging jackets and pants

Royal Orleans (New Orleans) 1981
Distributors of votive bisques, china tableware (see also: United China & Glass)

Royal Typewriter Co. (???) 1938-39
Sold typewriters through ads depicting Snow White and Seven Dwarfs

Royalty Designs, Inc. (Miami, FL) 1954-56
Lamps

Rubber for Molds, Inc. (Chicago) 1948-49
Rubber masks, hand puppets

Rugby Rugs (see: Quetta Carpet (sales) Ltd.)

Russ Toggs, Inc., div. of Juniorite (NYC) 1970-71
Adult swimsuits

Russell Mfg. Co. (Leicester, MA) 1945-86
Card games, miniature card games, play money, Disneyland train

Russell Mills Inc. (Alexander City, AL) 1965-73
Sleepwear

S. & R. Infants Wear Co., Inc. (NYC) 1958-59
Sleeping bags

Saalfield Publishing Co. (Akron, OH/NYC) 1931-37, 67-69
Illustrated books, puzzles and painting books

Sackman Bros. Co. (NYC) 1933-35, 38-39
Costumes and masks

Salant & Salant, Inc. (NYC) 1967-71
Boys' shirts

The Salem China Co. (Salem, OH/NYC) 1934-39
Chinaware

Sales Affiliates, Inc. (NYC) 1943-44
Instruction books

Salient, Inc. (E. Longmeadow/Holyoke, MA) 1951-52
Children's wallets and purses

Samsonite Corp. (Denver, CO) 1972
Plastic indoor and outdoor skates

Sandess Mfg. Co. (Philadelphia) 1950
Advertising materials

Eli L. Sandler & Co. (NYC) 1971-72
Scatter rugs, textile wall hangings (see also: Lysander Tufted Products)

Sandura Co., Inc. (Philadelphia) 1940-42
Floor covering

Santly-Joy, Inc. (NYC) 1946-48
Music publishers

Sar-A-Lee Co. (Cleveland, OH) 1949-50
Mayonnaise, salad dressing, sandwich spread, French dressing

Savage Shoe Co., Ltd. (???) 1949-50
Children's Shoes

Savoy-Reeland Printing Co. (NYC) 1931
Printers of Mickey Mouse material

Sawyers, Inc. (Portland, OR) 1955-68
3 dimensional color reels and viewers (see also: Tru-Vue, View Master)

Henry Schanzer and Sons, Inc. (NYC) 1933-34
Sweaters, shawls

Scharco Mfg. Corp. (Mt. Vernon, NY) 1952-53
Plastic high chair, plastic covered mattresses, crib bumpers, play yard pads

Alfred Schiftan, Inc. (NYC) 1987
Framed and unframed foil prints

Schmid Bros., Inc. (Boston/Randolf, MA) 1970-87
Handcarved music boxes, Christmas tree ornaments, pewter and silver figurines, musical Christmas balls, musical mugs, musical key chains, ceramic music boxes, character thimbles, bookends, salt and pepper shakers, napkin rings, gardening set, jam pot and pitcher, china mugs, bowl and plate sets, lead crystal figurines and plates, pewter plates, musical ceramic figures, commemorative plates and bells, bookends, ceramic giftware

Joseph Schneider, Inc. (NYC) 1936-38
Wind-up toy

John F. Schoener, Inc. (Reading, PA) 1937-42
Hollow chocolate moulded figures

A.H. Schreiber Co., Inc. 1936-41, 58-59, 81-83
Children's wear (slips, panties, and petticoats), swimwear

Schumann China Corp. (NYC) 1932-34
Chinaware, pottery and earthenware

Schutter Candy Co. (Chicago) 1940-41
Candy bars

A. H. Schwab (St. Louis, MO) 1975-77
Sandboxes, picnic tables, peg desks, workbenches, peg chests, chalk boards, cork boards, indoor/outdoor seesaws, slides & swings, toy chests, step-stools, artist easel, children's director's chair, doll furniture

Scott and Bowne (Bloomfield, NJ) 1935-37
Advertising booklet for "Scott's Emulsion"

Sculptors Guild Ltd. (St. Louis, MO) 1981-83
Sculptured mirrors with and without stained glass

Seagren Products, Inc. (Brooklyn, NY) 1946-48
Cake decorations

Sears, Roebuck and Co. (Chicago) 1960's-87
Special Winnie the Pooh license

Seasonal Fruit Packing Co. (LA) 1956
Fruit juice serving sets

Seattle Luggage Corp. (Seattle) 1947-48
Children's luggage

Seiberling Latex Products Co. (Akron, OH/NYC/Chicago) 1934-42
Rubber toys, hot water bottles

Selandria Designs/Walter Fleisher Co. (Van Nuys, CA) 1987
Melamine spoons and forks, bowls, plates, mugs, acrylic glasses, goblets, vinyl placemats comprising of 1-6 of above

Selchow & Righter Co. (Bay Shore, NY) 1987
Disney Family Edition of Trival Pursuit

Selco Knitwear Company (NYC) 1968-69
Sweaters

Selfix Products Co., Inc. (Chicago) 1961-63
Wall toothbrush holders

Semca Time Corp., div. of Hamilton Watch Co. (Long Island, NY) 1970-71
Clocks (wall, desk, alarm, and travel)

Seneca Textile Corp. (NYC) 1933-34
Piece goods (cretonne, chintz and marquisette)

Sentinel Plastics, div. of Gulf and Western Corp. (Bronx, NY) 1972-74
Mirrors, picture frames, wall organizers

Service Industries, Inc. (Chicago) 1937-38
Masonite cut-outs

Seven-Up Company (St. Louis, MO) 1957
Buttons with Zorro logo (celluloid) supplied by Green Duck Co.

Seward Luggage Co. (Dayton, OH) 1975
Luggage

Shane Mfg. Co. Inc. (Evansville, IN) 1965-66
Winnie the Pooh dress shirts (Sears)

W. Shanhouse and Sons (NYC) 1955-57
Mickey Mouse and Davy Crockett cloth and vinyl jackets

Sharose Consultants, Inc., div of Arco Ind. Ltd. (Westbury, NY) 1985-86
Rack and novelty toys, umbrella shower, hand-held indoor/outdoor shower

Sharp & Dohme (Pittsburgh) 1947-48
"Sucrets"

Shaw Creations (NYC) 1987
Umbrellas

Evan K. Shaw Company (LA) 1945-55
Ceramic figurines

Sheaffer Eaton, div. of The Texton Corp. (Pittsfield, MA) 1982-85
Kaleidoscope ballpoint & rolling ball pens

Shelbud Products Corp. (New Rochelle, NY) 1972-73
Pin-wheel, badminton set, paddle ball, table tennis set, kazoos, flashlights

Shelby Cycle Co. (Shelby, OH) 1949-50
Bicycles

Shelcore Inc. (NYC/S. Plainfield, NJ) 1976-87
Battery operated phonograph, record carrier, nesting blocks, peek-a-boo picture toy, inflatable infant toys, stack blocks

Sherman Bros. Rainwear Corp. (NYC) 1933-34
Raincoats

Louis Sherry, Inc. (Long Island City, NY) 1941-42
Ice cream containers, window displays

Sherry Mfg. Co., Inc. (Miami, FL) 1969-70, 82-87
Character T-shirts and sweatshirts associated with the name of a resort or geographic location

Shillcraft (Baltimore, MD/Montreal, Quebec, Canada) 1973-79
Disney character rug kits

A. & H. Shillman Co., Inc. (Baltimore, MD) 1972-85
Rug kits (latch hook, direct mail)

M. & S. Shillman, Inc. (Brooklyn, NY) 1987
Fashion and baby doll clothes, doll accessories

M. Shimmel Sons (NYC/Brooklyn, NY) 1958-60, 65-67
Toys, Zorro rings

Shirtees, Inc., div of Pilgrim Sportswear, Inc. (NYC) 1955-56, 59, 68
Children's knitted polo shirts (slip-overs & cardigans) pajamas, infants' creepers, Davy Crockett T-shirts

Philip Shlansky and Bro., Inc./Donnybrook Coat Corp. (NYC) 1938-39
Suits and coats

Shutzer Mfg. Co., Inc. (NYC) 1976-77
Men's and boys' jackets and vests

Arthur Siegman, Inc. (NYC) 1941-42
Men's neckwear

Leonard Silver International, Inc. (Boston) 1979-81
Three dimensional, silverplated savings bank

Silvercraft of California (LA) 1946-48
Children's silverware

Silvestri Art Mfg. Co. (Chicago) 1968-71
Store displays, Christmas decorations

Max Simon & Associates (LA) 1967-68
Handkerchiefs

Simon & Schuster (NYC) 1947-58
Little Big and Giant Golden Book series, record albums, books

Simplicity Pattern Co., Inc. (NYC) 1944-46, 86-87
Patterns

Singing Needles div of William Carter Co. (Leola, PA) 1969-71
Sleepers

Skil-Craft Corp., sub of Western Publishing Co. (Chicago/Racine, WI) 1976-77
Craft kits

Skyway Products, Inc. (Brooklyn, NY) 1972-73
Kites, jet plane flyer, frisbee

M. Slifka & Sons / aka **Windsor Belt Co.** (NYC) 1932, 47-57
Boys' leather belts, suspenders, ties, tie slides

Sloan & Co. (NYC) 1934-40
Jewelry in precious metals, solid gold, platinum and silver jewelry

Slumbertogs, Inc. (NYC) 1960-61
Pajamas and nightgowns

Small World Greetings, Inc. (LA) 1987
Vinyl memo holders, checkbook covers, address books, credit cardcases, diaries, die-cut name-card holder

Smart Deb. Frocks (NYC) 1930-40
Junior dresses

Smart Set Togs (NYC) 1959-60
Girls' sportswear, creepers

Alexander Smith & Sons Carpet Co. (Yonkers, NY) 1935-37
Wool, cotton or jute carpets and rugs

Smith Enterprises, Inc. (Rock Hill, SC/Denver, CO) 1968-85
Easter baskets, Halloween and Christmas novelties

Smith, Hogg, & Co., Inc. (NYC/Boston/Chicago) 1935-37
Bed linen, towels, terry cloth beach and bath robes, bath mats, wash clothes and napkins, "feeders"

Smith and Peters (Philadelphia) 1938-42
Candy

The Smockery (Englewood, NY) 1939-40
Dresses (not children's)

Foster D. Snell Sales Corp. (NYC/Rochester, NY) 1931-32
Cigarette snappers, door stops

Snuggle Rug Co., aka **Rock Run Mills, Inc.** (Goshen, IN/NYC) 1932-34
Infants' bags and crib covers of the "Snuggle Rug" and "Bunting" types

Solar Electric Corp. (Warren, PA) 1956-57
Electric light bulbs and lamp bases

Sondra Mfg, Co., Inc. (NYC) 1966-70
Velour shirts (Sears)

MICKEY MOUSE

Soreng-Manegold Co. (Chicago) 1934-38
Lamps, sewing kits, yarn holders, lampshades

Soroka Sales, Inc. (Pittsburgh) 1964-65
Framed pictures

South Berwick Shoe Co., Inc. (South Berwick, ME) 1966-67
Shoes

Southeastern Foods, Inc. (Andalusia/Brundidge, AL) 1947-53
Salad dressing, mayonnaise and sandwich spread

Southern Dairies, Inc. (Washington, D.C.) 1936-40
Ice cream and dairy products

Southern Music Publishing Co. (NYC) 1942-50
Music publishers

Southwestern Household Equipment Co. (Chicago) 1945-46
Toy tools, brooms

Space Face (Laguna Hills, CA) 1983
Expandable polyethylene Space Face visors

Spartans Industries, Inc. (NYC) 1968-70
Socks, hosiery

Spatz Bros. Inc. (NYC) 1955-56
Mickey Mouse and Davy Crockett raincoats (see also: Weatherman Corp.)

Spear Products Co. (NYC) 1946-49, 1958-61
"Jack-in-the-box" and "Jack-on-the-box"

Specialty Advertising Service, Inc. (Long Island, NY) 1954-59
Mickey Mouse press badges and cards (for Vick Chemical Co.), plastic rings (for General Mills), Hardy Boys Rings (for International Shoe Co.), puppet (for General foods Corp. — Jello div.), drinking mugs (for General Foods Corp. — Baker's Instant Choc. Mix)

Spec-Toy-Culars, Inc. (Long Island City, NY) 1957-58
Musical toys

Spectra Star Kites (Pacoima, CA) 1987
Kites

Speidel Corp. (Providence, RI) 1938-41
Costume jewelry

Sponge Clean Products (NYC) 1972-73
Placemats, tablecloths

Sponge Specialties Corp. (E. Rockaway, NY) 1972-???
Polyurethane foam jigsaw puzzles, building blocks, block puzzles, story block, bowling sets, play pads, sponges, bath mats, bath mitts

Sporting Shoe Co., Inc. (NYC) 1947-49
Children's leather sandals, bedroom slippers, rubber boots and rubbers

Sportline, div of Beatrice Foods Co. (Shawnee Mission, KS) 1981
Sleeping and slumber bags

Springs Industries, Performance Product Division (NYC) 1987
Children's bed tents

Stadium Sport-Headwear Co. (NYC) 1939-40
Beachwear accessories (hat, gloves, scarfs)

Stance Industries (Hauppauge, NY) 1982-84
Children's and adults' comb and brush sets

Standard Brands, Inc. (NYC) 1940-41, 67
Sold Royal Desserts through ads depicting Pinocchio

Standard Brief Case Co., Inc. (NYC) 1934-35
Children's brief cases

Standard Home Products (Holyoke, MA) 1964-67
Shoe polish

Standard Knitting Mills, Inc. (Knoxville, TN) 1966-71
Ski pajamas

Standard Oil Co. of California (???, CA) 1939-49
Preference for Standard gasoline, oil and services is shown in ads depicting Walt Disney characters

Standard Oil Clothing Co., Inc. (NYC) 1937-38
Raincoats

Standard Plastic Products, Inc. (Plainfield, NJ) 1963
Children's luggage, doll cases, cosmetic cases, pillows, wallets

Standard Toykraft Products (Brooklyn/NYC) 1939-41, 62-63
Paint and needlework sets

Stark Brothers Ribbon Corp. (NYC) 1934-35, 40-41
Ribbons and bandeaus

Stationers Specialty Corp. (NYC) 1938-39
Blotters

D.F. Stauffer Biscuit Co., Inc. (York, PA) 1983-86
Cookies and biscuits

Stayon Products Company (Greenville, SC) 1965-73
Blanket sleepers, crib sheets pillowcases, etc.

Stehli & Co., Inc. (NYC) 1939-40
Printed Rayon Crepe

Margarete Steiff and Co., Inc. (NYC) 1931
Stuffed dolls (perhaps imported by Geo. Borgfeldt)

A. Stein and Co. (NYC) 1934-35
Rubber baby clothes

Stelber Cycle Corp. (Elmhurst, NY) 1966-67
Tricycles

Barney Stempler and Sons, Inc. (NYC) 1938-41
Garment hangers

W.L. Stensgaard and Associates, Inc. (Chicago) 1938, 41-62
Store displays and promotions

Stephens Products Company, Inc., aka **Philson In.** (Middletown, CT) 1953-57
Automatic picture gun set, Donald Duck projector, Davy Crockett picture projector with toy-length film strips

Sterling Novelty Products Co. (Chicago) 1975-82
Coloring tablecloths, window decorations

Steven Mfg. Co. (St. Louis, MO) 1961-63
Kaleidoscopes (including Wonderful World of Color and Babes in Toyland), periscope (Pinocchio), Inventor sets

Stevens Industries, Inc., aka **Cinderella Foods** (Dawson, GA) 1948-50
Peanut butter

J.P. Stevens and Co., Inc. (NYC) 1954-55
Lady and the Tramp crib sheets, pillow cases, printed fabrics

Stick a State Publishing Co., Inc. (Chicago) 1970-71
Stick a State map

Style Undies, Inc. (NYC) 1960
Slips, petticoats, and panties

Stonite Co., Inc. (NYC) 1930-32
Mickey Mouse door stops, cigarette snuffers

Storkline Furniture Corp. (Chicago) 1938-41
Juvenile furniture

Storktowne Products Inc. (Chicago) 1965-70
Winnie the Pooh robes (Sears)

The Straits Corp. (Detroit, MI) 1934-35
Toy airplanes, motor boats, lamp shades

Strathmore Co./Watkins-Strathmore (Aurora, IL) 1943-46, 55-58
Magic slate blackboards, magic slate T.V. set

F.J. Strauss, Co., Inc. (NYC/North Bergen, NJ) 1976-84
Water color paint boxes, telescope, binoculars, kaleidoscope, harmonica, Jr. sports sets and Paint 'n Puff, crayons, glitter pail sets

Strombeck-Becker Mfg. Co. (Moline, IL/NYC) 1955-59
Mickey Mouse and Davy Crockett stage coach model kit, trackless train, "Man in Space" ship, Casey Jr. locomotive, horse and rider wooden push toy

Strombecker Corp., div of Chemtoy (Chicago) 1982-87
Bubble pipes and kits, play putty, jack and ball sets

H.J. Strotter, Inc. (NYC) 1987
Plastic patio accessories, ice bucket, trays, glasses, etc.

Strutwear Knitting Co. (Minn., MN) 1940
Pajamas

Stry-Lenkoff Co., Inc. (Louisville, KY) 1984-87
Invisible ink sets, magic pen sets, magic pen postcards

Studio Art Embroidery Co. (Union City, NJ) 1949
Schiffli embroidered edges, laces, and all-overs

Studio Design, Inc., T/A Rainbow Art Glass (Neptune, NJ) 1979-83
Tiffany style lamp shades, Tiffany wall lights and kits

Sugar Foods Corp. (NYC) 1976
Individual condiment servings

N. Sumergrade and Sons (NYC) 1965-72, 75
Baby comforters with pillows, slumber bags, bed pillows

Sun Hill Industries, Inc. (Stamford, CT) 1982-87
Egg art, Easter egg decorations

Sun Oil Company/Sunoco (Philadelphia) 1938-46
Sold gasoline and oil through ads depicting Mickey Mouse, Donald Duck, etc.

Sun Products Corporation, div of Wellington Leisure (Madison, GA) 1985
Inflated riding ball, foam life vest

Sun Rubber Company/Sun Products Corp. (Barberton, OH) 1941-58, 72-86
Latex, rubber and vinyl toys, rubber fire truck, tractor, car, airplane, Cleo tub toy, Donald soap dish, Huey, Louie and Dewey tub toy, rubber figures of Mickey, Minnie and Donald, dipped latex figures of Mickey, Donald, Pluto, Dumbo, and Davy Crockett soft vinyl doll, balls, inflated riding balls, castle playhouse, life vest, spring suspended ride-on

Sunworthy Wall Covering/Borden (Brampton, Ontario, Canada) 1987
Decorative wall coverings

Super Novelty Candy Co., Inc. (Newark, NJ) 1955-58
Novelty packages of candy, Davy Crockett prize box (candy and toy), Davy Crockett bag of pops

Superior Bedding Co. (LA) 1945-48, 66-67
Mattresses, etc.

Superior Toy and Mfg. Co., Inc. (Chicago) 1981-87
Fun showers, gum ball machines and pocket gumball dispenser

A.D. Sutton and Sons, Inc. (NYC) 1970-72
Fabric and vinyl luggage, pillows, 7" plastic figurines

L.S. Sutton and Sons, Inc. (NYC) 1973-???
Novelty decorated pillows

Swift and Co. (Chicago) 1938-39, 55-58
Snow White and Seven Dwarf flower seeds could be obtained by sending the company 10¢ and the printed end from Allsweet Oleomargarine

Synergistics Research Corp. (NYC) 1979-83
Velcro target games and hand puppets

T.N.P. Jewels and Design Co. (NYC) 1977
Silver and gold charms, earrings, rings, pendants, necklaces, belt buckles, key chains and figures

O.C. Tanner (Hinsdale, IL) 1971-72
Jewelry

Tara Toy Co. (Glendale, NY) 1981-82
Miniature toy desk accessories and organizers

The Tarrson Co. (Chicago) 1977
Mosaic picture kit

Thomas P. Taylor Co. (Bridgeport, CT) 1931-32
Blouses, pajamas, playsuits, dresses, etc.

Telemovie Co. (Hollywood, CA) 1932
8mm film for use in toy motion picture machines

Tennessee Valley Associates (Nashville, TN) 1943-45
Shoo flies, rocking horses

Terry Products Co. (Kannapolis, NC) 1956
Terry cloth kimono (infant) play pen pad & outfits

Testor Corp. (LA) 1981-82
Plastic model and paint kits

Tex Togs Inc. (El Paso, TX) 1965-73
Winnie the Pooh slacks and shorts (Sears)

Texas Infants Dress Co. (San Antonio, TX) 1939-40
Children's dresses

Texas Star Flour Mills (Galveston, TX) 1937-38
Flour bags

Texas Works, Inc. (Fort Worth, TX) 1987
Ice cube trays and ice sculpture trays

The Thermagraph Company (NYC) 1943
Hot iron transfers

Thermo Products Inc. (Albany, NY) 1955-56
Melamine dinnerware

Thinshell Products (Chicago) 1938-39
Licensed use not known

George H. Thomas & Co., Inc. (Cincinnati, OH) 1953
Frozen fruits and vegetables

James Thompson and Co., Inc. (NYC) 1982
Plastic decoplaques

Thompson Ice Cream Co. (Chicago) 1940
Cups

Thorens, Inc. (NYC) 1938-42
Swiss music boxes

Thornton Glove Co., Inc. (Totowa, NJ) 1972-???
Children's gloves

Three Little Girls, Inc. (NYC) 1949-50
Dresses

Thyra of California, Inc. (Canoga Park, CA) 1964-65
Shoes

Tiger Electronics (Mundelein, IL) 1982
Battery-operated cassette tape players

Tiger Fabrics, Inc. (NYC) 1965-66
Cotton fabric for use in piece goods (Sears)

Tiger Home Products (Princeton, NJ) 1979-81
Wall hooks

Tigrett Industries, Inc. (Jackson, TN) 1960-63
Toys

Tillery Container Co. (Kansas City, MO) 1945-47
Puzzles, savings banks

Time and Place, Inc. (NYC) 1970
Tops & jeans

Timely Toys (Chicago) 1945-46
Wooden rocking toys

Timex Corp. — see Ingersoll-Waterbury Co. and US Time

Charles Tobias Bro. & Co. (Cincinnati, OH) 1933-40
Boys' hats and caps

Tomart Publications div of Tomart Corporation (Dayton, OH) 1985-87
Illustrated collector's catalogs and price guides

Tommee Tippee Playskool, Inc. — see Playskool Mfg. Company

Tomy Corporation (Carson, CA) 1982-87
Hand-held and table-top electromechanical/electronic toys and games, painted figures, vehicles sold at theme parks, TRON playsets, plastic wind-up toys, plush doll characters from The Black Cauldron

Topco Toys, Inc. (NYC) 1982
Soap sponge and holder, toothpaste dispenser, vinyl door knob covers

Topps Chewing Gum, Inc. (Brooklyn, NY) 1955-56, 58-59, 63, 79
Davy Crockett, Zorro, and Black Hole trading cards

William Tory Company (NYC) 1961-62
Jewel boxes

Touraine Co., Inc. (NYC) 1955-56
Skirts, blouses & sportswear

Toy Kraft Company (Wooster, OH) 1933-37
Wooden pull, push, and sand toys

Toy Tinkers, Inc. (Evanston, IL) 1937-39
Mickey Mouse and Snow White series "Tinkersand" picture sets

Transogram Company, Inc. (NYC) 1939-42, 45-71
Paint and crayon sets, games, banks, roly-poly, 8mm projector and films, kazoos, magnetic xylophone

Travis Fabrics, Inc. (NYC) 1955-56

Printed synthetic fabric, tricot dish rags

Tre-Jur (NYC) 1968
Dusting powder, cologne, molded soaps (re-release of Snow White book set with plastic lid)

Treat Hobby Products (Fullerton, CA) 1983
Trading cards and stamp collecting kits

Treville, Inc. (Orange, NJ) 1981-84
Hair ornaments & accessories

Triangle Paper Bag Mfg. Co. (Covington, KY) 1958-59
Paper shopping bags

Triboro Quilt Mfg. Co. (NYC/White Plains, NY) 1970-86
Baby & youth blankets, cotton quilts, robes, pram suits, jumpsuits, bunting sets, blanket sleepers, infant jackets and snow suits, diaper stacker

Tri-Chem, Inc. (Harrison, NJ) 1984-85
Liquid embroidery craft sets (sold via home parties)

Trifari, Krussman & Fishel, Inc. (NYC) 1937-39
Novelty jewelry and rhinestone & non-precious metal charms

The Trimart Co. (NYC) 1945-46
Framed felt pictures

Trimfit, Inc. (NYC) 1971-73
Terry cloth sleep/play sets

Trimfoot Company, Inc. (Farmington, MO) 1949-58
Children's slippers, sandals and shoes (49-54), MM & Davy Crockett felt slippers, baby & children's shoes, cowboy boots, moccasins (55-56)

Trimz Company, Inc. (Chicago) 1947-48
Wallpaper & boarders

Trojan Maid, Inc. (NYC) 1936-39
Clothes

Tropix-Togs, Inc. (Miami) 1972-77
Shirts and sweat shirts

Troy Sunshade Co. (Troy, OH) 1935
Carrier bags and aprons

Truitt Brothers, Inc. (Binghamton, NY) 1932-35
Shoes

Tru-Vue, Inc. div of GAF Corp./Sawyers, Inc. (Beaverton/Portland, OR) 1950-56, 68-71
Toy film viewers, film strips, slide sets, 3-D film cards and viewers

Tucker Garment Inc. (Springfield, MA) 1956-57
Play aprons

Tudor Metal Products, Inc. (NYC) 1960-64
Xylophones, electric vibrating games

Jack Turk, Inc. (NYC) 1955-56
Infant and children's nightwear

Robert Tutelman Company (Somerset, PA) 1968-87
Woven pajamas, robes, cotton pajamas, shirts

Harry Tuttman & Son (NYC) 1950-51
Children's dresses, skirts

Tuxton Cravats (NYC) 1944-45
Neckwear

Twentieth Century Novelty Casting (NYC) 1957
Tie and slide

Tyco Industries (Moorestown, NJ) 1987
Telephones

U.S. American (LA) 1983-84
Drinking glasses and ceramic coffee mugs

U.S. Carbide Tool Company (St. Louis) 1946-47
Lamps

U.S. Electric Mfg. Corp. (NYC) 1935-38
Flashlight cases and batteries

U.S. Lock & Hardware Co. (Columbia, PA) 1934-40
Jack sets

U.S. Plastics Company (Pasadena, CA) 1953-55
Plastic pull toys and mobiles

U.S. Plywood Corp. (NYC) 1969-71
Glues and adhesives

U.S. Printing and Lithograph Co. (Chicago) 1949-50
Gift box wrap

U.S. Time Corporation — see Ingersoll-Waterbury Co., Timex, United States Time Corp.

The Ullman Company (Brooklyn, NY) 1977-81
Placemats

Bernhard Ulmann Company, Inc. (Long Island, NY) 1953-59
Unfinished art needlework for embroidering, crocheting and/or knitting, terry cloth products (also Davy Crockett-1955)

Uneeda Doll Co., Inc. (Brooklyn, NY) 1960-62
Dolls from Pollyanna, Babes In Toyland, & Pinocchio

Union Ice Cream Co. (Nashville, TN) 1940
Cups

Union Wadding Company, Inc. (Pawtucket, RI) 1970-82
Yo-yos, pre-seeded roll-out flower & vegetable gardens, Christmas tree accessories, spinning tops

Unisonic Products Corporation (NYC) 1981-85
Electronic calculators and talk back computer, clock pen clock picture frame, calculator and wallet sets

United Biscuit Co. of America (Chicago) 1934-36
Crackers and biscuits

United China & Glass Company / aka **Royal Orleans** (New Orleans) 1979-84
China, porcelain and ceramic giftware

United Felt Company (Chicago) 1961
Pillows

United Merchants & Manufacturers, Inc./ Ameritex (NYC) 1975-84
Piece goods, fabric

United Precision Plastics, Inc. (Erie, PA) 1966
Plastic codophone toys made for H.J. Heinz

United States Time Corporation — see: Ingersoll-Waterbury Co., Timex (NYC) 1945-71
Watches, clocks, ballpoint pens

United Trading Co. (LA) 1971
Plush toys

United Wall Paper Factories (Jersey City, NJ) 1935-37, 44-50
Wall paper boarders

United Wallpaper Co. div DeSoto Chemical Coating Inc. (Des Plaines, IL) 1961-63, 65-66
Wallpaper (Sears)

United Wallpaper Inc. (Chicago) 1944-50
Wallpaper

Universal Lamp Company, Inc. (Chicago) 1969-71
Blow molded lamps

Universal Novelties Corp. (Chicago) 1947-49
Donald Duck electric scissors set

Utility Chemical Company/Utico Corporation (Paterson, NJ) 1984-86
Swimming pool accessories

Valdeco, Inc. (Fresno, CA) 1987
Pinwheels

Valentine Textile Corp. (NYC) 1937-38
Cloth

Valtex Fabrics, Inc. (NYC) 1963-64
Cotton fabric yard goods for home use

Vance Laboratories, Inc. (NYC) 1967
Teflon-coated pan in shape of Mickey Mouse for cooking eggs, pancakes, etc.

Vanguard Corporation (Chicopee, MA) 1949-53
Plastic inflatable toys, jingle balls, play rings

Vanity Fair Electronics Corp. (Brooklyn, NY) 1955-56
Phonographs pogo sticks, inter-com, Geiger counter, plastic figure with sound

Van Kirk Chocolate Corp., Ltd. (Canada) 1949-50
Chocolate candy

Varsity House, Inc. (Columbus, OH) 1970-74
Knitted shifts, large T-shirts, sweat shirts

Velva Sheen Manufacturing (Cincinnati, OH) 1986-87
Souvenir T-shirts and sweatshirts

Lillian Vernon Corp. (Mt. Vernon, NY) 1977-81
Christmas tree and year-round brass and gold finish ornaments

Vernon Potteries, Ltd. (LA) 1940-42
Vernon Kilns ceramic figures (some molds later purchased and used by Evan K. Shaw)

Viceroy Mfg. Co., Ltd. (Canada) 1949-50
Rubber car, fire truck, tractor & airplane (Made Donald Duck airplane not made in U.S.)

Vick Chemical Company (NYC) 1956
MM World Reporter press card, badge, & map (supplied by Rand McNally Specialty Adv. div) premiums

View-Master — see: G.A.F. Corp/Sawyers, Inc.

Vita Corp. (Mamaroneck, NY) 1951-52
Greeting cards

Vogue Needlecraft Company (NYC) 1931-32
Stenciled pillow tops for embroidering, dresser scarfs, card table covers, luncheon sets, breakfast sets, etc.

Volupte, Inc. (NYC) 1933-34
Compacts, vanity cases

Volz & Fawcett (NYC) 1931-32
MM handkerchiefs

Vroman-Shaver Ice Cream Company (Toledo, OH) 1953
Ice creams and sherberts

Wahlborg Printing Company (Chicago) 1968-71
Party kits, gift wrap

Waldburger, Tanner & Co. / **Waldburger & Huber in US** (NYC/St. Gall, Switzerland) 1930
Handkerchiefs

Waldill Sales Co. (NYC) 1965-66
Disneyland Drazy-Krass Trackless Train (Sears)

Wallace Berrie & Company (Van Nuys, CA) 1984
Plush rag dolls, bean bags, & PVC figures (also see: Applause)

Wallace Silversmiths (Wallingford, CT) 1972
Silver and silverplated spoons, forks, cups, and porriger sets

Rolf Wallach (NYC) 1936-37
Imported scarfs

Wamsutta Mills, Inc. sub of M. Lowenstein & Sons (NYC) 1968-87
Sheets, pillowcases, beach/bath towels, wash clothes, bed spreads, slumber bags, comforters, waste paper baskets, bathroom tumblers, shower curtains, tissue holders, printed cloth, laundry bags, pillow shams, curtains and drapes

Watkins-Strathmore Company (Racine, WI) 1958-68
Magic slate items, activity sets, puzzles

Waynewood, Inc. (Hazelwood, NC) 1966-67
Crib and youth mattresses, bumper pads (Sears)

Wear-A-Blanket Inc. (NYC) 1965-66
Blanket sleepers (Sears)

Weathermac Corp. (NYC) 1955-56
Davy Crockett fur hats

The Weatherman (Chicago) 1946-53
Weather vane (plastic)

Weather Tamer (Chicago) 1972
Children's jackets and snow suits

Wecolite Co., Inc. (Teaneck, NJ) 1982-85
Straight & flex plastic drinking straws

Wee Willie Tog's Ltd. (NYC) 1977
Boys' sportswear

Albert Weiss & Co. (NYC) 1970-71
Women's belts

Louis Weiss / Louis Weiss Umbrellas, Inc. (NYC) 1933-43, 45-58
Umbrellas and raincoats

Eleanor Welborn Art Products, Inc, (Seaside, CA) 1955-56
Ceramic dinnerware, decorative plates

Welby div Elgin National Industries, Inc. (Chicago) 1976-85
Wall clocks

Welded Plastics Corp. (NYC) 1955-56
MM Clubhouse, Davy Crockett fort, MM hat, card construction set, magic etching set, plastic Mousecaps with movable ears

Weldon Mfg. Corp. (NYC) 1946-49
Boys' pajamas

Wells div of Benrus Corp. (Attleboro, MA) 1972-73
Sterling silver statuettes, charms, charm bracelets, banks, paperweights

Wells Lamont Corp. (Chicago) 1958-68
Gloves, gauntlets, mittens

Wen-Mac Corporation (LA) 1963-64
Make-it yourself construction sets

E.K. Wertheimer and Sons, Inc. (NYC) 1942-43, 60-61
Jewelry

Stanley Wessell & Co. (Chicago) 1950-55
Litho and molded plastic wall plaques

Westab, Inc. div of Mead Corp. (St. Joseph, MO/Dayton, OH) 1956-57, 68-74
School tablets, pocket pads

Western Art Leather Company (Denver) 1938-39
Souvenir pillows

Western Printing & Lithographing — also see Western Publishing Co., Inc. & Whitman Publishing Company (Racine, WI/Poughkeepsie, NY/St. Louis) 1944-87
Producers and publishers of books, publications, and comic books; games, jigsaw puzzles & stationery in 1951

Western Publishing Company, Inc. (Racine, WI) 1970-87
Golden books, toy books, Gold Key Comics, tray puzzles, boxed puzzles, coloring books, magic slates, sticker fun books, paperback punch-out playsets, board games, books, craft & hobby items, dominoes, checkers, weather thermometers, crayons, boxed paint & water sets (also see: Skil-Craft Corp.)

Western Tablet and Stationery Corp. — also see Westab, Inc. (St, Joseph, MO) 1939-41
Tablets

Westfield Products (Waterloo, IA) 1964
Glass mugs, bowls, and tumblers

White and Whyckoff Mfg. Co. (Holyoke, MA) 1937-39
Stationery and greeting cards

Whitman Publishing Company (Racine, WI/NYC/Chicago) 1933-87
Books, cut-outs, games, playing cards, bridge tallys, stand-up figures, sticker fun items, stationery, picture puzzles, coloring books, magic slates,

craft and hobby items, dominoes, die-cuts, erasable drawing sets

Whitney Mfg. Co. (NYC) 1939-41
Labels and tags

Whitson Food Products Company (Denton, TX) 1949-50
Canned meats, beans and sausages

Wilbur-Suchard Chocolate Company (Philadelphia) 1933-34, 72
Chocolate candy

Wilco Company (LA) 1953-55
Aerosol snow bomb

William Rogers & Son aka **International Silver** (Meriden, CT/NYC/Chicago) 1931-39
Children's silverware, cups, feeding plates, pushers, etc. Some packaged with other toys and wooden figures. Available from Post-O cereal for 10¢ and a box top

The Williams Mfg. Co. (Portsmouth, OH) 1972-74
Children's shoes

Williamsburg div Dressner & Rabinowitz (NYC) 1972
Boys' trunks, girls' swimwear, and Terry cloth cover-up

Williamsburg Knitting Mills (Brooklyn, NY) 1966-69
Swimsuits

Rollin Wilson Co., (Memphis,TN) 1936-37
Bow and arrow sets

Wilson Sporting Goods — Wonder Products is a div (Collierville,TN) 1972
Spring suspended and rocker ride 'em toys

Wilton Enterprises, Inc. (Chicago) 1972-86
Cake pan kits, sugar molds, and plastic mold kits

Windmill Productions, Inc, (NYC) 1976-82
Calendars, including Nite-glow

Windsor Textile Co., Inc. (Chicago) 1961-62
Towels (Sears)

Winer Sportswear, Inc (NYC) 1968
Jackets (Sears)

Winthrop-Atkins Company, Inc. (Middleboro, MA) 1968-70
Pantograph, magnetic game, mystery writing set

Withington, Inc. (West Minot, ME) 1955-57
Davy Crockett blow gun, bow & arrow set

L. Wohl & Co., Inc. (NYC) 1956-57
Infants' and children's dresses

Bernhard Wolf (NYC) 1938-39
Handkerchiefs

Wolf Detroit Envelope Company (Detroit) 1950
Paper bottle collars

Wolf Envelope Co. (Cleveland, OH) 1939-41
Bottle collars

Wolf Mfg, Co. (Waco, TX) 1958-59
Embroidered clothing

Wolverine Toy Company, Inc, (Pittsburgh/Boonville, AL) 1970-83
Toy kitchen sets, ironing board sets, coin-sorting banks, pin ball games, bag toss target game,quiz game

Wonder Products Company sub of Wilson Sporting Goods (Collierville,TN) 1972
Spring suspended and rocker ride 'em toys

Wonderknit, Corp. (Lindhurst, NJ) 1952
Shirts, cardigans, ensembles, pajamas, trunks, terry knits (except robes and towels)

G.G. Wood Co. (Girard, PA) 1975
Director chairs

Woodall Industries, Inc. (Detroit) 1962-63
Lamidall panels

W.R. Woodard Co., Inc. (LA) 1939-40

Blouses

Woodhaven Metal Stamping Co., Inc. (Brooklyn, NY) 1938-39
Children's toy sweepers and vacuum cleaners

Woodlets, Inc. (Buffalo, NY) 1982
TRON air fresheners for car use only — supplied by Sent Pak, Inc. (Baltimore)

Worcester Toy Company div of Plascor, Inc. (Worcester, MA) 1972-79
Housekeeping, sand, and garden toys; tea sets

World Citrus West, Inc. (Fullerton, CA) 1981-86
Donald Duck orange juice

World Toy Mfg. Corp. (NYC) 1939-41
Dolls

Worlds of Wonder (Fremont, CA) 1987
Mechanical talking plush Mickey Mouse, packaged with a book and cassette

W.S. Wormser Co. (Chicago) 1968-71
Slacks, robes, boys' pajamas

Wornova Mfg. Co. (NYC) 1932-38
Costumes, masks

J.L. Wright, Inc. (Chicago) 1938-39
Salt and pepper shakers

John Wright, Inc. (Wrightsville, PA) 1972-73
Metal giftware, cast iron bookends, Mickey Mouse metal flag holder

R. John Wright Dolls (Cambridge, NY) 1987
Snow White collector dolls

William Wrigley, Jr. Co. (Chicago) 1938-39
Doublemint offered a McCall's dress pattern for making a Snow White inspired frock

Philip Wunderle (Philadelphia) 1936-42
Candies

Yacht Sales and Service Co. (Oakland, CA) 1938-39
Count Sakhnoffsky to make designs for boats

Yankee Homecraft Corp. (E. Natick, MA) 1966-67
Model casting kits, "Knit-Wit knits," "pom-poms" yarn kits

Yogg & Company (Millburn, NJ) 1968-69
Face masks

Young Squire (NYC) 1968-70
Boys' sport coats and blazers

Youngland Inc. (NYC) 1987
Infant and girls' constructed dresses

Youngstown Pressed Steel Co sub Mullins Mfg. Corp. (Salem, OH) 1942-43
YPS Plaks die-cut laminated paperboard plaques to color and assemble

Harry C. Zaun (NYC) 1937-39
Gas discharge lamp containing glowing elements known as a "Glow Lamp"

Zebco, div of Brunswick Corp. (Tulsa, OK) 1982-86
Fishing rod, fishing reel, fishing rod and reel combination outfit, tackle box

Zee Toys, Inc. (Long Beach, CA) 1983-87
Inflatable pool and beach toys, pools, inflatable toys and games, inflatable children's furniture, play tunnels

Zell Products, Corp. (NYC) 1933-34
Banks

The Zephyr Group, Inc. (Torrance, CA) 1985-87
Children's suspenders

Zimmer Paper (Indianapolis) 1940-41
Licensed use not known

Jay V. Zimmerman Co. (St. Louis) 1949-50
Donald Duck "Living Toy" ring made for Kelloggs

Zonite Products Corp. (NYC) 1939-40
Advertising materials

Zwicker Knitting Mills (Appleton, WI) 1970-71
Gloves

MICKEY MOUSE

12—One Col. Drawing
(Mat 05¢; Cut 30¢)

Tomart's DISNEYANA — Volumes 1, 2, & 3

This book is a supplement to the first three volumes in this series. It lists items of major collecting interest from the 30's up to 1987 not found in the original set.

The first three books provide the basic information on collecting Disneyana and over a hundred classifications for which no update is included in this volume. Tomart's Illustrated DISNEYANA Catalog and Price Guide can be purchased from your favorite book seller or direct from the publisher — Tomart Publications, P.O. Box 2102, Dayton, Ohio 45429. The cost is $24.95 per volume, plus $1.50 per book for postage and handling. Ohio residents add 6% sales tax.

VOLUME ONE HIGHLIGHTS —

America On Parade	Christmas
American Pottery	Clocks
Animation Cels	Coins and Medallions
Banks	Cookie Jars
Books	Disneykins
Brayton's Laguna Pottery	Disneyland
Chinaware	Dolls

VOLUME THREE HIGHLIGHTS —

Paint sets	Salt & Pepper shakers
Pinback buttons, badges & tabs	Sheet music
	Soap
Plates — collector	Stamps
Postcards	Toothbrush holders
Posters	Trains & handcars
Puzzles & Puzzle sets	Watches
Radios & Phonographs	Windup Toys
Records	

VOLUME TWO HIGHLIGHTS —

Donald Duck products	Lamps & nightlights
Figures — all types	Lunch boxes
Fisher Price Toys	Maps
Games	Mickey Mouse Clubs
Disney Goebel figurines	Mickey Mouse Magazines
Gum cards & wrappers	Model kits
Hagen-Renaker ceramics	Music boxes